SIN AND FORGIVENESS

'This is a guide for the perplexed, a map through the moral maze of a world full of conflicts, some with the capacity to destroy worthwhile life on earth. At a time when terrible atrocities and barbaric acts are still committed across the globe in the name of religion, race, language, and nationalism, this wise and humane work explores how the practical application of the concepts of sin and forgiveness, as understood in the Judaeo–Christian tradition, are expressed in a secular society. Drawing upon a lifetime's practical experience, and the insights of psychology, literature, philosophy and science, this powerful book challenges our collective and personal responsibility to construct humane and peaceful moral processes. This is a timely antidote against ethical aimlessness. It is a work that needs to be read widely and considered deeply.'

Lord Anthony Lester QC

'A profound and important book. In this compulsively readable and passionately argued book, Kay Carmichael has helped us to forge a new ethic for a confused world.'

Richard Holloway, former Primus of the Scottish Episcopal Church

'In this challenging book Kay Carmichael makes use of the rich experience of her personal and professional life to raise important questions about the conditions in which forgiveness may be appropriate in a post-traditional society. She concludes that moral principles are created as a result of people working together collectively rather than as individuals. In the public arena it is much less important to focus on the issue of personal forgiveness and much more helpful to deal with justice, especially a justice which is based on restoration rather than on retribution. This is a book which is much needed in the uncertain world in which we now live.'

Baroness Vivien Stern CBE, Senior Research Fellow,
International Centre for Prison Studies, London, UK

Western attitudes to crime were in the past rooted in concepts of sin, and therefore of hopes for redemption and forgiveness. So what happens – to offenders and society as a whole – in a world where people no longer talk of sin but of evil? If hopes of redemption go too, will revenge take the place of forgiveness?

Kay Carmichael explores these dilemmas in this topical and provocative book. She traces the stories of Myra Hindley, Mary Bell, Sarah Payne, James Bulger and his killers, comparing public responses to such crimes. Art and literature are examined for the light they throw on the evolution of our ideas about sin and forgiveness – from Rembrandt to Nathaniel Hawthorne, Samuel Beckett, Dali and writings inspired by the Holocaust. Turning to our own day, Carmichael discusses the emergence of structural sins or 'iniquities' in which we may all find ourselves involved: poverty, slavery, violence and war are her themes. Her analysis leaves her sceptical about many contemporary appeals for forgiveness, but hopeful about ideas of restorative justice.

Explorations in Practical, Pastoral and Empirical Theology

Series Editors: Professor Leslie J. Francis, University of Wales, Bangor, UK and Professor Jeff Astley, University of Durham and Director of the North of England Institute for Christian Education, UK

Theological reflection on the Church's practice is now recognized as a significant element in theological studies in the academy and seminary. Ashgate's new series in practical, pastoral and empirical theology seeks to foster this resurgence of interest and encourage new developments in practical and applied aspects of theology worldwide. This timely series draws together a wide range of disciplinary approaches and empirical studies to embrace contemporary developments including: the expansion of research in empirical theology, psychological theology, ministry studies, public theology, Christian education and faith development; key issues of contemporary society such as health, ethics and the environment; and more traditional areas of concern such as pastoral care and counselling.

Other titles published in this series:

Ordinary Theology
Looking, Listening and Learning in Theology
Jeff Astley
ISBN 0 7546 0583 3 (Hbk)
ISBN 0 7546 0584 1 (Pbk)

In what eternity of the mind will
South America or Belsen be put
with the sun on Sgurr Urain
and its ridges cut in snow?

Sorley MacLean, *The Lost Mountain*

Traveller, there is no path,
Paths are made by walking

Antonio Machado

Sin and Forgiveness

New Responses in a Changing World

KAY CARMICHAEL
Writer and Activist,
Glasgow, Scotland

ASHGATE

© Kay Carmichael 2003

Published by
Ashgate Publishing Limited
Gower House, Croft Road
Aldershot, Hants
GU11 3HR
England

Ashgate Publishing Company
Suite 420
101 Cherry Street
Burlington, VT 05401-4405
USA

Ashgate website: http://www.ashgate.com

British Library Cataloguing in Publication Data
Carmichael, Kay
  Sin and forgiveness : new responses in a changing world. –
  (Explorations in practical, pastoral and empirical theology)
  1. Forgiveness – Religious aspects – Christianity 2. Sin
  I. Title
  234. 5

Library of Congress Cataloging-in-Publication Data
Carmichael, Kay.
  Sin and forgiveness : new responses in a changing world / Kay Carmichael.
     p. cm. – (Explorations in practical, pastoral, and empirical theology)
  Includes bibliographical references. (alk. paper)
  1. Sin. 2. Forgiveness of sin. I. Title. II. Series.

BT715 .C29 2003
241' .3–dc21

2002034536

ISBN 0 7546 3405 1 (Hbk)
ISBN 0 7546 3406 X (Pbk)

Typeset in Times by LaserScript Ltd, Mitcham, Surrey
Printed and bound in Great Britain by MPG Books Ltd, Bodmin, Cornwall

Contents

List of Illustrations

Acknowledgements

This book is dedicated to those children, women and men often described as 'sinners', who have horrified us by their shocking deeds. From them I have learned how intense can be their desperate need for human contact, for love and approval, and how those deprived of these basic human experiences can behave in the most terrible and bizarre ways. I have learned to recognize the courage of those among them who develop a capacity to live in more humane and creative ways; and to respect those people, both professional and non-professional, who with a loving understanding of the difficulty, for all of us, of being a human being have helped them achieve that.

I particularly want to thank David Jasper of the International Society for Religion, Literature and Culture, who sustained me both intellectually and spiritually in this work. I have also been very fortunate in having the editorial help of Jeanne Brady, to whom I am grateful. Staff at Ashgate Publishing have also been most supportive.

I thank my beloved husband David Donnison, source of my comfort and joy and of the conversation which runs, as Jung described love, like a golden thread through our lives. Finally my wonderful daughter Sheena Hussain, whose skill, clarity and constant optimism steered me through a maze of formatting and technical confusion.

Introduction

It is important to acknowledge the personal factors that have influenced my attempt to understand the nature of sin and forgiveness in a post-Christian society. Brought up by a Roman Catholic mother who believed the 'Protestant' Bible to be a dangerous, heretical work and an infrequently glimpsed Protestant father, I had an early exposure to West of Scotland theological disputes. At a domestic level these frequently centred round accusations of sin and very little forgiveness. There was none of that generosity so movingly described by Newlands.[1] This produced in me a somewhat confused set of responses which, in spite of my efforts to understand and clarify them, may sometimes be reflected in the following pages.

My original notion was that, in the western world, the movement away from adherence to religious institutions towards a secular society would require a reformulation of our understanding of sin and forgiveness. In the past, religious institutions, because of their claim to understand the divine will, have been accepted as the definers of sin and the holders of the gift of forgiveness. For significant numbers of people in the western world this belief no longer applies. The movement away from accepting the authority of religious institutions can be seen as part of a wider cultural shift, affecting all our institutions. This has been described as a new paradigm,[2] brought into being by the development of the information technology which is replacing the industrial society that has been with us for the last three hundred years and which, in its time, had replaced a primarily agricultural society.

Each paradigm shift brings with it changes which cause confusion, pain and anxiety – particularly for those who have a vested interest in the old society – as well as new opportunities. The move from agriculture to industrialization brought changes in family life, religion, culture, politics and business, as peasants were driven off the land to feed what Blake described as the 'dark satanic mills'.[3] We have still not, as a society, properly responded to many of the problems created by that shift. The emerging paradigm of the information society is bringing ever-newer changes which are causing further confusion, pain and anxiety. Anthony Giddens makes the point that now we have to decide about traditions which need to be saved or recovered, 'what to try to sustain and what to discard'.[4] As part of a global rather than a European perspective he suggests that the phrase post-traditional may be more helpful than post-modern when considering issues of

---

[1] George Newlands, *Generosity and the Christian Future*, SPCK: London 1997.

[2] For a more detailed discussion see Fritjof Capra, *The Tao of Physics*, Fontana: London 1975 which offered the first popular statement of this thinking.

[3] William Blake, *Complete Writings*, ed. Geoffrey Keynes, Oxford Paperbacks: Oxford 1972, p. 481.

[4] Anthony Giddens, *Beyond Left and Right: the future of radical politics*, Polity Press: London 1994, p. 48.

social change.[5] I am only concerned in this work with addressing those aspects of these changes which influence our attitudes to sin and forgiveness.

For those brought up in the Christian tradition to which I was introduced, sin and forgiveness are linked to notions of guilt, shame, the need to atone and in doing so to be cleansed. These aspects of feeling, sometimes not clearly articulated, are contained within a wider assumption that the goal of the Christian is to achieve perfection. In childhood I was indoctrinated into a medieval view of the world. God, the devil, saints and demons were active players in the daily events of my life. I believed in every word of the Nicene Creed. I believed that in taking communion I literally took God into my mouth and that if I did this when there was even a venial sin on my soul my mouth would be burned. I believed in every detail of the hell Bosch painted. Every night before sleep I was taught to cross my arms and prepare myself for death, hoping for heaven but fearing hell. The devil was an active participant in daily life offering temptation, but I was protected by a guardian angel whose purpose was to give protection against his strategies. I believed God saw and knew everything I did and thought. I prayed to the Virgin Mary with certainty that my prayer would be communicated directly to her son. I was taught that my goal was perfection, I had to keep my body pure and I had to guard my senses. I lived in an aura of guilt which could only be eased by the confession of my sins followed by priestly absolution which would cleanse my soul. Both Hieronymus Bosch's *Garden of Delights* and James Joyce's *Portrait of the Artist as a Young Man* spoke to my condition.

In later life I found myself constantly confronted with ways in which my personal struggle to separate myself out from this medieval theology interacted with wider changes in modern thought. At the same time I wanted, needed, to retain the sense of meaning, awe and wonder that this primitive religious view had offered me in its myths, music, art and ritual. Inevitably, as part of an earlier move away from that view, I had explored the powerful secular religions of Marxism and psychoanalytic theory, finding in both many of the attributes of the lost sense of meaning and power. Each in different ways has proved unable to satisfy my inner life so the search has had to continue. For reasons also associated with my early life, that search focused on questions of sin and forgiveness. In doing that I have been forced to consider both Christian and secular ways of dealing with these questions.

At times, while writing, I have been overwhelmed with a sense of the absurd. This arises both from a sense of my own temerity at trying to make sense of concepts which are rooted in the most mysterious aspects of those impulses which define our humanity, and from what I see as the extraordinary attempts humans make to reinforce the structures in which they believe. This latter practice was summed up for me in the newspaper photographs of Pope John Paul II, an old man nearing death, dressed in extraordinary garments, who believes himself to be God's representative on earth and himself to be infallible, holding up a Bible heavily encrusted with a precious metal while asking for forgiveness for sins on behalf of the Church:

Wearing the purple garments of lenten mourning, the Pope sought pardon for seven categories of sin: general sins; sins in the service of truth; sins against Christian unity;

---

[5] Ibid., p. 87.

against the Jews; against respect for love, peace and cultures; against the dignity of women and minorities; and against human rights.[6]

The sins for which he was asking forgiveness and the language in which forgiveness was asked had been carefully edited by those cardinals who had objected to the whole enterprise on the grounds that such a statement would bring the Church into disrepute. Conservatives in the Curia, the Vatican's bureaucracy, had argued that an apology for past misdeeds would 'erode the foundations of church authority'.[7] A team of theologians had spent three years drafting a report titled *Memory and Reconciliation: The Church and the Mistakes of the Past*. This was designed to be the centrepiece of the Vatican's jubilee celebrations dedicated to repentance and renewal, and was first issued by the Vatican on 12 March 2000.

The public statement might instead have been an extract from a play by Dario Fo and the theatre of the absurd. This term, coined in 1961 by the critic Martin Esslin, was an attempt by him to define a form of theatre which rejected naturalism and instead used a variety of dramatic techniques which defied rational analysis and explanation. In this way it tried to express, by implication rather than by direct statement, the 'absurdity' of the human condition.

This was reflected in the Pope's theatrical performance. There was in his statement no mention of individuals, no identification of those church men or women who committed these sins. No one was held to account, nor was there any statement that these errors of the past would not be repeated in the future. Nor was there any talk of reparation. So the pursuit of heretics continues though they are no longer burnt at the stake, merely silenced or excommunicated; the humiliation of women continues in the denial of their right to priesthood and their right to control their reproduction; anti-Semitism may slumber but has not disappeared; the sexual abuse of children by the clergy, which was not even mentioned, continues to be reported although now taken more seriously by church authorities.

But the apology is more than a gesture: as the Irish writer Sean O'Conaill has said, 'an unprecedented acknowledgement about disastrous historical errors of ecclesiastical praxis ... it will remain as the best evidence ... of a progress of descent from the hubristic insanities of Christendom'.[8] He sees however that although the exercise was aimed at the purification of memory, it has left untouched crucial errors of doctrine and praxis which lie ready for repetition.[9] One important question it raises is: in whose name is the Pope asking forgiveness? Have we any right to ask forgiveness for other people? This has been one of the central questions Jewish survivors have raised in relation to the Holocaust or Shoah.[10] The document *Memory and Reconciliation ...*, which provides the theological framework for the

---

[6] Rory Carroll, *The Guardian*, 13 March 2000.

[7] Rory Carroll, *The Guardian*, 4 February 2000.

[8] *The Irish Times*, 25 April 2000.

[9] O'Conaill believes that all the errors admitted by the Church were due to the Church's alliance with the State, which is 'the ultimate source and locus of coercive power'. This, he says, has neither been fully acknowledged nor abandoned.

[10] Shoah, a Hebrew word meaning 'desolation', has come to be the preferred term for the Holocaust by Jewish scholars who feel that 'Holocaust' has lost much of its significance through overuse.

Pope's action, emphasizes a distinction between the sins committed by the Church's sons and daughters and the Church itself, which he claimed remains holy and immaculate. This presumably means that the Church itself has no need of forgiveness. This has relevance to my later discussion of structural sin.

The whole episode can be seen as a metaphor for the confusion that surrounds the issues of sin and forgiveness. It can also be seen as a metaphor for the way in which the Catholic Church and other denominations are forced to recognize that the apparently unshakeable assumptions of the last two thousand years have become eroded. When I am drawn into the sense of the absurd I turn to writers like Camus and Ionescu. I can associate myself with Camus' attempt in *The Myth of Sisyphus* to explore the human situation in a world of shattered beliefs. This deeply religious non-believer made the point:

> A world that can be explained by reasoning, however faulty, is a familiar world. But in a universe that is suddenly deprived of illusions and of light, man feels a stranger. His is an irremediable exile, because he is deprived of memories of a lost homeland as much as he lacks the hope of a promised land to come. This divorce between man and his life, the actor and his setting, truly constitutes the feeling of Absurdity.[11]

A Lost Homeland

I had experienced not only the loss of a personal god and with that loss the powerful deprivation of ritual, mystery and meaning offered by that most theatrical of institutions, the Catholic Church, but also the subsequent losses of belief in progress, science and other political faiths. All the stories in which I had invested meaning had run out of meaning for me. What alternative could there be but a sense of absurdity? Martin Esslin quotes Ionescu's definition: 'Absurd is that which is devoid of purpose ... Cut off from his religious, metaphysical and transcendental roots, man is lost; all his actions become senseless, absurd, useless.'[12]

For those who have lost such a homeland there is a common problem of finding an alternative. To live in isolation can stretch human capacities to breaking point. Camus, at one point, was asking the question, why since life had lost all meaning should not man seek escape in suicide? He offered the thought that one's most important decision every day is deciding not to commit suicide; it is to explore other options which might have meaning for a wider human condition. We have seen one solution to this in the explosion of consumerism which appears to have offered alternative meaning to so many lives. Is there anything more absurd than living and working in order to spend time and money in shops?[13] Yet the thrill of

---

[11] Albert Camus, *The Myth of Sisyphus*, trans. Justin O'Brien, Penguin Books: Harmondsworth 1975.

[12] Quoted in Martin Esslin, *The Theatre of the Absurd*, Penguin Books: Harmondsworth 1974, p. 23.

[13] For a quick commentary on consumerism see Chris Horrocks and Zoran Jevtic, *Baudrillard for Beginners*, Icon Books: Cambridge 1996, which contains this response to the question of 'You want us to consume? OK, let's consume always more and anything whatsoever – for any useless and absurd purpose' p. 140. Baudrillard sees the entire society as organized around consumption and display of commodities through which individuals gain prestige, identity and standing.

shopping may be a substitute for religious experiences, with malls and garden centres replacing churches. In my own lifetime I have watched friends move from conventional religious belief to a search for alternatives which could ease the sense of alienation. The true need, to combine mythos and logos, is not to be found in a shopping mall, but the religious impulse may be met in post-traditional causes assumed to be secular.

The theatre of the absurd, while offering no solutions to these questions, nevertheless offers a useful mental framework within which to work. It can be seen as a return to the original religious function of the theatre, confronting us with our myths and making us aware of our fragile and mysterious place in the universe. Its plays do not tell stories as we have understood stories but in Esslin's view communicate a pattern of poetic images. He gives the example of Beckett's *Waiting for Godot*, pointing out that while things happen in the play, the happenings do not add up to a plot or a story: 'they are an image of Beckett's intuition that *nothing really ever happens* in man's existence'. Esslin sees the whole play as being a complex poetic image, a complicated pattern of images and themes woven together like a musical composition, not offering a line of development but rather a static situation, as an Imagist poem might, presenting a pattern of images and associations in a mutually interdependent structure. While I have tried to hold my thought processes within a linear structure I have a sense that the interplay of the currently conflicting perceptions of sin and forgiveness fits better into Esslin's notion of patterns of images and associations: 'Nothing happens, nobody comes, nobody goes, it's awful.'[14]

The subject of the play is not Godot but waiting, a defining aspect of being human as we wait for events, for other people, for understanding and for death. It is perhaps the first lesson a child learns and in later life may resent most. Esslin describes how a performance of Godot in a prison was understood more intuitively by that audience that any other the theatre company had encountered.[15] It seems also to be a powerful metaphor for our time as we wait for some resolution of the dilemmas confronting us in our loss of belief in religion, politics, the law, science and the future. We are waiting for a new story which can help us make sense of the world in which we find ourselves.

Each play in the theatre of the absurd presents itself as a projection of its author's personal world, whether it be Beckett, Fo, Ionesco or Genet. Unlike Greek theatre, the medieval mystery plays and the later humanist theatre where there was a generally accepted metaphysical system, here we find no such accepted cosmic system of values. This reflects another truth of our time, living as we do in a complex, pluralist, multicultural world. As with Dali, the Symbolists, or abstract painters, we are being offered access to a succession of private visions of the world or else to the view that there is no vision. According to Joseph Campbell, the individual is increasingly seen as 'an end and entity in himself'.[16] This may be an additional factor in our sense of uncertainty. Perhaps we see ourselves, like Vladimir and Estragon, as waiting for Godot.

---

[14] Samuel Beckett, *Waiting for Godot*, Faber & Faber: London 1959, p. 41.

[15] Martin Esslin, *Theatre of the Absurd*, p. 19.

[16] Joseph Campbell, *Myths to Live By*, Paladin Books: London 1985, p. 17.

However, unlike them, we can choose to create a new ending and decide to do something rather than wait for someone else to write our script for us. The theatre of the absurd is not concerned to offer a story with a moral lesson. If we seek a morality we have to create it for ourselves but – and here is the rub and this is where we have to move on from the theatre of the absurd – it has to be done in cooperation with those with whom we live. But that in itself is not enough. The search for morality, while its roots may lie in pragmatism, requires us also to draw from the human drive for transcendence of the mundane. To tap into this resource we have to learn from the individual vision of the artist and from the mystic.

Issues of sin and forgiveness constantly involve us in the lives of others and we have to take them with us on this journey. Perhaps the work of the theatre of the absurd, and a sense of absurdity or loss of meaning, has only continuous resonance for those who continue to hope that some external power, whether it be science or religion, will provide meaning. There may be no meaning externally prescribed. If we consider the possibility that on the next stage of the journey we will have to formulate our own 'meanings' and hence ideas of what constitutes sin and wherein lies the responsibility for forgiveness, our lives may become harder but more hopeful. The journey we are on involves the thought offered in Plato's *Republic* when discussing morality: 'what is at stake is far from insignificant: it is how one should live one's life'.[17]

The Stories by which we Live

Humans seem always to have told stories or painted pictures which told stories. These were cooperative ventures that reflected group identity and activity. Theories include the possibility that this has been an attempt by people from earliest times to make sense of their existence, give meaning to their lives and gain some control over their world. Edmund Leach relates this to the development of a sense of 'otherness' from nature, when they recognized themselves as different and needed to understand that difference. He views cooking, and painting on cave walls, as transformative acts which eliminated danger and brought the world under control.[18] Language would later do the same through song and poetry; dance was, and still is, powerful.

Joseph Campbell took that thought further. 'People' he told Bill Moyers,

> say that what we're all seeking is a meaning for life. I don't think that's what we're really seeking. I think that what we're really seeking is an experience of being alive, so that our life experiences on the purely physical plane will have resonances within our own innermost being and reality, so that we actually feel the rapture of being alive.[19]

---

[17] Plato, *Republic*, trans. Robin Waterfield, World's Classics, Oxford University Press: Oxford 1993, 352e, p. 40.

[18] Edmund Leach, *A Runaway World?*, The Reith Lectures 1967, British Broadcasting Corporation: London 1968.

[19] Joseph Campbell, *The Power of Myth*, with Bill Moyers, Doubleday: New York 1988.

That rapture of which Campbell speaks is mediated to us through linking our experience with a story that offers it a mythological context. 'Mythology', Campbell writes, 'is apparently coeval with mankind.'[20] He claims more. He believes that the fundamental themes of mythological thought (that which underlies our stories) have remained constant and universal, not only through our current historical awareness, but also over the whole extent of human occupation of our planet from the development of consciousness onwards. Two fundamental realizations have emerged: first, the inevitability of individual death, and second, the endurance of the social order. From the combination of these two levels of awareness have grown the great symbols and rituals that form the structures of our individual and social awareness.

I am arguing that we are now at an interim stage of the human journey, midway between past and future stories. Kuhn claimed that significant shifts took place when the old story – he called it a paradigm – could no longer answer new questions that were being asked.[21] That is what is happening now. We are leaving behind the stories that no longer speak to us, the traditions that no longer serve our needs. But there are significant religious and other symbols and themes which constantly recur in human lives and these have to be recognized and respected. These themes include the need to be accepted within our social group. This in turn creates an aspiration to be 'good' which can be distorted into a drive for perfection. Because of the sense of guilt or shame when we fail to meet group membership criteria we develop strategies to ease these feelings of discomfort and fear of punishment.

These strategies can involve the search for a scapegoat to carry responsibility for our failures to be good which we describe as sins. They also involve a search for forgiveness, which gives reacceptance by the group. These various themes and strategies are embodied in rituals, procedures regularly followed, not only in public ceremonies but also in private rituals of daily life to enable us to shape and transform the above themes.

This complexity of drive and response has been the stuff of drama whether in the rituals of African villages, the Greek amphitheatres or Pope John Paul II performing in the great basilica in Rome. It is central to the practice of religion and is central in Judaism and Christianity to the processes of the confession and cleansing of sin. Ritual is of central importance to all of us and I am aware that John Paul's ritual of forgiveness was part of this ancient tradition. Had I been looking at a North American Indian shaman performing similar cleansing ceremonies I would be more detached and appropriately respectful. I would acknowledge the intention and value its symbolism. I would value the recognition of guilt and the attempt of the leader of a community to cleanse his co-religionists. Nearing his death, John Paul has taken this responsibility on his own shoulders. The words 'Father, forgive them, for they know not what they do' hovered around him. But another view of the matter is that in the Crusades, in the Inquisition, in the pogroms the perpetrators knew very

---

[20] Campbell, *Myths To Live By*, p. 15.

[21] Thomas S. Kuhn, *The Structure of Scientific Revolutions*, 3rd edn, International Encyclopaedia of Unified Science: Foundations of the Unity of Science, Vol. 2, No. 2, University of Chicago Press: Chicago 1996.

well what they were doing. Those involved were following their own stories based on a corrupted version of the Christian story. This raises another question for us – how do we judge if a story is 'good' or 'evil' when we no longer have an authority making the decision for us?

We can now, from this distance, look at the context from which our understanding of sin and forgiveness has developed.

The story we inherited

In the Hebrew Bible both sin and forgiveness are mediated through the relationship between the human and the divine. The divine is encapsulated in the concept of God. Sin is defined as an offence against God; forgiveness is a gift God offers in return for repentance. This heals the relationship which has been destabilized by the sin. Sin was seen as alienating the human from God and as a result separating the sinner from God's community, disordering the inner life of the sinner and in effect disordering creation itself. To illustrate this alienation James McLendon quotes Psalm 51:4: 'Against thee, thee only, have I sinned.'[22] Damage in relationships between human beings is always secondary to relationships between God and humans. This is reflected in the order of the statutes and judgements of the Covenant made through Moses.[23]

The widespread nature of sin is reflected in the common terms used in the Hebrew Bible to describe offences against God: *awon*, crookedness or self-abuse; *chethah*, the anti-social breaking of boundaries; *peshah*, rebellion against the Most High. All three of these terms are translated in the Greek Septuagint by *hamartia*, missing the mark or veering off the straight and narrow. This became the New Testament term we translate as sin.

Sin and forgiveness are linked by the disorder and imbalance that result from sin. No community can tolerate this as a permanent feature so a process of forgiveness has to be put in place to restore order and balance. Reparation of the damage done, through forgiveness, is considered to be always available through God's mercy. This thought played a central role in both Jewish and, later, Christian understanding of the history of God's relationship with humans. The various Hebrew and Greek words used in both the Hebrew and Christian Bibles describe the divine action which removes or covers over sin. The history of Israel has been described as 'the history of a forgiving God in search of a repentant people'.[24] This in a sense identifies the nature of forgiveness as it was understood by the people of Israel. It was the whole community who sinned and who repented together in ritual form within a context of sacrifice, atonement, repentance and mercy. It was the whole community whom God forgave in this hierarchical relationship.

---

[22] *A New Handbook of Christian Theology*, eds Donald W. Musser and Joseph L. Price, The Lutterworth Press: Cambridge 1992, p. 442.

[23] Deut. 5. The importance of obedience to these commandments is emphasized in Matt. 19:17.

[24] Enda McDonagh in *A New Dictionary of Christian Theology*, eds Alan Richardson and John Bowden, SCM Press: London 1983, p. 214.

The new story of Christianity

In Christianity the concept of sin initially followed the pattern of Ten Commandments adapted from the Mosaic law but, from the sixth century on, the Church began to develop a more sophisticated view which was reflected in a list of cardinal sins and cardinal virtues.[25] Paul, in spreading the message of Christianity, chose to emphasize the effect on the human race of the story of 'The Fall' of Adam and Eve told in Genesis 3. From this story he deduced that 'by the sin of our first parents',[26] the human race had been deprived of immortality and innocence. The 'original sin' had been transmitted to every person in every subsequent generation. Augustine was later to develop this view in his theology. The continuing message of the narrative of the Fall has been that God is not responsible for a sinful world, but that such a world is due to humans using their free will which is a gift of God. Humans have failed to meet his hopes for them. As Paul argued, sin is in us.

A new paradigm of forgiveness emerged within Christianity. Hannah Arendt made the point that 'the discoverer of the role of forgiveness in the realm of human affairs was Jesus of Nazareth'.[27] Forgiveness became a major theme of his teaching: the new factor was the importance of interpersonal forgiveness reflected in the Lord's Prayer. Baptism,[28] a traditional form of cleansing which Mark describes as beginning Christ's mission, became a Christian sacrament. Along with this developed the sacrament of the Eucharist, which represented the great sacrifice of Jesus who died to cleanse the sins of all who believed in him, which was the basis of atonement theology.

Experience of the compulsive nature of sin and the loss of expectation of Parousia led to an extension of ecclesiastic involvement in the processes of sin and forgiveness. A period of public penance and public absolution was later replaced by private confession and absolution. In this way the Church through its practices reinstated the hierarchical nature of forgiveness over the more egalitarian group processes of the early Church. Protestantism challenged this granting of God's power to the ministry at the time of the Reformation; direct access to God was claimed. Both these views however developed an individualistic cast of thought and we are now seeing these effects in the variety of religious interpretations available. When Arendt made her point about Jesus and forgiveness she followed it up by stating 'the fact that he made this discovery in a religious context and articulated it in religious language is no reason to take it any less seriously in a strictly secular sense'. The thing is real, she is saying, even if it does sound religious. Shriver uses this to conclude that both religious and secular thinkers have underestimated the empirical importance of forgiveness in social and political life.[29]

---

[25] See Morton W. Bloomfield, *The Seven Deadly Sins: An Introduction to the History of a Religious Concept, with Special Reference to Medieval English Literature*, State College Press: Michigan 1952.

[26] Romans 5:12–21.

[27] Hannah Arendt, *The Human Condition*, University of Chicago Press: Chicago and London 1958, pp. 238–39.

[28] Mark 1:4–9.

[29] Donald W. Shriver, Jnr, *An Ethic for Enemies: Forgiveness in Politics*, Woodstock Report, March 1996, No. 45, p. 3 See also Donald W. Shriver, Jnr, *An Ethic for Enemies: Forgiveness in Politics*, Oxford University Press: Oxford 1995.

This I suggest is what we have to address on a world scale as well as at the interpersonal level. This book is a modest attempt to explore some of the issues involved. One of the difficulties in this attempt is the lack of a structure within which to place ideas. This is another example of the interim space we occupy. Biblical literature, either listened to or read or looked at in murals and paintings, used to be part of everyone's moral education and the stories they told were part of everyone's culture. That this is no longer so was illustrated in spring 2000 when Neil MacGregor, Director of the National Gallery, London, set up an exhibition called *Seeing Salvation: The Image of Christ in Western Art*. Recognizing that a more secular general public is no longer able to 'read' these paintings in the way that a religiously sophisticated public once could, he set out on an educational tour of the United Kingdom to retell the story which lay behind the paintings. The book, *The Image of Christ*, which accompanies the exhibition, is quite clear in its message on the cover. It writes of the great paintings in the National Gallery and elsewhere of Christian subjects:

> to many people who come to see these works, who do not share these religious beliefs, their content can seem puzzling or irrevocably remote ... This book, and the exhibition it accompanies, express the confidence that modern secular audiences can engage with the masterpieces of Christian art at an emotional as well as a purely aesthetic or historical level.[30]

In other words, the story matters in that it gives access to the inner life. MacGregor wanted more than a cognitive understanding of the Christian story he was retelling.

Secular religions developed their own stories, paintings, songs and banners. MacGregor illustrated this by including and comparing a drawing by Käthe Kollwitz, the inspired secular recorder of German poverty, with a Holbein drawing of the dead Christ. In the secular drawing there was a dead man, obviously based on the Holbein, but this man was surrounded by his hungry family.[31] Secularists too had their saints and martyrs – and their demons. Most of all they too had their saviours, who would lead their people to the Promised Land. These secular religions inspired the same passions as religions of Christianity. They offered hope, comradeship, a sense of belonging and consolation to their adherents. The saviours have mostly been discredited, the paintings seen as tawdry; the banners are now only to be found in museums or trades union offices, brought into the public view only for special occasions. The words of the hymns and songs that supported the ideas have mostly been forgotten and are known only to small groups who come together in conference halls – and even they do not always know the words.

The shift of consciousness, among Europeans, away from a morality based on the belief in an anthropomorphic god has been slow but steady. There seems indeed to be an ebbing and flowing tide of belief in the source of morality although the general direction is of steady decline in church attendance and of belief in a

---

[30] Gabriele Finaldi, *The Image of Christ*, National Gallery Company Limited: London 2000.

[31] The drawing, *The Downtrodden* (Zertretene), 1900, The National Gallery of Art, Washington, Rosenwald Collection, is reproduced in *Prints and Drawings of Käthe Kollwitz* selected and introduced by Carl Zigrosser, Dover Publications, Inc., New York 1969.

personal god. We have seen in the western world two particular periods of outright challenge to Church-defined morality which are seen as liberating but also attacked as self-indulgent: the 1920s and early 1930s, and then the late 1960s and early 1970s. The focus of the challenge in both cases was the human body and the right of the individual, particularly individual women, to take responsibility for their sexual behaviour. The sexuality of women and their sinfulness has always been intimately linked with general standards of social morality, so it was not surprising that both these periods were seen by some as examples of the collapse of all civilization in Europe. Others saw it as a logical consequence of the availability of contraception which developed from the widespread distribution of condoms to soldiers in the First World War following the invention of latex. Even greater freedom was given to women in the 1960s following the invention of the contraceptive pill. Previously the fear of pregnancy had been allied with the strictures of the Church. Without that fear, the Church was largely ignored.

Since the 1960s the authority of the Church in matters of morality has been steadily diminishing. People, both church members of all denominations and non-church members, have increasingly been creating their own definitions of what is and is not sinful behaviour. Some of these have been reinforced by legal changes. Abortion and homosexuality, both now legally recognized, are seen as sinful by only a minority of Christians.[32] Sexual harassment, previously not seen as something to be taken seriously, is now not only seen as sinful by religious people but is also illegal. Sex before marriage and illegitimacy, once sinful,[33] are now taken for granted. The case for keeping God out of morality was spelt out by Bishop Richard Holloway in his book *Godless Morality*.[34] He argues that we need a purely human public morality undistorted by religious zealotry.

Sin, as we have understood it in the past as an offence against God, and that which alienates us from God, no longer dominates public awareness. Humans continue to hurt and damage themselves and each other. In decreasing numbers we seek forgiveness for this behaviour from a supernatural source; when injured ourselves, we are increasingly more likely to seek help from the law than from the solace of our own beliefs. Justice is increasingly regarded as the most significant value in a secular and democratic society and when we fail to find easement from that source we are more likely to turn to secular counsellors than to the pastors of the churches. In the following chapters I hope to explore these issues in more depth.

What clearly emerges, however, is that this increasingly secular society has not abandoned its aspirations, perhaps I should say need, for transcendence and opportunities to experience the rapture of being alive. Some of this comes with the physiology of being human. Falling in love, making love, holding one's newly born child, laughing with friends, reconciliation with enemies, listening to music, getting

---

[32] In spite of this it was July 2002 before Alan Duncan, MP, became the first Conservative Member of Parliament who felt able to publicly declare himself as 'gay'.

[33] Until the 1970s on the island of Lewis, 'fornication' required public humiliation on the penitence stool. For more detailed reports see Morris Pottinger, *Parish Life on the Pentland Firth*, White Maa Books: Thurso 1997.

[34] Richard Holloway, *Godless Morality*, Canongate: Edinburgh 1999.

drunk, stoned out of one's head or dancing are only some of the ways in which people break out of the constraints of the self.[35] At another level people appear to be increasingly drawn to esoteric, even bizarre, explorations of spiritual states in an attempt to understand the mystery of being alive and the inevitability of suffering. There is a new and growing sense of the web of unity that links all life on the planet. In seeking to understand the nature of sin and forgiveness, I have also had to recognize their unity and that nothing and no one can be considered in isolation from anything or anyone else. Everything and everyone is connected – the story, the story-teller and the reader; the picture, the painter and the viewer; the musician, the music and the listener.

Method

Inevitably much of what I write is speculative since academic attention seems not yet to have turned to the questions that concern me. The sociologists of religion who might appear to be those most concerned mainly focus on trends in belief and church attendance rather than the implications of this for the inner life of human beings. Their studies carry little interest for the pure theologian since number-crunching disciplines bear little relation to questions of transcendence. I approach this from the perspective of a social scientist whose main concerns have been in the field of social policy and its impact on individual lives. On occasion I find it necessary to stray over the borders of individual and social psychology. This base in the social sciences goes hand in hand with a consistent interest in the theory and practice of religious thought. That concern derives from my own religious upbringing and my sense that institutional Christianity, in its current expression, is failing to address issues of both individual and community responsibility for reassessing what is understood as sin or, along with that, exploring the changing nature of forgiveness. There are individuals and groups who, both inside and outside the institutions of Christianity, are exploring these questions and I discuss these in this book. Part of understanding the Christian approach involves recognizing that Christianity is a religion of apocalypse, concerned with what will happen at the end of things, and therefore moral issues are always secondary to that thought.

The intention of this book is to explore the way in which the practical application of the concepts of sin and forgiveness, as understood in the Judaeo-Christian tradition, are expressed in what is increasingly described as a post-Christian society. Because some of the issues I have been examining are not yet to be found in the work of academics, I have been thrown back to some extent on magazine and newspaper reportage for glimpses of post-Christian attitudes to sin and forgiveness. Underlying my approach is the conviction, which I have not always been able to express as fully as I would have liked, that song, theatre, painting and poetry tell us more about the issues than the comparative clumsiness of words can possibly communicate.

---

[35] Aldous Huxley discussed this phenomenon in his study of religious hysteria, *The Devils of Loudon*, Chatto & Windus: London 1952.

The method I have used is first, in Chapter 1, to take a number of narrative case studies which describe individuals who carry the double burden of what would, in any Christian context, be seen as sin but who in addition are viewed by the State as guilty of crimes for which they are held responsible by the secular institutions. These are analysed in terms of individual and public responses to their offences and the implications of this for their reacceptance within their communities. These case studies are followed, in Chapter 2, by considering whether art and literature may offer a more subtle, complex and humane approach than the categorical judgements currently in play.

The tone then changes as, in Chapters 3 and 4, I turn attention to changing perceptions of sin and forgiveness. This involves a discussion of how, following both intellectual enquiry and social changes, attitudes to many Christian beliefs began to change. This widening of belief, combined with a widening of social experience and information, has led to an understanding of sin that appears to be new, but is really an echo of the past, that is, sin as being a failing of community; sin in which we are all involved and for which we all share responsibility.

I return to the case study narrative method in Chapter 4 to describe ways in which a number of people who see themselves as sinned against have resolved either to find forgiveness out of their religious or spiritual understanding, or to conclude that forgiveness in isolation from restitution was not an appropriate response to their particular situation. This section introduces the question of a stronger emphasis on restorative justice as a significant element in developing and changing attitudes to forgiveness.

Up to this point the issues discussed are, in the main, those of breaches in relationships between individual human beings. Focusing on these, the work explores some attempts, not to discuss the nature of sin, but simply to help wounded people find forgiveness for their oppressor through psychological techniques. Claiming an ecumenical approach, the Institutes of Forgiveness in which these therapies are based appear primarily concerned with the damage lack of forgiveness does to the victims' health and spiritual life. This work goes hand in hand with a flood of self-help literature which I describe as quasi-theological since it combines popular psychology with a powerful undercurrent of Christian belief.

In the final chapter, Chapter 5, I then turn to what I describe as iniquities in order to separate the discussion from what has previously been seen as individual sin. In a world dominated by a global economy and global communication, we are becoming aware of a range of iniquities which include poverty, sexism, racism, violence, war and slavery. The common factor in all these appears to be a disregard for suffering and dignity. The question of what is the sin and who are the sinners is bewildering because of the complex interlocking of our global economies. Increasingly global communication brings us information directly challenging to anyone seeking to live an ethical life. I focus in this chapter on three issues: poverty, slavery, and violence associated with war.

I then ask some questions – how do we live together in this pluralist world which offers us no compelling meta-narrative we can share? This is equally relevant to the individuals described in Chapter 1 who are facing exclusion from their communities and those oppressed groups excluded from the normal decencies and human rights of the wider society. Is it possible to recreate some kind of community in which we accept responsibility for each other, or has the distorted individualism of the later Christian tradition with its corrupted and selective language, along with other defunct theologies, caused irreparable damage? That thought is intolerable and I suggest some possible approaches through which we may find our way back to some of the values which are expressed both in the Sermon on the Mount and the Communist Manifesto.

Throughout the work I use what I understand as the fundamental assumptions of Judaism and Christianity in their perception of sin and forgiveness. I also make a distinction between Christianity and the Christian tradition, the latter having been shaped by the institutions which have grown up to interpret – and on occasion overwhelm – the language and thought of the Christian message which can be found in the Christian Bible.

I regret that I have not been able to consider these issues in relation to the great religions of the East. It would have been impossible to do them justice within one book and disrespectful to make only occasional references to them. I hope however that those whose faith does not derive from the Judeo–Christian tradition and those who have no faith find they can join in the discussion set forth here.

Narratives of a Modern Dilemma

Introduction

The intention of this chapter is to offer four case studies. They are the stories of Myra Hindley, Mary Bell, James Bulger and Sarah Payne. What these stories share is that they are each concerned with the killing of children and the public reaction to those killings. In two cases an adult was responsible for the killings, in two cases the children were killed by other children. In each case the reaction of the public, as expressed through the media, has been a significant factor in the possibility of forgiveness for the offenders and their reintegration into the community. Also in each case the public perception combines the religious concept of killing another human being as a sin and the civil perception of the same action as a crime. This double perception appears to have significantly confused the discourse which has surrounded the individuals involved. The stories are given in the order in which the crimes were committed.

The first case study tells the story of the woman Myra Hindley who was convicted of the murder of children and was imprisoned for nearly forty years. She was repeatedly denied any hope of release and died in prison on 15 November 2002. Her story is rather longer than the others since it includes a summary, rarely available, of an offender's own view of her situation. The second tells the story of Mary Bell who, when she was a child, killed two small boys, was convicted, released after twelve years, but is still pursued and reviled by the press. The third and fourth stories differ in that they are publicly perceived, not as the story of the murderers, but as stories of the victims, James Bulger and Sarah Payne, who have been given an iconic status of innocence and their murderers demonized. Each story may be viewed as a failure of the Christian tradition to offer any acceptable resolution to the relationship of these children and adults to their communities.

The Story of Myra Hindley

Myra Hindley's story is presented both from a public perception of the circumstances of her background, the trial, her subsequent imprisonment and from her own account of those events. The discussion is centred around issues of image and reality, both the emotional images projected on to Myra Hindley and the pictorial image which has been used as a signifier of her evil capacities and secondly, in so far as it can be understood, the reality of her as a human being. Why, I ask, was the question of this woman's redemption contested so passionately by so many people and what is understood by 'redemption'? Was the assumption that she could only be granted freedom if she was spiritually redeemed?

In 1966, Myra Hindley, then 23 years of age, was jointly charged with her partner Ian Brady, 27, with the murder of three children. At the trial, which took place from 19 April to 7 May of that year, Hindley was charged separately that, knowing that Brady had killed one of the children, she 'did receive, comfort, harbour and maintain Brady'. Both pleaded not guilty; both were found guilty and sentenced. Brady was given three concurrent life sentences for the three murders he had committed, Hindley two concurrent life sentences for the murders in which she had been involved and a concurrent seven-year sentence for being an accessory to the third murder. What was not known at that stage was that Brady and Hindley had committed another two murders, which had not yet been linked to them.

Brady and Hindley had refused in any way to cooperate with the police and in court; sitting together in the dock, they maintained a united air of calm for most of the time. Hindley's composure broke down when an audiotape recording Brady forcing a 10-year-old girl to take something in her mouth was played. She put her head in her hands and wept, saying, 'I am ashamed.'[1] The attorney general spoke about the 'perverted sexual element' although no one knew what had actually happened other than that pornographic photographs of the child had been taken. On the tape the child, Lesley Ann Downey, was heard by the court pleading with Hindley for help – an appeal which she was heard to brusquely reject.

Psychiatric evidence was submitted and the judge, Mr Justice Atkinson, in his summing-up was able to say, 'from first to last in this case there has not been the smallest suggestion that either of these two are mentally abnormal or not fully and completely responsible for their actions ... If what the prosecution says is right, you are dealing here, are you not, with two sadistic killers of the utmost depravity?'[2]

There seems little doubt that had this trial taken place before 1965 both the defendants would have been hanged: this was the first case involving multiple murders to be tried since the Abolition of the Death Penalty Act had been passed in 1965.

The case became known as the 'Moors Murders' because the bodies of the children had been buried on the Yorkshire moors. *The Times* reported the trial daily, in detail. The issues around capital punishment were still very much alive; many, including the police, were opposed to the new legislation and community opposition was reinforced as the detailed story of the murders became public. The jury was made up entirely of men, four women having been rejected. It was thought by some observers that 'the three weeks of horror ahead might have been a greater strain than many women could have contemplated'.[3]

Police cars appearing to be transporting the accused to court were attacked with hatred by relatives of the victims. Two of these relatives were forbidden to attend the trial in case they tried to attack Hindley in court. From the beginning it was she who was the focus of hate. When the trial ended, about 250 people gathered outside the court to jeer and boo the police van in which Brady and Hindley were removed.[4]

---

[1] *The Times*, 21 April 1966.

[2] Ibid., 6 May 1966.

[3] Pamela Hansford Johnson, *On Iniquity*, Macmillan: London 1967, p. 10.

[4] Jean Ritchie, *Myra Hindley: Inside the Mind of a Murderess*, Angus and Robertson: London 1988, p. 120.

The intensity of feeling around these murders continued to be an issue for the justice system since any attempt to release Hindley was vehemently opposed by the family of the victims and significant numbers of the general public.

More than thirty years later Myra Hindley still languished in prison. Brady, who was later diagnosed as schizophrenic, was transferred to a special hospital for the criminally insane. He has consistently refused visitors and is quite clear that he wants to spend the rest of his life locked up. Indeed he has requested the right to commit suicide. Not so Myra Hindley. She appealed time after time to be given parole. A succession of Secretaries of State for the Home Office rejected her appeals; Jack Straw, acting minister at the time of Hindley's death, had been given the right by the judiciary to decide that she might die in prison but she had appealed to the European Court against this decision.

Between them, *The Guardian* and *The Observer* newspapers published a total of over eighty articles about Myra Hindley between 1966 and 1999. Normally interest ends with the end of the trial. One article written in October 1995, 'A Mind To Crime', discussing whether violent criminals could be cured, described Hindley as a psychopath. She reacted angrily to being labelled in this way and wrote to *The Guardian*[5] saying that numerous psychiatric and psychological tests had shown she had 'no evidence of a mentally disordered mind'. *The Guardian* replied to Hindley inviting her to justify her letter and asking, 'If she had shown no psychopathic tendencies, what had made her commit these crimes?' She responded by writing an essay of 5,000 words, which was published in full.[6]

Myra Hindley's Apologia

While in prison Hindley studied for a degree with the Open University and the essay she wrote reflects her academic understanding of the psychological and sociological influences of early life experience on adult behaviour. She begins her essay with the statement that she makes no excuses for her behaviour in the years she spent with Brady and takes full responsibility for the part she played in the offences. She wrote, 'I ... will not attempt to justify the unjustifiable.' She also claims to have grown up 'a normal happy girl, with religious convictions, who would never be cruel to animals and children'. In making the latter point she is disassociating herself from the *Guardian*'s charge that she had a psychopathic personality. Put crudely, she is saying that she was bad rather than mad. An outside view might consider her relationship with Ian Brady to be significantly abnormal.

Myra Hindley was the elder daughter of an unskilled, working-class, Manchester family. Born in 1942, in wartime Manchester while her father was in the army, she was mostly cared for by her grandmother while her mother worked. When her father returned after the war the arrangement continued and, when a second daughter was born, 4-year-old Myra was moved in full time with her grandmother. Her parents lived near and as she got older she seems to have moved between the two households. She describes her father as a violent and tyrannical drunkard:

---

[5] *The Guardian*, 4 October 1995.
[6] Ibid., 18 December 1995.

'When my mother berated him for the state he was in, he began knocking her about, and when I tried to prevent him, I was hit too.'

She develops this point by saying, 'Through witnessing and being on the receiving end of so much violence within my own family, I was given many lessons in dominance and control, which was possibly the foundation stone on which I built my own personality.' She learned, she says, not to show feelings and to keep her emotions under control, 'to build up layers of protective buffers, to tremble, rage, cry and grieve inwardly'. This would perhaps explain her impassive appearance during the trial, an impassivity that was presented by the media as evidence of her inhumanity. She claims that her 'fatal ability' to control her emotions was probably one of the main ingredients in her relationship with Ian Brady. She never showed her feelings to him any more than she had shown them to her father. Brady saw this as a virtue.

She describes how she became engaged at 17 to a boy she had known since childhood but withdrew from this at the prospect of living the kind of life she saw being endured by the women around her: 'I wanted a career, to better myself ... I ... dreamed and made plans and kept everything to myself.'[7] When she, now aged 18 and trying to improve her prospects, changed jobs and met Ian Brady, she describes herself as 'emotionally immature, relatively unsophisticated and sexually inexperienced − I was still a virgin and intended to be so until I married'. She claims an 'immediate and fatal attraction' on her part. This was reinforced by his treatment of her which alternated between approval and rejection, a phenomenon known in brainwashing techniques as a way to reinforce dependency and anxiety to please in a prisoner, a child or in an insecure partner. She was, she says, 'utterly obsessed by him. He had ... a magnetic-like charisma into which my own personality, my whole self, became almost totally subsumed.'

Brady ridiculed her religious beliefs with arguments she couldn't counter. At the trial the Crown 'plainly acknowledged that the younger Miss Hindley had been indoctrinated by Brady', that he had introduced her '... to corrupting literature and the idea of murder and that he initiated, planned and committed the crimes in which she participated'. On one occasion she had tried to break away from him but his influence was too strong and, after the first murder, the secret they shared bound them more closely. It was however only when they were both on remand before the trial that he said in a letter[8] that he loved her − a notion he had always dismissed as sentimentality. Afraid of annoying him she had never told him that she loved him but now poured her feelings out in letters. His danger of life imprisonment and new helplessness seems to have produced in her a determination in her own words 'to nurture him and encourage him and sustain him'.

She recognizes that without her cooperation the crimes could not have been committed since it was she who was instrumental in procuring the children, who would have been less likely to go with a man. In rejecting the label of psychopath she is forced to accept the label of bad. She does this, but only for her past behaviour and claims redemption for herself in the new person she has become.

---

[7] Ibid., 4 October 1995.

[8] This letter was written in German, which they were both learning because of Brady's obsession with everything connected with the Nazis.

This work of redemption, she claims, has not been easy but has involved years of confronting not only 'one's offending behaviour but one's inner self'.[9] She found the public expression of remorse difficult, as do many prisoners convicted of serious crimes.[10] She much prefers to think of herself 'as repentant before Christ in the same way as Peter, after denying him three times, wept bitterly, repented and begged forgiveness'.

In her essay, Hindley wrote that she believed that her release would have been more likely if she had been diagnosed with a mental disorder of which she could be seen to have been cured. Instead she 'was labelled as an enigma, someone whom people could not comprehend'. The tabloids, she claimed, had turned her into 'an industry, selecting me as the public icon/evil monster, Medusa-like image, which holds the projected hatred, fear and fury of the nation's psyche...'. Although she was judged and she believed 'rightly convicted and sentenced', trial, judgement and sentencing by the tabloids continued with highly emotive arguments and, whenever the question of her release surfaced, they presented 'you the jury' polls to their readers. The newspaper, *The Sun*, described her among other things as 'the symbol of the nation's revulsion at all those who prey on innocent children'.

Two days after the 1966 trial ended the judge wrote to the then Home Secretary:

> Though I believe Brady is wicked beyond belief without hope of redemption[11] (short of a miracle) I cannot feel that the same is necessarily true of Hindley once she is removed from his influence. At present she is as deeply corrupted as Brady but it is not so long ago that she was taking instruction in the Roman Catholic Church and was a communicant and a normal sort of girl.

It was only the production at the trial of the horrifying audio tape made by Brady while they were maltreating the child, Lesley Ann Downey, before she was killed, that made clear the full extent of Hindley's involvement. Previously it had been argued that she had only helped him dispose of the bodies, but even before the trial public feeling was directed against her rather than Brady. The tape, which caused Hindley distress when it was played, has taken on a mythical status like her picture – both artefacts have been given a life of their own. Freedberg[12] discusses the fusion that can take place between an object and what it represents; this was seen later in the public response to the police photograph of Myra Hindley.

---

[9] Hindley appears to be using the word redemption in two ways. The first sense is religious in that her old self, the sinful self, has been redeemed by Christ to create a new person. But in the second sense she seems to imply a more clinical therapeutic redemption where through years of confrontation with her 'inner self' she has come to understand why she behaved as she did.

[10] I found this repeatedly when working with male prisoners serving life sentences. They seem to think either that it is too superficial a way to deal with their own feelings about what they have done or else that no one will believe them.

[11] We have no idea of the judge's meaning of the use of the word 'redemption'. It may be the Oxford Dictionary definition of 'man's deliverance from sin and damnation' or it may be a looser meaning that he will repent and never commit another crime, thus making him available for parole.

[12] David Freedberg, *The Power of Images*, University of Chicago Press: Chicago and London 1989.

People in court, including the police, who heard the tape recording of the child crying, protesting and asking Myra Hindley, whom the child called 'Mum', to help her, say they will never forget it. Hardened crime reporters have said that listening to it was one of the most frightful experiences of their lives.[13] It is often referred to, even by people who have not heard it, as a reason for never being able to forgive her or release her. It had identified her as a woman who tortured children.

It is possible that if Hindley had not met Brady she would have married and led a perfectly ordinary if rather discontented life, seeking transcendence in more prosaic forms. Instead she was able to project onto this very psychologically disturbed man, Brady, all the power, excitement and meaning earlier relationships had failed to give her. The two became inseparable and it was as if he was able to lock into her mind the ideas with which he was obsessed. She had her first sexual experience with him and he became the centre of her life. God and what she understood as religion were abandoned and replaced by Ian Brady and his view of the world. It could be argued that Hindley took part in the murders simply to gain his approval.

Her experience of prison, because of the reaction of other prisoners to her, was of a profound sense of isolation. A turning-point came with her inclusion in a small special unit for long-sentence prisoners which gave opportunities for women and staff to communicate more freely and get to know each other. They cooked their own meals, could sit out in a small garden and spend their time reading or talking. This was, in a simple form, a therapeutic community of the kind that might have been offered in the early Christian Church. She responded to this by entering into relationships. Initially they were focused on sexual attraction; homosexuality was and is very much a part of prison life, and Myra Hindley became actively lesbian.

Learning of this from the constant leaking of information about her, the press used it to reinforce her image of evil and passionate sexuality. In fact over the years a number of these relationships were loving and reciprocal and may have been an important factor in her emotional growth. The first of these was with a prison officer who had for many years been a Carmelite nun. The poetry Hindley wrote for her was full of religious imagery in which we can see the same need for a passionate connection such as she had shared with Brady of whom she had said: 'Within months he had convinced me that there was no God at all (he could have told me the earth was flat, the moon made of green cheese, that the sun rose in the West and I would have believed him). He became my god, my idol, my object of worship and I worshipped him blindly, more blindly than the congenitally blind.'

By her third year in prison she was writing to a visiting chaplain, 'I'm still desperately trying to make my peace with God ...'. Nine years after the trial she was transferred to another prison where she met an experienced Jesuit prison chaplain who had an important effect on her spiritual life. He introduced her to the Jesuit programme of 'The Spiritual Exercises', which she began to practise. Letters she wrote to friends and former prisoners with whom she kept contact make frequent religious references. She described her life as a Via Dolorosa and identified herself as the one carrying the cross. It was after this transfer that she began to write a 21,000-word plea for parole to be sent to the Home Secretary. The

---

[13] Johnson, *On Iniquity*, p. 14.

rest of her life was one of struggle to be taken seriously as a reformed person, who was entitled to be reinstated as a member of the community.

What was remarkable was that despite 36 years of intense press persecution Hindley did not collapse into a passive acceptance of her fate or of her guilt, although beginning in the autumn of 1999 when aged 57 she was reported as being in renewed ill health.[14] She refused to see herself as an evil person beyond forgiveness, and continued to challenge the right of the State to keep her in prison for the rest of her life. Over the years she attracted support from a number of people who argued vehemently on her behalf. This capacity to attract middle-class support, in particular from some people known to have strong religious convictions or who were ministers of religion, reinforced popular prejudice against her.

Her additional offence was that she crossed class boundaries by virtue of being wicked rather than by being talented. The powerful anti-liberal, anti-middle-class symbolism lying behind the word 'do-gooder' for those who have supported her release was used to add fuel to the fire of hatred and to excite thoughts of revenge should she be released. Relatives of her victims in some cases made elaborate plans to kill her should she ever be released. They saw release or forgiveness for her as impossible and claimed that if she were released no child would be safe from her.

Image and reality: a discussion

Was there in fact any reason not to forgive or release this woman? These are two separate questions. Criminals, even those given a life sentence who have not been forgiven by their victims or by the public, are regularly released on parole yet with Myra Hindley the two issues of forgiveness and release were rendered co-dependent. It seemed impossible to separate the crime and the woman.

The press mounted what was in the 1960s an unprecedented campaign against this woman, a campaign which gained support among the tabloid readers and voters. This led Hindley to claim that she was a political prisoner. There is a sense in which this is true: it is politically useful to have one person to whom a government can point in order to reinforce their claim to be 'tough on crime'. It is also politically expedient to have one area of populist feeling to which the government is seen to have sided with the tabloids rather than the broadsheets. But there was more to Myra Hindley than that. She claimed also, as we will see later, to be the innocent sacrificial victim, the crucified Christ, the classical scapegoat carrying the sins of the world. It is true that she served this purpose. As long as Myra Hindley was held in prison, all other women murderers were safe from the intensity of hatred she had aroused. She was right when she described herself as holding the 'projected hatred, fear and fury of the nation's psyche'. She may have been absolved by her confessor; that may be what gave her confidence in her redemption but to compare her with Christ savours of blasphemy ... until we remember that the High Priest claimed that Christ was guilty. He too could have claimed to be a political prisoner whose crucifixion placated the mob.[15]

---

[14] *The Herald*, 14 September 1999.
[15] John 18:19–37; 19:4–12.

From the beginning the official police 'mug shot', on which Marcus Harvey's painting, *Myra*, is based, has been part of the argument. It shows a woman with bleached blonde hair, heavy dark eyebrows, thick mascara and lipstick with shadows under her eyes and a sullen look; she could be 40 years of age rather than the 23 she was when it was taken. More recent photographs show a woman looking younger than her 60 years, with short brown hair and a pleasant expression – the kind of woman you might encounter in a bookshop or at an evening lecture. The first picture invites us to imagine a tough, emotionally hardened and sexually experienced woman of low social status. The other, taken after 20 years in prison, offers a more middle-class image of someone friendly, intelligent (by this time she had taken an Open University degree) and attractive in a low-key way. Another, taken with a woman prison governor and her dog in a garden, offers a variety of messages about a woman comfortable with authority, fond of animals and the natural world. These are rarely seen.

In an article published in the January 1998 issue of the *London Review of Books*, Marina Warner offers the thought that 'Protestant scepticism about the power of pictures has been weakening for a long time, and a new Catholic confusion between image and reality has been in the ascendant.' The Puritan iconoclasts of the sixteenth and seventeenth centuries hacking their way through religious images in cathedrals and churches feared that worshippers believed the image and what it represented to be one and the same. This was the 'Catholic confusion' to which Marina Warner is referring. The capacity of statues and paintings to tell stories and to inspire devotion was thought to outweigh any moral danger of idolatry. Warner appears to be arguing that the blurring of image and reality, aided by the increasing popularity of films and television, is now not challenged.[16]

She uses this thought to illustrate the reaction to Marcus Harvey's painting, which was shown in the Sensations Exhibition at the Royal Academy in 1997. The police photograph, widely circulated and used by the press whenever yet another article about her was published, had gained an iconic quality long before Marcus Harvey decided to use it as the basis for his painting. Instantly recognizable, carrying the same impact as Warhol's famous portrait of Marilyn Monroe, Hindley's epitomized evil as Monroe's embodied sexuality. Marcus Harvey, using Hindley's 30-year-old photograph as a basic image in his painting, covered it with handprints of a 4-year-old child (Fig. 2). The result was immediate and awful: the message clear. In point of fact none of the children killed was as young as four years of age; the image was constructed by the artist in a way which emphasized the innocence of the victims and therefore the evil of the killer.

It aroused fury and protest from a variety of sources. People who had kept their hatred of Hindley alive since the trial, one of them a relative of one of the victims, attacked the picture directly, throwing ink and eggs at it. Others who thought she had suffered enough and should now be released were appalled at the idea that a human being was being exploited in this way. Myra Hindley herself protested. Warner describes Harvey's portrait as a classic example of a *pittura infamante* – a portrait intended to defame, where the image enters the argument and fixes the

---

[16] Marina Warner, 'Peroxide Mug-Shot', *London Review of Books*, Vol. 20, No. 1, January 1998.

identity of its subject. Whenever this portrait of Hindley is seen, it tells the story of its subject as an evil woman. It could be seen as giving a theological message.

The Hindley portrait takes its place in the long history of attacks on paintings which demand a response. Here Freedberg's view is that in some cases damaging the representation is thought to damage the person whom it represents: 'At the very least, something of the disgrace of mutilation or destruction is felt to pass on to the person represented.'[17] Furthermore, 'The dishonour paid to the image ... does not simply pass to its prototype but actually damages the prototype.'[18] Hindley remained a *cause célèbre* for the media and her every action watched. The public was constantly reminded of the horrendous nature of her crimes and encouraged in the view that she could neither be released nor forgiven. One newspaper, *The Sun*, which long campaigned against her release, polled its readers when her last appeal was being considered and, unsurprisingly, the great majority voted to keep her in prison.

As was said earlier, a succession of Home Secretaries had rejected her appeals, the most recent leading to the judicial decision in December 1997 that the Home Secretary is entitled to decide that she must die in prison. On the other hand the judges agreed, to the horror of the victim's families, that cases like Hindley's must remain open to review. One mother said, 'She is an evil woman and should rot in hell.' The other, who is dying of cancer, said, 'I will rest in peace and I'll tell you, I will haunt that woman from my passing on. From that minute, if there's such a thing as haunting and ghosts, I will be on her shoulder, morning, noon and night.' But in October 2000, the Lord Chief Justice, interviewed in the *New Statesman*,[19] appeared to infer that she 'may hope for freedom and that the handling of her case reeks of injustice'.

It is clear that more than thirty years after the death of their children the parents' hatred of Hindley has not eased. Those children who would by 2002 have been in their late forties are unchanged in memory for their parents, whose pain seems unabated, kept alive in the furnace of their anger. It is clear from reading the tabloid newspapers over the years that the relatives continue to receive massive public support to nourish that anger as the story of the Moors Murders is passed from generation to generation. The death of Myra Hindley evoked an ugly flare-up of public feeling; notions of the possibility of redemption and forgiveness were singularly lacking from the discourse.

It was on Myra Hindley alone that the burden had fallen of proving her humanity, her membership of our community, a being with free will capable of both sin and redemption. She was seen only as being capable of sin which is unredeemable. The notion of a sin for which there is no forgiveness is well established and subject to a range of interpretations. It allows for what may be a need for the human imagination to maintain an undefined, reserved area for the inconceivable. It can also be a need for reassurance that there may be some acts which even we, evil, guilty creatures though we may see ourselves as being, would

---

[17] Freedberg, *Power of Images*, p. 413.

[18] Ibid., p. 415.

[19] *New Statesman*, 16 October 2000, p. 18. It is interesting to note that this issue of the *New Statesman* used the 1966 iconic photograph of Myra Hindley on its front cover.

not commit. The sin for which there is no forgiveness offers us a boundary which we cannot imagine ourselves crossing.

The Story of Mary Bell

In 1968, two years after the trial of Myra Hindley, an 11-year-old child, Mary Bell, was tried in a public court and, along with another, 13-year-old Norma, accused of manslaughter after the deaths of two small boys in Newcastle upon Tyne. She was sentenced to detention for life; the other child was acquitted. The writer and commentator on the nature of evil, Gitta Sereny, attended the trial and over the next two years researched and wrote the classic study, *The Case of Mary Bell*.[20] Her central concern was to understand the question: what makes a child kill another child? She came to believe that only when such a child became an adult would it be possible to hope for an understanding.

Twenty-seven years after her conviction, her release on parole and after her mother's death, Mary Bell agreed to talk to Sereny. She talked about her childhood, the murders of the children, the public trial and her twelve years of detention. The result was published as *Cries Unheard*.[21] The story that unfolded was deeply painful. This girl's childhood had been one of gross emotional, physical and sexual abuse. Her mother, clearly unstable, had emotionally rejected her from birth, was suspected of having tried to poison her in infancy and, working herself in prostitution, had violently forced the child, from her pre-school days, into mainly oral sexual activity with her male customers.

The result of this abuse was a deeply disturbed, if intelligent, child whom no one in her environment recognized as needing help. What emerged about the murders was the absolute inability of this child to understand the concept of death. The psychiatrist interviewing her for the court reported that she 'showed no evidence of mental illness or severe subnormality, or subnormality of intelligence', but had a 'severe disorder of personality ... [which] required medical treatment'.[22] The court prosecutor described her as '... a most abnormal child: aggressive, vicious, cruel, incapable of remorse ... a dominating personality with a somewhat unusual intelligence and a degree of fiendish cunning that is almost terrifying ...'. Mary was found guilty on two charges of manslaughter, the other child was found not guilty, the implication being that she had been under Mary's domination.

The trial judge, after pronouncing sentence, made a formal statement that if it had been possible he would have made a hospital order so that Mary could have gone to a mental institution to receive treatment under a restriction order. This was not possible since there was no suitable hospital available. All that was left to him was a sentence of detention for life. The first seven years of this were spent in an approved school. She was fortunate in finding a humane headmaster with whom she could make a relationship. This was particularly important in view of her earlier abuse by men.

---

[20] Gitta Sereny, *The Case of Mary Bell*, Pimlico: London 1998.

[21] Gitta Sereny, *Cries Unheard: The Story of Mary Bell*, Macmillan: London 1998.

[22] Three years later, in 1971, reassessing Mary on behalf of the Home Office, he wrote an entirely positive opinion of her and recommended that she should be considered for release by 1975.

At 18, Mary could have been released but, against the advice of those professionals who had worked with her, was sent to an adult prison for the next seven years. This was not a helpful experience for her but she was stronger now and more able to cope. She was released on parole in 1980 and given a new name and a new identity. Later she entered into a relationship which led to her having a baby daughter. Since her release she has committed no offence.

When the news of Sereny's book was published, frenzy broke out in the press to find out where Mary was living so that she could be interviewed. Mary's daughter, now 14, was suddenly confronted with her mother's history; Mary had been waiting until she was older to tell her the truth. It emerged that tabloid newspapers had been stalking her for 18 years since her release in spite of a court ruling to protect her identity for the sake of her daughter. The press claimed that they had the moral duty to hunt Mary down when it emerged that she had accepted a modest amount of money from Sereny to help her put a deposit on a house. Sereny said she had felt morally compelled to share some of the profits from the book and not use Mary as she had been used in the past. The result was a witch-hunt by the tabloid press; even the Prime Minister and Home Secretary, when asked, condemned Mary for taking the money rather than condemning the tabloids for besieging her home and family. Mary and her teenage daughter had to be taken to a safe house.

Discussion

Free for 18 years, deemed by law to have paid the penalty for her crime, Mary Bell had previously disappeared into the freedom of anonymity. This disappearance also gave the parents of the dead children the possibility of freedom from the pain of the past. Both had suffered greatly. The mother of one of the boys said, 'Mary Bell died when she left prison and took on a new identity. I thought of her as dead; I tried to have a decent life. I started to learn not to hate her, because she had died and become someone else. Now Gitta Sereny has resurrected her. Why?'[23]

Sereny's motivation is clearly expressed in the conclusion to her book. She wanted to show how such a terrible story comes about, with all the many flaws it uncovers – primarily within the family, but also within the community. Relatives, closing ranks against outsiders, tend to protect their own, unmindful or unaware of the consequences; neighbours close their ears to manifestly serious troubles next door. Over-extended police officers underrate the potential dangers in conflict between parent and child and almost invariably side with the parent against the child (unless children, on the rare occasions that they do so, complain of sexual abuse). Social workers protect their relationship with parents at the expense of children, and overworked primary-school teachers are seriously undertrained in the detection of disturbance in their charges. We do not look carefully at our neighbours' children: 'Above all, we do not listen to them – forgive me for repeating it yet again – or hear their cries.'[24]

These are good reasons for Sereny writing the book and it contains important messages for the kind of steps that could be taken to prevent future tragedies. What

---

[23] *The Observer*, 3 May 1998.
[24] Sereny, *Cries Unheard*, p. 374.

she offers is also a commentary on community responsibility. What the consequences of the book's publication present are questions about a community's response to 'sinful' behaviour in a child. Although led by *The Sun*, all the newspapers, tabloid and broadsheet, seized the opportunity to retell the story of the murders and repeat, even with apparent disdain, the phrases describing the child Mary as 'cruel', 'inhuman', a 'beautiful icon of evil'. Sereny is the only consistent advocate she has had.

The Story of James Bulger

In 1993, two 10-year-old boys, Robert Thompson and Jon Venables, both with learning difficulties, and behaviour and school attendance problems, abducted and killed a 2-year-old boy, James Bulger. Like Mary Bell they were publicly tried and convicted. Unlike the previous two case studies, the story associated with them is known by the name of the victim rather than the offenders. The child's mother was shopping with him in an arcade. While her attention was distracted he wandered off and was led away by the two boys. Holding his hands, they made their way out of the arcade, apparently aimlessly through the town and ended up on a railway siding where they appear to have treated the child as an object to be explored and then left on the track to be run over. Opinion is divided as to whether this was deliberate torture and cruelty or childish ignorance and emotional disturbance.

The reaction to this happening swept the country, in part because a video film of the two children leading the toddler out of the shopping arcade to his death was continuously presented on television with photographs from it in all the newspapers. When the public trial was over and the boys sentenced, the poet Blake Morrison was moved to write a book.[25] He describes how, at the trial, he discovered a sad ritual of condemnation with two bewildered children at its centre. For a month the police and witnesses described the 'how' of what had happened. Morrison sought to understand the 'why'. He opens with a quotation from *Macbeth*:

> ... From this instant,
> There's nothing serious in mortality.
> All is but toys, renown and grace is dead,
> The wine of life is drawn ...

And the book reflects that sensitivity.

The public response was massive condemnation of these children. They were described as 'monsters', and when the news of their detention was first announced the press besieged the school they attended, trying to interview their classmates.[26] The main trigger for this was the continuous representation in newspapers and on television of the video camera footage. There was something desperately appealing and distressing in knowing what the result had been of this apparently innocent image. James became an icon of innocence. An industry of making harnesses with

[25] Blake Morrison, *As If*, Granta Books: London 1997.
[26] David James Smith, *The Sleep of Reason: The James Bulger Case*, Century: London 1994, p. 169.

reins for toddlers exploded in order that parents could hold on to their children while shopping. Tabloids, as well as demonizing Jon and Robert, gave the impression that no child would ever be safe again.

When sentencing the boys to detention during Her Majesty's Pleasure, the trial judge, Mr Justice Morland, said, 'The killing of James Bulger was an act of unparalleled evil and barbarity . . . your conduct was both cunning and wicked.'[27] He went on to say that the secure detention should be for 'very, very, many years, until the Home Secretary is satisfied that you have matured and are fully rehabilitated and are no longer a danger to others'.

In order to confront the 'why' not addressed at the trial, Morrison went to the children's hometown of Liverpool seeking explanation in their family background. Even with Morrison's poetic and sympathetic understanding and identification with the difficulties of parenthood, it is clear that childhood for these boys was one in which violence, ugly relationships and neglect were part of the fabric. But what is even clearer is that the parents as well as the boys were living in what one reporter described as 'an environment of social and economic deprivation, of trashy television and cultural poverty, inadequate social services, failed schooling and general confusion'.[28]

For eight years these two boys were held in a secure unit and, ironically, they were given opportunities denied them in the horrifying, cruel conditions of their earlier lives. The professionals caring for them, impressed by their personal and emotional growth, began to prepare for their release. This involved giving them new identities, carefully manufactured histories, and preparing new lives for them in different parts of the country. Fearing the same media response as with Mary Bell, their lawyers asked the High Court to impose a permanent injunction banning the media from revealing the slightest detail of their lives. The photographs of these two boys at the age of ten were still being endlessly recycled in the media's iconography of evil in the same way as Myra Hindley's 1966 photograph.

In the year 2000, the lengths of sentence appropriate for the two boys came up for review. Lord Woolf, who had been given this task, opined that they should be considered for parole in 2001, when they would be 18 years of age. In his view they had benefited morally and educationally from their custodial regime and would only deteriorate if, as would be necessary after the age of 18, they were transferred to an institution for young offenders where they would be exposed to corrupting influence. He showed a sensitive, understated understanding of the personal and social factors involved in the original offence.

His view aroused outrage from the tabloids and participants in radio 'phone-in' programmes. Every detail of the most horrendous aspects of the murder was repeated and the word 'evil' lavishly used both as a noun and an adjective. Jamie Bulger's mother, perhaps understandably, pressed for them to be imprisoned for many more years; his father threatened that if the boys were released, he would hunt them down wherever they were hidden.[29] A few voices were raised in defence of the

---

[27] Ibid., p. 226.

[28] Audrey Gillan, *The Guardian*, 1 November 2000.

[29] They have been given new identities and may not even be able to live in this country, so violent is the reaction against them. They will have to reinvent themselves.

boys, arguing a more complex, but largely ignored case, not only for their release but questioning if they should have been exposed to the rigours of criminal law in the first place.

The response of the media to the request for an injunction against media reporting about the two boys after their release was immediate and punitive. James Bulger's mother became part of the tabloid campaign to prevent the injunction. Her claim was that justice required that these boys should also serve a long prison sentence, while the newspapers claimed that the injunction was an attack on the freedom of the press. Hate campaigns seem to sell newspapers. In the event the injunction to protect the boys' identity was granted. This was later extended to preserve their anonymity for life on the grounds that they are seriously at risk of death or injury if their identity or whereabouts become public knowledge. This is due to the fact that in human rights issues British courts have now to take into account case law from the European Court of Human Rights in Strasbourg. Under article 2 of the convention, the State is obliged to protect an individual's right to life. The boys were released on parole in the year 2001.[30] They were the first to be granted a permanent injunction to protect their identities. Mary Bell and her daughter had only been granted strict but temporary injunctions. However, by 2003, they had already been given, out of necessity, three new identities by the UK Home Office, and their lawyers then felt it appropriate to claim a permanent injunction for Mary and her daughter. This was successful.

Discussion

These two case studies share some characteristics. The three children principally involved came from backgrounds which did little to develop in them a sense of the importance of caring for themselves or for others. Each child had been exposed in different ways to forms of violence and neglect. Each of them showed disturbances of behaviour which were either not recognized or else ignored by those adults who might have been expected to seek help for them. What Sereny said about the failure of adults, both neighbours and professionals, in recognizing and intervening in the distresses of Mary Bell's childhood applies equally to the childhoods of Robert Thompson and Jon Venables. One is left with a sense of families living in isolation in a fractured community.

It also seems clear that none of these children should have been dealt with by a public trial. Britain, unlike many other European countries, has clung to a very low age of criminal responsibility. In 1933, the age of criminal responsibility was raised from seven to eight; in 1963, when the Children and Young Persons' Act was revised, it was raised to ten. The ages of these three children ranged from ten to twelve and the impression of most watchers at the trial was that none of them had any idea of what was happening around them. Nor does it seem likely from the evidence that they fully understood the effect of their actions on the children they killed.

---

[30] *The Guardian*, 9 January 2001.

The Story of Sarah Payne

We turn now to a story of a child killed by an adult. In the summer of 2000, the body of an 8-year-old child, Sarah Payne, was found dead, 20 days after her disappearance from a field near her home where she had been playing with her brothers. Throughout the disappearance, her parents, particularly her mother, made dramatic appeals on television for her recovery and after a high-profile funeral launched a campaign for a law to be passed in this country, similar to the American 'Megan's Law', which entitled citizens to be told of any paedophiles living in their area. The British law would, they hoped, be called 'Sarah's Law'. This story of Sarah Payne is really the story of the consequences of her murder.

In the last weeks of July and the early weeks of August 2000, the issue of paedophilia dominated the news media. This word, torn from its original meaning, is popularly used to describe the sexual abuse of children. The *News of the World*, noted for its salacious content, had a new young editor anxious to make her name. On 23 July she decided to publish, every week, lists of the names and locations, as well as photographs, of known paedophiles. This task was carried out under the heading of 'Naming and Shaming'. This slogan was borrowed from a government-led campaign intended to improve standards of service in public utilities like health and education. It was thought that the public shaming of services that were not meeting desirable standards would mobilize staff to improve performance. The *News of the World* claimed that the government was failing to protect children and by naming and shaming the paedophiles, it would force them to take action.

Their stated intention was to alert parents to the possibility that men – there was no mention of women[31] – who had a history of sexually abusing children were living in their community. The implication for parents was that all their children were at risk and urgently needed protection. This fear required them to buy the *News of the World* until the total number of descriptions – about 10,000 – was published. This would take several months. In addition the newspaper ran a campaign to compel the government to give members of the public open access to these names. Their petition to this effect collected 300,000 signatures. The newspaper's language throughout the campaign was luridly emotive: paedophiles were evil perverts lurking round every corner ready to pounce on beautiful, innocent, unsuspecting children. As in medieval times, the Devil was stalking the world.

The result could have been anticipated, and indeed was, by *News of the World*'s critics. Aggressive groups gathered to attack those with names or appearances similar to those published, whom they thought were paedophiles although they had no evidence of this. In every case those whom they attacked were innocent. In one case a paediatrician was attacked because the word was thought to describe a paedophile. The paedophiles understandably went to ground; this result of the campaign caused serious concern to the police and probation service who had been supervising their behaviour. Mothers took their young children on marches, and

---

[31] There is a small proportion of women who sexually abuse small children sometimes in quite terrible ways, like inserting sharp objects into the vagina of a girl child or more commonly stimulating or damaging the penis of small boys. These, like the activities of male paedophiles, are mostly carried out by women against their own children, or in the case of men, stepchildren, and happen within the home.

were heard coaching them to shout slogans asking for sex killers to be killed themselves.[32]

The police described those individuals who attacked the paedophiles as mainly young men between the ages of 16 and 20, who seemed to be enjoying the violence. The broadsheet newspapers, police and probation officers, as well as agencies concerned with childcare, tried day after day to offset the hysteria and bring a note of reason into the picture but those efforts were overwhelmed by the moral panic created by the newspaper.

An unhappy dichotomy exists which separates those who read the broadsheets and have been educated to middle-class attitudes of reason and detachment to issues like sex attacks on children, from those who read tabloids like *News of the World* and live in communities where their children are more at risk from such attacks. We are not now talking about sexual abuse within families, which is equally distributed across the social classes. We are talking about opportunistic attacks on young children who may, for a variety of complex reasons to do with social deprivation, be less protected and more vulnerable to approaches from strangers than middle-class children. These are those most likely to make up the average of eight killed every year, a figure which is relatively static and bears no relationship to the numbers of children being abused without being killed.

Discussion

It is not surprising that it is the members of poorer communities who respond with fear, outrage, aggression and grief when yet another of their children is damaged in this way. Paedophiles being rehoused after serving a prison sentence are not allocated to the leafy suburbs. They are inevitably placed in less desirable housing estates which already have a higher than usual proportion of disadvantaged families, for example, single parents or the unemployed. Nor is it surprising that the public style of the response is irrational and becomes a focus not only for the particular issue involved but also for the anger and humiliations that make up such a large part of the lives of those excluded from social advantage.

The group, Residents Against Paedophiles, led seven nights of vigilantism on the run-down neighbourhood of Poulsgrove, in Portsmouth, England. The spokeswoman for the group claimed that this kind of behaviour was the only way in which they got attention. In a newspaper interview she said, 'How else is anyone going to listen to a common person like me?' This statement of powerlessness needs to be acknowledged. She also talked to the interviewer about the drive behind her anger: she had been abused at the ages of five and six by her paternal grandfather and was later abused while in the care of the local authority. She admitted that she had never dealt with her feelings about being abused and didn't expect she ever would. Since no one had ever been available to help her, that is not surprising.

Young children in a family or in a community can be a symbol of hope, the hope that perhaps their lives can be better than those of the adults. It is a myth that regenerates with every child born into a community, and particularly poor

---

[32] BBC, *Today* programme, Radio 4, 9 August 2000.

communities, who lavish what they can on their children until hope is exhausted. The wanton death of a child threatens the myth for everyone. Such a murderer is not just a sinner. The *News of the World* touches on a deep nerve when it describes such a person as a monster. The intention may be to increase their circulation figures but what they print is based on a deep understanding of what experience has taught them will arouse strong feelings.

The two episodes of children killing children, instead of raising massive public awareness of the questions that needed to be asked about why children committed these horrifying acts against other children, appeared from the popular newspaper, television and radio responses to be focused almost entirely on issues of punishment and revenge. Notions of redemption were derided, the word 'evil' was heard everywhere – applied not only to the behaviour of these children but to the children themselves. The notion that a moral rejection of their behaviour could be compatible with concern and compassion, together with a refusal to blame the children, seemed too far an emotional step to take.

For some, a painful consequence of the public failure to address the underlying meaning of these episodes has been the loss of the myth of childhood innocence. The myth had also been threatened by the increased publicity that surfaced in the 1990s about the pervasive nature of sexual abuse of children. It is difficult to look at the reality of our new knowledge about the sexual abuse of children. Fathers have become self-conscious about the way in which they physically handle their children and men who previously would have thought nothing of talking innocently to a small child in the park restrain themselves for fear their motives would be misunderstood.[33] These murders of children by children took the loss of innocence a step further – children themselves could no longer be trusted. Public discourse concentrated, not on rehabilitation of the children whose history showed them to have been exposed to deeply damaging experiences before they committed these murders,[34] but on the conviction that they were incapable of redemption.[35]

Conclusion

We have looked at four case studies which have involved the deaths of children. In only one of these has there been any presentation of the Christian case for redemption and forgiveness of the offender, and this has been presented only by the offender herself, Myra Hindley, and a few of her supporters. In all of the cases public reaction has focused on hatred and revenge. There has been little or no attempt on the part of the State as it is represented in the justiciary or its public

---

[33] For a disturbingly honest discussion of this see Morrison, *As If*, Chapter 10.

[34] Martha Klein in *Determinism, Blameworthiness, and Deprivation*, Clarendon: Oxford 1990, asks the question: 'How can someone be morally responsible for his acts if he is not responsible for the desires and beliefs which motivate him?' She also refers to the research work of John Bowlby in his seminal work, *Child Care and the Growth of Love; based on the report on Maternal Care and Mental Health; abridged and edited by Margery Fry*, Penguin Books: Harmondsworth 1953.

[35] This was precisely the dilemma that faced Myra Hindley and those who wished to see her released before her death.

servants to moderate this reaction in any way. In some cases, particularly those of Mary Bell, Robert Thompson and Jon Venables, comments made at the trial seem to have fanned the flames. The most vicious statements have come from the press, particularly the tabloid press, but even the broadsheets, while superficially less condemnatory of those responsible for the killings, have failed at every level to challenge the condemnation. It was only when the attacks on paedophiles – or rather those who were thought to be paedophiles – were moving toward mob rule that the more responsible papers reacted sharply against the *News of the World*.

No moral leadership was offered by any of the Christian denominations. A moral vacuum was created into which feelings of anger, hatred and revenge were poured. No public voices were raised from the churches preaching messages of redemption and forgiveness. Lord Longford, one of the few to offer support to Myra Hindley which was openly based on a Christian conviction and who publicly advocated mercy for her, was ridiculed. There may have been others who shared his view but what action they took appears to have been in private rather than in the market-place. Statements quoted in the press about those who committed the murders being 'evil', 'devils', 'deserving to burn in hell' seem not to have evoked a response, in public at least, by any church representative.

Individual 'Christian' responses tended to be fiercely punitive and supportive of the more dramatic tabloid headlines. There was one exception. In an Episcopalian church in Scotland the vicar chose to preach a sermon on forgiveness of sin. Using Myra Hindley as an example he asked the question: if she cannot be forgiven, where is forgiveness for the rest of us? Is there a line above which some stand and others fall below? This brave act of putting his head above the barricades resulted in him being reported to the Bishop by a member of the congregation.

Richard Holloway[36] suggests that tabloid newspapers have replaced the church institutions which once exerted real authority over us but have now lost their power. It was they who first enforced sanctions and later shame and social banishment reinforced by social stigma. This is certainly how the tabloids have operated in the case studies I have described. If this is so, what has happened to the concept of redemption which has been central to the Christian faith? We have seen little sign of it; the consistent emphasis has been on the permanence of evil. Love, mercy, tenderness and compassion, or even a serious scientific attempt at rational understanding of causes, seem to have no part to play in this modern discourse.[37]

These humans pursued by the press may indeed be considered as the sacrificial victims onto whom we can for the moment concentrate all the pollution that threatens us. We are also forced to recognize that as a community, in what is increasingly being described as a post-Christian society, we are in an uncomfortable period which may be described as transitional but is certainly confusing for many. Adam Phillips, the psychoanalyst, offers the thought that in Britain psychoanalysis

---

[36] Richard Holloway, *Godless Morality*, Canongate: Edinburgh 1999, p. 30.

[37] The absence of serious analysis of causes may be partly due to an academic tradition which has firmly separated analytical statements which are seen as 'respectable' from moral statements which are seen as inferior. The market-place is not seen as suitable for academic, let alone 'moral' or 'ethical' thought.

is 'redescribed Christianity'.[38] Certainly what attempts have been made to understand and even to forgive the offenders in these murders have been based on a psychological rather than a religious approach.

The certainties which in the past gave the State the power to hang men and women and even children for murdering a fellow human being have been eroded. As a community we moved from a debate on revenge, based very often on a reading of the Hebrew Bible, to a debate on deterrence, assumed to be a scientific mode (dealing with the question whether capital punishment deterred people from crime), to a debate on whether capital punishment could be a tolerable feature of a civilized society – in other words, the new question became part of a new debate on the morality of hanging. This had only a tangential relationship to the view expressed by groups like the Quakers, drawing on the Christian Bible for authority. The power to hang men and women was withdrawn from the State because the majority of members of Parliament had become convinced that this was not 'civilized' behaviour. They were claiming authority from social and political rather than religious sources.

What was not fully realized was that hanging was not the only thing abolished. With it went the rituals that had for the bereaved and for the wider citizenry brought the issues exposed by the act of murder back into balance; the murder of one's fellow citizens is a deeply destabilizing act. In previous centuries the Church and State had combined to provide rituals which met most human crises or rites of passage. Hanging was one such ritual where the prisoner went to his death in the company of the hangman and prison governor representing the State and a chaplain representing the Church. Order was restored in this way. New questions are being raised about the relationship of the State and the Church and the appropriateness of them combining in public affairs.

The vacuum created by the abolition of hanging indicates that we have not yet acquired a new language and new rituals to help us cope with the age-old questions of justice, sin and redemption as they apply to Myra Hindley, Mary Bell, Robert Thompson, Jon Venables, or Roy Whiting, found guilty of the murder of Sarah Payne in December 2001. Whiting was given a life tariff, with 'life to mean life'. What we have now is a punitive emphasis on marginality and abnormality. The paradox is that this very marginality has placed our offenders as central figures in the drama, in the same way as Christ's marginality placed him as the central figure in the drama of the crucifixion.

These stories remind us of the important point at which a shift in the perception of a problem occurs. It was anticipated by Dostoevsky in his story-within-a-story of *The Grand Inquisitor*.[39] We read in this of the clash of values presented when Jesus appears among the crowd attending the great church ritual of the *auto-da-fé*. His love and compassion are seen by the Grand Inquisitor as a dangerous challenge to the authority of the Church. Jesus has to be eliminated in order to preserve the power of the Church. We are however now living in a time when the Church no

---

[38] Adam Phillips, *Promises, Promises: Essays on Literature and Psychoanalysis*, Faber & Faber: London 2000.

[39] Fyodor Dostoevsky, *The Karamazov Brothers*, Oxford University Press: Oxford, 1994, Book Five, p. 309.

longer appears to have the authority it secured by allying itself with the State. We appear to be facing a vacuum which is being filled by crude responses that are fuelled by vengeful instincts and commercial interests.

The philosopher Raymond Gaita reminds us that there are 'voices in our culture that speak of different possibilities' and looks to Sophocles' *Oedipus the King* where the chorus combines moral severity with pity.[40] They sum up the dilemma facing many of us struggling to find a response:

> I pity you but I can't bear to look.
> I've much to ask, so much to learn,
> So much fascinates my eyes,
> But you ... I shudder at the sight.[41]

We do indeed shudder at the sight of murder, cruelty and torture – all of which we have seen acted out in these stories. But is it not also right to shudder at the damaged and broken lives of the perpetrators of those horrors and at the brutality of the responses to their behaviour and the character of socially disintegrated and excluded communities which make such behaviour more likely? Do we shudder at the person, whether it be the murderer or the paedophile, do we follow the advice of a previous Prime Minister, John Major, who advised us to understand less and condemn more, or do we re-examine our ancient human commitment to forgiveness, redemption and reintegration?

In the next chapter we will have an opportunity to look at some of the alternatives offered in art and literature.

---

[40] Raimond Gaita, *A Common Humanity: thinking about love and truth and justice*. Routledge: London and New York 2000, p. xiii.

[41] Sophocles, *The Three Theban Plays*, trans. Robert Fagles, Penguin Classics, Penguin Books: London, 1984, p. 238, lines 1439–42.

2

Responses to Sin and Forgiveness
in Art and Literature

Introduction

In this chapter I consider some responses in art and literature to sin and forgiveness. I offer one example from art in the seventeenth century and the rest from literature written in the nineteenth and twentieth centuries. The first two examples, Rembrandt's painting of *The Return of the Prodigal Son*[1] and Hawthorne's novel *The Scarlet Letter*,[2] are set in a context which would clearly define itself as Christian but which was moving away from some earlier understandings of what that implied. Simon Wiesenthal's *The Sunflower*[3] then poses a range of responses from the Jewish, the Christian and the atheistic traditions following the profound cultural shock of what has come to be known as the Holocaust. The three examples which follow, Margaret Atwood's *The Handmaid's Tale*,[4] Bernhard Schlinck's *The Reader*[5] and Alice Walker's poem, 'Goodnight, Willie Lee, I'll See You in the Morning',[6] grow from a period which has moved uneasily from seeing itself as Christian to an uncertainty about its beliefs and a search for a new basis of moral judgement – a period sometimes described as post-Christian.

Rembrandt and the Parable of the Prodigal Son

The story of the prodigal son performs two functions simultaneously: it conjures up an image and is charged with emotion. In Jungian terms, this would identify it as an archetype, that is, the image is charged with numinosity or psychic energy: 'it becomes dynamic, and consequences of some kind must flow from it'.[7] The story is recognized as a literary masterpiece: phrases from it have become part of many languages. Both painters and story-tellers have used it as an artistic source. It has also been used as a basis for a variety of theological interpretations by such varying figures as Jerome, Ambrose, Tertullian, Calvin and Luther. More recently it has

---

[1] Rembrandt, *The Return of the Prodigal Son*, in the Hermitage Museum, St Petersburg.

[2] Nathaniel Hawthorne, *The Scarlet Letter*, The World's Classics, Oxford University Press: Oxford 1990.

[3] Simon Wiesenthal, *The Sunflower*, Schocken Books: New York 1998. This edition includes a symposium edited by H.J. Cargas and B.V. Fetterman.

[4] Margaret Atwood, *The Handmaid's Tale*, Vintage: London 1996.

[5] Bernhard Schlink, *The Reader*, trans. Carol Brown Janeway, A Phoenix Paperback, Orion Books Ltd, London 1997.

[6] Alice Walker, *Goodnight, Willie Lee, I'll See You in the Morning*, The Women's Press: London 1995.

[7] Carl G. Jung, *Man and his Symbols*, Aldus Books: London 1964, p. 96.

been the subject of psychological and secular interpretations. It touches the essence of human fears and hopes, miseries and joys. Its theme is echoed in Flannery O'Connor's short story 'Redemption' and Clint Eastwood's film *Unforgiven*, while in northern Uganda, the Church has been using the parable in an attempt to bring about reconciliation with the Acholi people, who were subjected to horrifying violence.[8]

Luke's story of the parable of the prodigal son as told by Jesus

The parable of the prodigal son appears in the New Testament as follows:

> And he said, A certain man had two sons: and the younger of them said to his father, Father, give me the portion of goods that falleth to me. And he divided unto them his living. And not many days after the younger son gathered all together, and took his journey into a far country, and there wasted his substance with riotous living. And when he had spent all, there arose a mighty famine in that land; and he began to be in want. And he went and joined himself to a citizen of that country; and he sent him into his fields to feed his swine. And he would fain have filled his belly with the husks that the swine did eat: and no man gave unto him. And when he came to himself, he said, How many hired servants of my father's have bread enough and to spare, and I perish with hunger! I will arise and go to my father, and I will say to him, Father, I have sinned before heaven, and before thee, And I am no more worthy to be called thy son: make me as one of thy hired servants.
>
> And he arose and came to his father. But when he was yet a great way off, his father saw him, and had compassion, and ran, and fell upon his neck, and kissed him. And the son said unto him, Father, I have sinned against Heaven, and in thy sight, and am no more worthy to be called thy son. But the father said to his servants, Bring forth the best robe, and put it on him; and put a ring on his hand, and shoes on his feet: And bring hither the fatted calf, and kill it; and let us eat and be merry; For this my son was dead, and is alive again; he was lost, and is found. And they began to be merry.
>
> Now his elder son was in the field: and as he came and drew nigh to the house, he heard musick and dancing. And he called one of the servants, and asked what these things meant. And he said unto him, Thy brother is come; and thy father hath killed the fatted calf, because he hath received him safe and sound. And he was angry and would not go in: therefore came his father out, and entreated him. And he answering said to his father, Lo, these many years do I serve thee, neither transgressed I at any time thy commandment: and yet thou never gavest me a kid, that I might make merry with my friends: But as soon as this thy son was come, which hath devoured thy living with harlots, thou hast killed for him the fatted calf.
>
> And he said to him, Son, thou art ever with me, and all that I have is thine. It was meet that we should make merry, and be glad: for this thy brother was dead, and is alive again; and was lost, and is found.[9]

Luke does not move directly into the story. He prefaces it with two others whose themes are loss, discovery and rejoicing. In the first it is a sheep that is lost, in the

[8] Dr Kevin Ward, 'The Armies of the Lord: Christianity, Rebels and the State in Northern Uganda 1986–1999', Paper presented to the British Association for the Study of Religion: Annual Conference, 6–9 September 1999, Stirling University.

[9] Luke 15:11–32.

second a piece of silver. These are material possessions and it is clear that while they are important they are not essential to the survival of those who have lost them. They would manage without them; nevertheless they are overwhelmed with joy at their recovery. But this has been a one-sided transaction. The sheep and the piece of silver are passive, they take no part in the drama: they wait to be found.

The parable of the prodigal son is of a different order. It is about relationships and about choice. It opens with the words, 'A certain man had two sons', and immediately we are thrown into a human drama. We remember Cain and Abel, we remember Jacob and Esau, we think of rivalry between brothers. The younger makes it clear he wants to take his share of his inheritance and leave. The story goes on to tell us in a severe and simple way how he lost all his money and was reduced to the level of the swine – a powerful image of destitution and degradation. With no one willing to help him he begins to think of his father and the comforts of home. We are told he 'came to himself' – in the tradition of the Hebrew Bible he 'returned' to himself – and in that moment of insight decided to go home and ask forgiveness. Now we come to the core of the story. Before he was near enough to be heard his father saw him 'and ran, and fell upon his neck, and kissed him'. This powerful and total acceptance, the essence of loving forgiveness, did not wait for repentance although the son tries to offer it. The emphasis is on an epiphanic rejoicing: 'For this my son was dead, and is alive again; he was lost, and is found.'[10]

But Luke goes on to describe a further dimension to the story. What does this ecstatic reunion say to the 'good' son who has stayed with the family and worked hard? We learn that he had been in the field when his brother returned. He presumably has caused his father no distress. Understandably he complains that his father has never given *him* a party and in his words we can sense that he feels he has been taken for granted and is resentful because of that. Does this mean that those who are obedient and obey the rules are given less consideration and are less valued than those who cause trouble?[11] This issue is not resolved in the parable since the father simply reaffirms the importance of the elder son's place in his life verbally while continuing to celebrate the joy of finding the one who was lost.

---

[10] This is a drama that is being played out on a daily basis in homes all over the world – often less happily than in this parable. Young people walk out and parents hear nothing of them, sometimes for years. The Salvation Army missing persons unit tries to find them, offering assurances that they will be received home with love and understanding. Every month the magazine, *The Big Issue*, has heart-breaking advertisements asking for information about lost and loved ones. When these lost ones are found they often say they were afraid that if they tried to contact their parents they would be rejected.

[11] This is also a modern dilemma. We read in the tabloids accusations that convicted prisoners and single parents get better treatment than the honest and moral citizen does. This concept of unconditional forgiveness has often been difficult for those who have attempted to live a moral life, obedient to the laws of God, to accept. The view of the elder son is compressed into the phrase, 'it's not fair'. We hear the same story in Northern Ireland where the Unionists feel they have been 'betrayed'. The modern battlegrounds for this issue are to be found in the legal system, the social security system and local authority housing allocations. Justice is not seen to be done when criminals, single parents, immigrants or the homeless are given what appears like special consideration. But the God of Israel, who was the God of Jesus, was seen as having two thrones, one of justice, one of compassion.

Rembrandt's interpretation of the parable

In the seventeenth century, Rembrandt gave us, repeatedly, the greatest visual representation of this parable in his paintings of *The Return of the Prodigal Son*. In the most widely reproduced, which hangs in The Hermitage in St Petersburg, we see in the background three shadowy figures, not identified, though one is thought to be the elder brother. Separate from them, in a pool of golden light, we see the shaven-headed, bedraggled, emaciated, foot-sore, younger son kneeling in front of his father – head bowed, not even able to look up at him. The father bends over him, gently laying his hands on the back of his distressed son. The viewer is given an impression of total acceptance and unquestioning love, what every child seeks from a parent. Clark[12] described it as having 'the completeness of some ancient symbol'. Nouwen[13] points out that Rembrandt has given the father a strong, muscular left hand and a more tender feminine right hand, an observation that Nouwen concedes has been recognized by other commentators. In this way the father offers both fathering and mothering to his repentant son. The great red cloak which the father wears can be seen as a sheltering tent or a womb to which he can return for rebirth. It is the great Christian humanist statement of God's compassion, mercy and forgiveness of sins.

Nathaniel Hawthorne's *The Scarlet Letter*

In this novel, first published in 1850, but set in Boston in the 1640s, Hawthorne creates and develops our perception of a woman, Hester Prynne, who by her sexual behaviour broke the rules of both Church and State in the Puritan theocratic society in which she lived. Arriving in the colony alone, in order to set up their home before her husband arrived, she became illicitly pregnant and gave birth to a child, clearly not her husband's. On release from her imprisonment by the magistrates, Hester was required as part of her punishment to stand and be seen with her child on a scaffolding in the market-place. While in prison, also as part of her punishment, she had been required to sew and wear permanently on her breast the letter A cut out of scarlet cloth, signifying her adultery. This letter A, the scarlet letter of the book's title, emerges as a fundamental symbol of the contradictions and multiple interpretations of Hester's 'sin'.

In 1640s Boston, as in post-Reformation Scotland or Geneva, religion and law were intimately connected. It was essentially a theocratic society. Those who had broken the civil laws or the laws of the Church could expect to be put in the stocks, whipped or hanged. To see others punished seems to be a universal attraction and the women, described by the narrator in this story as watching Hester walk to be publicly displayed on the scaffold, could have been sisters to those women who in the following century were to sit knitting under the guillotine in Paris, or in the twentieth century, those women howling at the prison van carrying Myra Hindley in Manchester. They call for Hester to be hanged or at least branded instead of being

---

[12] Kenneth Clark, *Rembrandt and the Italian Renaissance*, John Murray: London 1996, p. 187.

[13] Henri J.M. Nouwen, *The Return of the Prodigal Son: a story of homecoming*, Darton, Longman & Todd: London 1944, p. 99.

given what they see as a soft option of wearing a badge of shame on the bodice of her gown. They condemn her for having, by her sin, caused grief to their 'godly' pastor, the Reverend Mr Arthur Dimmesdale who is, we realize from this, the visible and outward sign of the town's virtue. Only one young woman, significantly with a child holding her hand, offers a word of sympathy.

When Hester first appears, the reader is immediately struck by her demeanour. This is no chastened sinner seeking forgiveness but a woman standing straight, refusing the restraining hand of the town-beadle, behaving as if the walk she had to take to the pillory for her punishment was taken of her own free will and not under compulsion. In her arms is the 3-month-old baby who is a public sign of the law she has broken. On her breast is another: the scarlet letter A.

But what a letter A! There is nothing modest or cringing about this either. It may have been meant to signify adultery but it also signifies artistry. It immediately challenges the authority of a single interpretation of the Word. With its elaborate and fantastic gold embroidery it appears decorative rather than shameful, matching the splendid clothes she is wearing. These clothes are themselves a challenge to this Puritan community. They recall rather the great liturgical garments of the society from which they had fled to worship in a different way. The narrator describes not only her beauty but also an underlying air of recklessness, a word which conjures a picture of someone who acts out of her will without counting the cost and who, when paying the cost, will not complain. Hawthorne's link with the ideas of the Transcendentalist movement, discussed later in this chapter, is immediately made clear to the reader.

Hester was required, as part of her punishment, to stand, and to be seen, on a scaffolding in the market-place above the crowd gathered round her. Foucault discusses the significance of exhibiting the offender to ensure that it brings the crime 'before everyone's eyes'.[14] This public exhibition of her body, her child and the symbolic wound of the scarlet letter involved the watching crowd in a conspiracy with the guilty verdict given by the magistracy. To be exposed against one's will is a violation of privacy, a kind of nakedness. Her beauty and the child in her arms gave Hawthorne a comparison with the Madonna and Child images so beloved of the Renaissance painters but he cannot resist pointing out that far from Hester's image being one of redemption, she and her child, even in their beauty, represented the darkness of sin. She is more the Magdalene than the Madonna. She is also the Scarlet Woman whose power in the form of the Catholic Church the Protestants feared so deeply. But in another sense she is none of these things. She is simply herself, complete in her own nature. Hawthorne describes Hester, in order to survive, as turning to her imagination, the essential resource of Romanticism, to protect herself by 'phantasmagoric forms, from the cruel weight and hardness of the reality'.[15]

From now on in this narrative we are constantly presented with the ambivalence of Hawthorne's feelings about Hester and her personality. At one level he seems to enjoy and approve of her striking individualism and her spontaneity, at another he

---

[14] Michel Foucault, *Discipline and Punish: the birth of the prison*, trans. Alan Sheridan, Penguin Books: London 1991.

[15] Hawthorne, *Scarlet Letter*, p. 57.

seems to emphasize the importance of public order and conformity which she is constantly challenging simply by being who she is. In this he reflects what must have been a real dilemma for the Puritan settlers. These early settlements were surrounded by uncontrolled nature, inhabited by North American Indians who were seen as savages. Conflicts between the European settlers and the indigenous peoples had resulted in attacks in which many settlers were killed; not just killed but mutilated in ways the Europeans saw as barbaric. Control of feeling, impulse and individuality within the community was a way of dealing with the frightening lack of control of life outside the town boundaries. That was where the powers of darkness and danger to the soul as well as the body were waiting to pounce. Hester was a threat at a subliminal as well as at the conscious level.

Hester's refusal to name the father of her child outraged the elders of the community, who are described by the narrator as sitting on a balcony overlooking the market-place and supervising the punishment. In her refusal she was both denying the right of the elders to ask this question and claiming the primacy of the natural, biological bond between mother and child. This amounted to a denial of the ownership of the child by the father and in the same way the denial of the ownership of woman by man, an ownership which was a fundamental tenet of Christianity in its identification with the Genesis story.

There is a long history of women refusing to name the father of their child – even in this day government welfare agencies deny aid to women who refuse identification. Hester's refusal is a challenge to both the religious and civil authorities. Mr Dimmesdale, the young, much loved and admired pastor referred to earlier, is instructed to 'exhort her to repentance and confession'[16] and to give the name of the man with whom she sinned. He appears reluctant to undertake this task but is driven to deliver a passionate appeal which alerts us for the first time to a powerful link between Hester and himself. Dimmesdale presents another burden Hester will have to bear even if she does not recognize it as such:

> ... I charge thee to speak out the name of thy fellow sinner and fellow sufferer! Be not silent from any mistaken pity or tenderness for him; for, believe me, Hester, though he were to step down from a high place, and stand there beside thee, on thy pedestal of shame, yet were it better so, than to hide a guilty heart through life. What can thy silence do for him except it tempt him – yea, compel him, as it were – to add hypocrisy to sin? Heaven hath granted thee an open ignominy, that thereby thou mayest work out an open triumph over the evil within thee, and the sorrow without. Take heed how thou deniest to him – who, perchance, hath not the courage to grasp it for himself – the bitter, but wholesome, cup that is now presented to thy lips.[17]

This bitter cup can also be seen as linking Hester to the Christ figure who, when on the cross, was given vinegar to drink. She, like Christ, and Myra Hindley, can be seen as a scapegoat carrying the sin of her community. This community must, if the intensity of its attack on her is anything to judge by, have been seething with repressed and acted-out lust. Indeed later in the story she becomes aware that others

---

[16] Ibid., p. 66.
[17] Ibid., p. 67.

may share what she has seen as a sin only she has committed; when she meets certain women her scarlet letter throbs in sympathy.

When Dimmesdale speaks, it is as if he is pleading with her to give him the courage to admit that he is the child's father so that he may stand beside her on the scaffold. He has been replaying the role of St Peter denying Jesus but needs her help to redeem himself. Hester's only response is to shake her head. When pressed by another clergyman, 'Speak out that name! That, and thy repentance, may avail to take the scarlet letter off thy breast', she replies, 'Never', and, 'looking into the deep and troubled eyes' of Dimmesdale, she adds, 'It is too deeply branded. Ye cannot take it off. And would that I might endure his agony as well as mine.'

This last statement is a sentiment that comes from a deep and protective love. It is more usually heard from a parent about their child and reflects a view that when we suffer the pain of sin we have caused pain to God. A 'stern' voice from the crowd, which she recognizes as her husband's, demands that she 'Speak; and give your child a father.' She again refuses, saying, 'And my child must seek a heavenly Father, she shall never know an earthly one!'[18] She is again rejecting the law of man and appealing directly to God. She is accepting her crucifixion. Dimmesdale's response is to say, 'Wondrous strength and generosity of a woman's heart! She will not speak!'

The reader, if not the audience in the town square, is left knowing that this is a passionate woman who has loved deeply and still loves deeply the partner in her downfall. She has rejected now, not only the Church and the civil authority, but any hope of reconciliation with her husband. She appears at this moment as the wild woman who makes no demands on anyone. She is the woman who runs with the wolves.[19]

We sense also, without any hard evidence, that Dimmesdale is that partner and that if he is, he is a weak fellow, unable to take responsibility for his own sins, willing at some level to see Hester as the Eve who tempted him but also as someone who could save him. He is caught in the constrictions of the religion to which he has committed himself but is unable to call on its power to offer grace and forgiveness. It becomes increasingly hard as we continue to read the book to understand how this man summoned up the sexual energy to mate with Hester. We feel she must have been a great natural source of warmth and comfort to which he was fatally drawn but wonder also what so passionately attracted her.

The rest of the story follows Hester's life wearing the scarlet letter. She withdraws to a small house on the fringes of the town, supporting herself and her daughter by her skilful embroidery, living modestly, a marginal figure, constantly exposed to minor humiliations as people feel free to stare at her or comment about her sin. Clergymen stop her in the street and lecture her, drawing a small crowd and, if she goes to church, she might find herself the subject of the sermon. In spite of this she resists the temptation to cover the scarlet letter with her hand. Occasionally the person seeing the symbol is Dimmesdale and for a brief moment she feels both joy that her sin was shared but also a renewed sense of her sinfulness.

---

[18] Ibid., p. 68.

[19] Clarissa Pinkola Estes, *Women Who Run With the Wolves*, Random House: London 1993. Estes argues that feminine wildness is both a positive and necessary quality for women to cultivate.

Her child, Pearl, becomes a lifeline preventing her abandoning hope of salvation and joining in the Satanic practices which we learn are part of the dark side of this 'godly' community. In time she becomes accepted in the town as she sheds her glamorous clothes and adopts a plain appearance. By helping those who are ill or even less fortunate than herself, she acquires a reputation for kindness and good works and her scarlet badge of shame becomes a symbol by which she is recognized and welcomed as one who comes to help and comfort those in distress.

The narrator comments: 'The letter was the symbol of her calling. Such helpfulness was found in her, – so much power to do, and power to sympathize, – that many people refused to interpret the scarlet A by its original signification. They said it meant Able; so strong was Hester Prynne, with a woman's strength.'

But he (and here we see again Hawthorne's ambivalence to his creation) goes on to describe how Hester rejects and refuses to respond to any open gesture of acceptance or warmth directed to her. He suggests that this might derive from pride rather than humility: '... society was inclined to show its former victim a more benign countenance than she cared to be favored with, or perchance, than she deserved'.[20]

This brings into the forefront of our thinking the likelihood that Hester had in fact never seen herself as a victim. What she had become was a mythic figure, a tragic hero coping magnificently with the consequences of an error of behaviour. The scarlet letter takes on a sacred quality; stories circulate in the town about its power. And she herself has developed in her appearance a kind of austerity that sets her apart from other women. By hiding her luxuriant hair and dressing in drab clothes she masks any outward show of her femininity, although the narrator makes it clear that he believes that it could be reawakened. She is the Magdalene, the reformed sinner, who is still seen as dangerous.

While Hester has been trying to make a life for herself and her child, her husband Chillingworth, still not having declared their relationship, pursues Dimmesdale for vengeance, under the guise of helping him. He and Hester have one meeting in which he confronts her with a Calvinist, predestined view of human destiny and suffering. By her sin of adultery she has set in motion a process nothing can change. Even if she had wanted to, there would have been no point in appealing for forgiveness for herself, or for her partner in sin. He has no power to forgive he says; he too is now trapped in the evil she has let loose. He leaves her with the sentence, 'Let the black flower blossom as it may.'

Dimmesdale's punitive conscience acts as an ally in his own destruction. Recognizing what is happening, Hester confronts Dimmesdale with the fact that she still loves him passionately and urges him to flee with her. He agrees but his conscience is unable to face the consequences of such an act. In a dramatic closing sequence, while Hester is listening outside the door of the packed church, waiting for him to join her, out of his guilt and his madness, Dimmesdale preaches the most brilliant and powerful sermon of his life. She hears the sub-text as a cry of pain: 'The complaint of a human heart, sorrow-laden, perchance guilty, telling its secret, whether of guilt or sorrow, to the great heart of mankind: beseeching its sympathy or forgiveness...'.[21]

---

[20] Hawthorne, *Scarlet Letter*, p. 162.
[21] Ibid., p. 243.

There is a procession after the sermon but when Dimmesdale appears at the door of the church he is hardly fit to walk. We are reminded here of Hester's appearance at the door of the prison, which opened the story but with a very different image. There we saw courage, here we see weakness. But as the procession reaches the scaffold he sees Hester and Pearl. Turning towards them, he calls their names. Pearl flies to him and Hester slowly approaches. At this moment, Chillingworth in his demonic mode tries to stop him finding the redemption he clearly is seeking. Dimmesdale rebuffs him and asks Hester's help to make the walk up the steps to the scaffold. There the three, Dimmesdale, Hester and Pearl, stand, united as a family in public for the first time, while Dimmesdale makes his confession to the crowd. He finishes with a dramatic rending of his clothes to show his naked breast – but the narrator refuses to tell us what was to be seen there. That is left to the imagination of the reader and the fantasies of the crowd watching, who later talk of a scarlet A gouged into his flesh. Meanwhile Dimmesdale escapes all, particularly Chillingworth, by dying.

But before he dies he forgives Chillingworth, rejecting that man's Calvinistic view of his own destiny. He asks Pearl to kiss him and by doing so she is released from her demonic inheritance and can release her mother and claim her own future as a loving woman. Dimmesdale says farewell to Hester but when she asks if there is hope for her that they might meet again in eternity he is as selfish as ever, denying her hope and concentrating on his own salvation. Hester is left unredeemed, isolated, the victim of her own will. She and Pearl leave the colony for many years but one day she returns alone, Pearl now respectably and successfully married, having escaped the sins of her parents. Hester replaces the scarlet letter on her breast and, to use Hawthorne's words, 'takes up her long forsaken shame'. Her sin and sorrow live with her until her death when she is buried beside Arthur Dimmesdale, still with no assurance that they will be reunited. On the slab which marked their grave, there was carved a heraldic device: 'On a field, sable, the letter A, gules.'

The word gules in heraldry means red: we are left, at the end of the story, with a final scarlet A over Hester's grave. We can consider the possibility that it might now have changed in meaning from adulteress to angel.[22]

Discussion

Although Hawthorne wrote about Hester Prynne with understanding and grace, he did not underestimate the threat a single, sexually active woman posed to this closed, patriarchal Puritan community. From the beginning of the novel, in ways

---

[22] The explanatory notes of the 1990 edition of the story in The World's Classics offer a possible source for the device as Marvell's 'The unfortunate Lover' which ends

... though
Forced to live in Storms and Wars:
Yet dying leaves a perfume here,
And Musick within every ear:
And he in story only rules,
In a Field *Sable*, a Lover Gules.

that would have had meaning for the highly literate and radical group with whom Hawthorne associated in the Boston of the mid-nineteenth century, he appears both fascinated and approving of Hester's individuality and nervously aware about her capacity as an anarchic woman to destabilize her society. The scarlet letter A which she wore on her breast was fantastically embroidered and appeared more as a decoration than as a symbol of shame.

She resolutely refused to give the name of her partner in adultery, who was in fact the highly respected community minister. Her arrival in the colony ahead of her husband demonstrated her independence and when her husband arrived unexpectedly while she was on the scaffold, and he, outraged and vengeful, withheld any knowledge of her, she made no attempt to claim his protection.[23]

Hawthorne gave her a background of having been brought up in England in a family of decayed gentility, and marriage to an older man, a scholar, with whom she had travelled and lived on the Continent of Europe. Such a background would ill equip any woman for the crude life-style of the early years of a Puritan settlement. She would be distanced emotionally and socially from the bigoted and less sophisticated crowd who surrounded her as she stood on the scaffold and in this way closer to the cultivated and educated women Hawthorne admired and mixed with in his own life. She is a pointer to the future rather than a representative of women of the period he is describing.

By repressing, as she seems to have done, passion and feeling, Hester has awakened her capacity for thought. The assumption made here is a very Augustinian and Calvinist one: that the body and feeling are a hindrance to the spirit. In an interesting passage the range of Hester's capacity to speculate on her situation and the nature of the rules of the society in which she finds herself is identified as more dangerous than the original sin which earned her the scarlet letter. To the authorities, thought, it seems, can be more dangerous than passion. The narrator even suggests that had it not been for her need to care for and educate her child, Hester's capacity to challenge and question conventional thinking might have led her to found a religious sect. But no such path is open to her; she is left only with the sadness of realizing that the entire system in which she lives requires to be destroyed and rebuilt.

The picture he paints is a subtle and complex mix of Eve, the Virgin Mary and Lilith. But while he recognizes the dangers such a woman can pose, his essential message is that Hester Prynne did not deserve to be treated in the way she was by the society in which she found herself. Hawthorne was described by one of his biographers, Lloyd Morris, as 'The Rebellious Puritan'.[24] His character, Hester Prynne, represents a more modern, more democratic and autonomous relationship with human destiny than was available to her in the Puritan setting in which he placed her. She believes passionately in the power of will, she believes in the power of feeling, and the right, and possibly duty, to express that feeling. She acknowledges her husband's right to be angry but draws back at the destructive

---

[23] Hawthorne's model for Hester may have been partly drawn from the life of Ann Hutchinson, a radical woman preacher, about whom he had written a sketch in 1830. In this he had stressed the danger she had posed to a colony in which public safety was incompatible with religious freedom.

[24] Lloyd Morris, *The Rebellious Puritan: Portrait of Mr. Hawthorne*, Constable: London 1928.

consequences of his hatred, consequences to himself as well as to others. She claims his ability to forgive, and the right of herself and her guilty partner to be forgiven by him, if not by God.

This view of Hester Prynne was the one which Hawthorne was working with when writing the novel. He had been for some years a member of the Transcendental Club, a group of American intellectuals, both men and women, who met informally for philosophical discussion at Ralph Waldo Emerson's house and elsewhere in Boston for some years starting in 1836. The Club was the embodiment of a movement of thought – philosophical, religious, social and economic – inspired in New England between 1830 and 1850 by the spirit of revolutionary Europe, German philosophy and the influence of Wordsworth, Coleridge and Carlyle. Its base was the Romantic Movement, which had flourished from around 1770 to 1848. Emotionally it expressed an extreme assertion of the self and the value of individual experience together with the sense of the infinite and transcendental. Hawthorne (1804–64) had a mixed response to the Transcendentalists and some of this ambivalence can be seen in the novel and in the character of Hester. *The Scarlet Letter* is seen as a classic enquiry into the nature of American Puritanism and the New England conscience, much preoccupied with the mystery of sin, the paradox of its occasionally regenerative power, and the compensation for unmerited suffering and crime. The American novelist Henry James wrote of *The Scarlet Letter*, 'it came out of the very heart of New England',[25] but it also communicates very powerfully the darkness at the heart of that tradition.

The conflict round which the novel revolves is between the law of man which was at the heart of the socio-political dimension and the law of nature which was given priority by the Transcendentalists. Hester's conflict is that she *is* nature – sensual, erotic in a society dominated by the law of man. She is a Lilith character defined in contrast to Eve, refusing like Lilith to lie under a man, claiming her freedom to disobey man's law. But in order to survive with her child she finds it necessary on the surface to behave like the Virgin Mary, docile, obedient, submissive, the reformed Magdalene (who is the alter ego of the Virgin Mary just as Lilith is the alter ego of Eve). Under the surface the passion of Magdalene lies quiescent but waiting to be reawakened.

The Scarlet Letter is an example of the novel as a literary genre which developed in the period of the democratic revolutions in America and in France. According to the literary historian, L.A. Fiedler,[26] the second half of the eighteenth century in Europe 'was marked by a violent outburst of all the main individualistic tendencies set loose by the Renaissance and the Reformation'. Porte[27] sees concern for 'the first person singular' as a dominant issue in American Romanticism and quotes Emerson as saying 'the mind had become aware of itself'. The invention of the novel was part of this. Porte also sees 'enthusiasm' as 'the great Romantic battle cry' and sees this as the source not only of Hester's sexual liaison with

---

[25] *The Oxford Companion to English Literature*, ed. M. Drabble, Oxford University Press: Oxford 1996, p. 449.

[26] Leslie A. Fiedler, *Love and Death in the American Novel*, Paladin: London 1960.

[27] Joel Porte, *In Respect to Egotism: Studies in American Romantic Writing*, Cambridge University Press: Cambridge 1991, p. 20.

Dimmesdale but also her attempt 'to undermine the foundations of the Puritan establishment'.[28]

The Scarlet Letter was in many ways a product of its time, being only one of a number of literary works dealing with conflicts between young women and the rigid Puritanism of Boston society. But it also foreshadowed some characteristics of our own century. Among other things it tells the story of a woman who sees herself as an individual and who is liberating herself from the fetters of an old social order but can only do this in non-verbal ways, thereby avoiding direct confrontation with the powerful of the society in which she lives: Hester and Myra Hindley have this in common. Hester's desire to proclaim a new order of equality of relationships between men and women is inhibited by her conviction that she is 'stained with sin' on account of her adultery and in this she is a prisoner of the setting in which Hawthorne places her – the Puritan community of the seventeenth century.

In spite of his rebellion against Puritanism, Hawthorne was very much a product of that tradition. It was this that fed his preoccupation with sin and with evil. His perception of life was that it was a moral journey with an essentially tragic meaning. That and his conviction that this journey was a lonely and individual experience was a classically Puritan position constantly reflected in *The Scarlet Letter*. He outlines four lives, four different journeys and four different responses to the central 'sin' of adultery. There is the hopeless and helpless Calvinism of Chillingworth which offers no forgiveness, and the contrite Dimmesdale finding forgiveness through confession and repentance, making what expiation is within his power. There is the child who, released by Dimmesdale's sacrificial death and confession that she is his child, can pursue a virtuous and successful life. Finally there is Hester, the woman who, in making her own path, makes also her own morality and appears to believe that love excuses everything.

Simon Wiesenthal's *The Sunflower*[29]

The Second World War and its aftermath became a forcing house for a reassessment of both public and private moral behaviour. Whereas previously it had been possible to offer separate assessments of attitudes to sin and/or forgiveness, a more complex inter-linking now emerged. The war can be seen as a watershed for interest in and understanding of what constitutes sin and forgiveness. Before this time it had been seen as an issue to be considered in the Church, in the Synagogue or in the Academy rather than in popular literature or a public forum. The realization that human beings were still capable of the barbarism that took place in the death camps as well as images of the devastation in Hiroshima and Nagasaki created uncertainty about the inevitable progress of human moral behaviour. Questions were asked with a new sense of urgency: what is a sin? What defines a victim and what defines a perpetrator? What does forgiveness mean and what limits does it have? The general

---

[28] Ibid., p. 25.

[29] The title refers to a German military cemetery where on each grave had been planted a sunflower. The author, then a prisoner of the Nazis, on seeing this realized that for him there would be no sunflower, only a mass grave.

discourse had now entered a stage where the individual's relationship with a religious saviour could not be taken for granted.

Of the many testimonies published after the Second World War, Simon Wiesenthal's *The Sunflower*[30] has most clearly opened up what it describes in its subtitle as both the possibilities and limits of forgiveness.

One day, while working as a camp prisoner in the grounds of a hospital, Wiesenthal was asked by a nurse if he was Jewish, and if so, to follow her. She led him to a room where a young German SS soldier was dying, and left them. The soldier, with something of the intensity of the Ancient Mariner, insisted on telling Wiesenthal, in detail, a gruesome story of how he had participated in the burning to death of a large group of Jewish men, women and children and how this had been preying on his conscience. Knowing he was dying, he wanted to make his last confession. He begged forgiveness from Wiesenthal because since he was a Jew, he could act as a surrogate for those he had killed. 'I have longed to talk about it to a Jew,' he says ... 'only I didn't know if there were any Jews left.[31] ... I know that what I am asking is almost too much for you, but without your answer I cannot die in peace.'

Wiesenthal describes how he sat thinking for a few minutes: 'Two men who had never known each other had been brought together for a few hours by Fate. One asks the other for help. But the other was himself helpless and able to do nothing for him ... At last I made up my mind and without a word I left the room.'

But uncertainty about his decision stayed with him although his friends in the camp supported him for varying reasons, some less thoughtful than others. The most reasoned argument came from Josek:

> 'I feared at first, that you had really forgiven him. You would have had no right to do this in the name of people who had not authorized you to do so. What people have done to you yourself, you can, if you like, forgive and forget. That is your own affair. But it would have been a terrible sin to burden your conscience with other people's sufferings.' 'But aren't we a single community with the same destiny, and one must answer for the other?', I interrupted. 'Be careful, my friend', continued Josek. 'In each person's life there are historic moments which rarely occur – and today you have experienced one such. It is not a simple problem for you ... I can see you are not entirely pleased with yourself. But I assure you I would have done the same as you did.' Arthur had simply said with satisfaction, 'One less!'[32]

The issue continued to trouble Wiesenthal and later, when a young Polish, Catholic, theology student, Bolek, was allocated to Wiesenthal's bunk in the camp he reopened the question with him. Bolek didn't see any difference in the attitudes of the great religions, by which he presumably meant the religions of the Book. He agreed that you can only forgive a wrong done to yourself but believed that the only important element in forgiveness was repentance. Since the German had truly repented he should have been forgiven. The confession itself may well have helped

---

[30] Simon Wiesenthal, *The Sunflower: On the Possibilities and Limits of Forgiveness*, Schocken Books: New York 1998. This edition includes a symposium edited by H.J. Cargas and B.V. Fetterman.

[31] The implications of that phrase alone are horrifying.

[32] Wiesenthal, *Sunflower*, p. 65.

him to die in peace. The story ends with Wiesenthal asking the reader what he or she would have done and he later put this question to a number of men and women who were not directly involved.

The 1998 edition of *The Sunflower* includes a symposium of comments from a group of 53 people, representing a range of religious views and none, who were asked to comment. Several refused to answer the question or to be drawn into any discussion of a philosophy of forgiveness. Many believed that one's response has to be an individual decision – for the Jewish community the inability to have a communal view on such an issue aroused much heart-searching and discussion. The two most consistent views presented were the Jewish and the Christian.

The Jewish view emphasized the inability to forgive on behalf of other people – such an act could only be a prerogative of God. The emphasis here, in most responses, was on retributive justice.[33] The Christians, while also believing that it is impossible to forgive on behalf of another, mostly say that they would have been concerned to comfort the young man with the thought that God would forgive him and that Christ had added forgiveness to the need for justice. They also emphasized the importance of love. Christopher Hollis, the former journalist and author, makes the strongest statement of this view: 'I have no doubt he should have said a word of compassion. The theology of the matter is surely clear ... The law of God is the law of love ... We are under obligation to forgive our neighbour even though he has offended against us seventy times seven.'[34]

Jean Amery, a non-religious Jew and former inmate of the same camp, said there were only two aspects to consider: the psychological and the political. 'Psychologically', he said, 'forgiving or non forgiving is nothing more than a question of temperament or feeling.' The implication of this for Amery was that whichever was done had little or no meaning. Politically too he considered the result irrelevant. He continued:

> Whether you are an agnostic or a believer, I do not know, but your problem belongs to the realm of guilt and atonement; so even if we cast it in an agnostic form, the problem is a theological one, and as such it does not exist for me, an atheist who is indifferent to and rejecting of any metaphysics of morality. I think that this does not concern individual forgiveness or individual intransigence. One can say: your dying SS man took part in the extermination; he knew very well what he was doing. He may come to terms with his God, if he believes in one, and may just as well die unconsoled. One can also say: What difference does it make? Let him rest in peace, in the name of God or of the Devil, and if my forgiveness matters to him, I'll give it. Politically it does not make any difference ... Politically I do not want to hear anything of forgiveness! Why does it matter to me? For one simple reason: what you and I went through must *not happen again, never, nowhere*[35] ... I refuse any reconciliation with the criminals, and with those who only by accident did not happen to commit atrocities, and finally, all those who helped prepare the unspeakable acts with their words.[36]

---

[33] This has been reflected to some extent in the hunting down and prosecution of Nazi survivors like Eichmann.

[34] Wiesenthal, *Sunflower*, p. 179.

[35] Amery's italics.

[36] Wiesenthal, *Sunflower*, p. 107.

Desmond Tutu, the Anglican Archbishop, who was giving his response at the same time as he was presiding over the South African Truth and Reconciliation Commission and attempting 'the process of seeking to bring healing and reconciliation to a deeply divided, wounded, and traumatized nation', takes the discussion on to a wider canvas: 'It is clear that if we look only to retributive justice, then we could just as well close up shop. Forgiveness is not some nebulous thing. It is practical politics. Without forgiveness, there is no future.' The thought that 'those who would be surprised to meet Hitler in heaven don't understand what it's all about' might have been designed for Tutu.

One contributor to the symposium, Harry Wu, was reminded of the 19 years he had spent in a Chinese prison labour camp where he was cruelly abused. His view was that it would have been inconceivable for such an encounter to take place in China. There could not have been any understanding by the Chinese that what the Communists did to their own people was wrong. He, no more than Wiesenthal, would not have been able to forgive the soldier on his deathbed but he adds that he would have been able to say to him: 'I understand why you were part of a horrible and vicious society. You are responsible for your own actions but everyone else in this society shares the same responsibility with you.' Wu now writes and lectures world-wide on slave labour camps, another issue of intolerable human behaviour that has come to light in the second half of the twentieth century in China and in the Soviet Union.

Discussion

Anyone seeking a definitive solution to the question of forgiveness in Wiesenthal's book will not find it. In the responses by contributors there is not even unanimity about the description of the German's actions as 'sinful' in a theological sense. This powerful story about a painful, personal dilemma is responded to by the 53 contributors to the symposium in ways which reflect only their own beliefs and experiences. What is not discussed, and what in my opinion may be one of the most important aspects, of the book, is that the young SS soldier, a member of Hitler Youth who had abandoned his Catholic background, a volunteer for the SS, whose mother was proud that he was fighting for the Führer and the Fatherland, was nevertheless capable of realizing the 'sinfulness' of what he had done to the Jews.

This man had been brainwashed into believing that each soldier must 'show himself a man … he must be tough … there was no place for humanitarian nonsense'. He was given literature about Jews and Bolsheviks, vicious cartoons, and told of Germany's need for room to live. He experienced the brutal horrors of the Russian campaign and survived believing the war would soon be over. Yet he had clearly retained some sensitivity to human suffering in spite of having obeyed brutal orders, the orders to drive two hundred Jewish men, women and children into a three-storey house, pour petrol and burn them to death. Talking to Wiesenthal he was seeing and hearing again in horror the hell he had helped to create: 'I can never forget – it haunts me ….' We are reminded of *The Rime of the Ancient Mariner*:

> Since then, at an uncertain hour,
> That agony returns,
> And till my ghastly tale is told
> This heart within me burns.[37]

This capacity, this sensitivity, this albatross that we carry, our wish, our need, to be good, to be forgiven, to cease to be the 'other', to be taken back into the human race, is also part of this story.

The army campaign, of which the young soldier was a part, carried on after the massacre, the soldiers never referring to what they had done, though some appeared uneasy. Following a battle, wounded and blinded, the soldier was shifted from hospital to hospital in unbearable pain but always remembering what had happened to the Jews: 'Believe me, I would be ready to suffer worse and longer pains if I could bring back the dead.'

This is where Wiesenthal asks us – what are the limits of forgiveness – and in doing so challenges the Christian view that there are no limits as long as there is repentance. What part does memory play for the victim and is it possible to forgive and not forget? Most important of all – is forgiveness relevant with or without atonement? And if it is relevant to whom does that relevance apply? Is it the victim or is it the perpetrator whose mental health is most at stake?

What we may most sharply need to address is Amery's response. He is not saying 'forget forgiveness because your question to me does not matter – is absurd in Sartre's sense.' He is saying 'forget forgiveness because other questions about how we manage our affairs, how we live together in the future after these barbaric acts, matter more.' I may agree but I am also forced to ask: rather than should he have been forgiven, why was this man able to hold on to some shred of humanity in spite of the strong conditioning to which he was exposed? What were the factors that enabled him to feel shame and guilt for his behaviour? How had some essential quality of compassion been able to survive and what can we learn from this in the way we deal with 'sinners'? Wiesenthal's book offers no answers but it has the grace of subtlety in that it takes us past the moment of decision and offers us an opportunity in hindsight to examine ourselves. When the war is over, how can people make peace with those whom they have been taught, or learned, to see as mortal enemies?

Margaret Atwood's *The Handmaid's Tale*

The Handmaid's Tale takes us a step further along the post-Christian path. Margaret Atwood has created a fable of a quasi-military, totalitarian, fundamentalist, religious patriarchy operating in a world which 'actively excludes a non human power or design'.[38] It is a grimly dystopian prophecy which sees Christian revolutionaries as having taken over the United States, renaming it the Republic of

---

[37] Samuel Taylor Coleridge, *The Rime of the Ancient Mariner*, in *Complete Poetical Works*, ed. Ernest Hartley, Oxford University Press: Oxford 1969, Vol. II, pp. 582–85.

[38] Atwood, *Handmaid's Tale*, p. 144.

Gilead. Men, in response to increasing sterility and a perceived need to maintain population levels, have reshaped this society. The story itself is comparatively simple but carries within it all the components of totalitarian nightmare. It envisages a society where women who claim sexual independence are brainwashed into becoming Handmaids – surrogate mothers to elite childless couples. Conception takes place during ritual ceremonies in which the husbands have sex with the Handmaids while the Handmaids lie between the legs of the wives. It uses quotations from the Hebrew Bible to reinforce the role of women as submissive bearers of those children so urgently desired.

Atwood's opening quotations refer to Genesis 30:1–3[39] and Jonathan Swift's 'A Modest Proposal'. This latter, a tract written in 1720 which gained great popularity, was Swift's despairing response to the gross poverty and degradation of the Irish population. In an attempt to shock he took the British government's inhumanity to what he satirically saw as its logical conclusion, to have 1-year-old children cooked and eaten to provide food and their skins used for ladies' gloves and fine boots for gentlemen. Atwood also presents us with the horror of the inhuman logic of a totalitarian society.

The novel describes the experience of one handmaid, Offred, named after her male master. Through the course of the novel, Offred gradually recovers her memories of her husband and child from whom she had been torn away by the state police, and discovers her individual voice and her capacity for opposition to the regime. The novel is a testament to the importance of holding on to memory as a source not only of pain, but of strength. It is also a testament to the right of the individual not to forgive and by doing so submit, but rather expresses the right, indeed the duty, to nourish one's anger as a source of resistance. This is a novel which offers no traditional image of redemption.

Discussion

The society described by Atwood is steeped in sinfulness, if by sinfulness we allow something more than either the criteria of the Ten Commandments or the Seven Deadly Sins – a condition which might better be described as iniquity. This definition of sinfulness is determined by a later, humanist and democratic view of the relationship between human beings. It is about the sinfulness of one human being exploiting another human being or one group of humans exploiting another group of humans. What is interesting is that Atwood, rather than write a purely secular story, has chosen to put it firmly into a theological framework of which she clearly disapproves. She appears to be saying that within this framework democracy and equality for women cannot be achieved. Within it she identifies the manipulation women need to employ to find any space for themselves and the hatred that lurks under their apparent submission.

In her novel Atwood writes of the difficulty of describing any experience with exactitude – even the experience of Offred in her story. The ending leaves us uncertain of her fate, not knowing whether she has been rescued by underground

---

[39] 'And she said, Behold my maid Bilhah, go in unto her; and she shall bear upon my knees, that I may also have children by her.'

resisters of the regime or is being taken for further punishment. In the following extract she seems to be suggesting that this difficulty can be compared with the complexity of forgiveness:

> It's impossible to say a thing exactly the way it was, because what you say can never be exact, you always have to leave something out, there are too many parts, sides, cross currents, nuances, too many gestures, which could mean this or that, too many shapes which can never be fully described, too many flavours in the air or on the tongue, half-colours, too many. But if you happen to be a man, some time in the future, and you've made it this far, please remember you will never be subjected to the temptation of feeling you must forgive, a man, as a woman. It's difficult to resist, believe me. But remember that forgiveness too is a power. To beg for it is a power, and to withhold or bestow it is a power, perhaps the greatest.[40]

Atwood has written, as well as a fable, a parody, which, in the paragraph I have quoted, separates out forgiveness from its traditionally understood Christian association of forgiveness as a virtue linked to redemption. In doing this she is reaching towards the end of the spectrum of the literature of forgiveness, already well established in the plays of the Middle Ages, in which forgiveness was either implicitly or explicitly part of the dramatic content and was actively related to a non-human or divine power. The narrator of Atwood's story, a prisoner of the regime, has no sense of a non-human power and holds on grimly to her tiny area of free will and her anger as a way of retaining some sense of her identity. Here we have the first indication of the liberating effects of anger as an alternative to forgiveness.

Bernhard Schlink's *The Reader*

We saw earlier Wiesenthal's attempt to come to terms with his own inability to forgive a German soldier. In a novel published in 1997, more than fifty years after Wiesenthal's moral struggle, Bernhard Schlink, a German professor of law and writer of novels, reopens, in a secular context, the question of the nature – and indeed the relevance – of sin and forgiveness as an aspect of the history of the Nazi period. The words 'sin' and 'forgiveness' are never used. The only words with any theological meaning to be used are 'guilt' and 'atonement'. The emphasis of the work is on a legal, humanist, educational and psychological understanding.

The narrator tells the story of a 15-year-old German boy, Schlink himself, who shortly after the end of the Second World War has a powerful emotional and sexual relationship with a 36-year-old woman. Its quality transcends the class and cultural differences between them. She is a tram conductor, he is the son of a professor of philosophy and plans to become a lawyer. He goes to her flat every day after school and they develop a ritual in which they shower, make love and he reads stories to her. The reading seems to be as important to her as the lovemaking. One day she is no longer there. He tries to trace her; her employers are as puzzled as he is at her

---

[40] Atwood, *Handmaid's Tale*, p. 144.

disappearance since they had, that week, offered her promotion. He is painfully forced to accept his loss.

Some years later, now a law student, he takes part in regular seminars as part of his professor's research project on the Holocaust camps. He, like his fellow students, has tried to make sense of Germany's wartime history and the part their parents played in that. There is also the question of their own role:

> What should our second generation have done, what should it do with the knowledge of the extermination of the Jews? We should not believe we can comprehend the incomprehensible, we may not compare the incomparable, we may not inquire because to inquire is to make the horrors an object of discussion, even if the horrors themselves are not questioned, instead of accepting them as something in the face of which we can only fall silent in revulsion, shame and guilt?[41]

The research involves weekly attendance at the trial of a group of women, formerly concentration camp guards, accused of allowing a group of Jewish women and children prisoners, in transit from the camp, to burn to death, locked into a church which was being bombed. Hanna, the woman he had loved, is one of the accused. He watches as if anaesthetized while in her responses she succeeds in antagonizing the judge and the court, giving confusing answers and asking awkward questions which make it appear she hadn't troubled to read the charges. The negative impression was reinforced when Hanna said that she had voluntarily joined the SS as a guard even though her previous employer, Siemens, had wanted to promote her to be a foreman.

The narrator begins to attend court every day, watching and listening obsessively, but numbly, as he tries to relate the woman he was watching to the woman he had known and the loving experiences he had shared with her. She and the other four women on trial had been guards in a small camp near Cracow, a satellite camp for Auschwitz. Women were constantly being transferred from the camp to the gas chambers but it emerged that Hanna had the habit, in the month before they were transferred, of having certain young girls as 'favourites'. These were brought to her in the evening and for them she arranged special privileges. The implication was that she was abusing them sexually before they were transferred to the gas chambers. In fact, it emerged, she was using them, not sexually, but to read aloud to her.

The main charge against all the women was that they had not unlocked the doors of a church which was being bombed and in which the women and children were being held overnight. The other four women, recognizing that Hanna's clumsy responses were irritating the judge, turned against her to save themselves, claiming that she had written the report of the incident and that this had been a cover-up. In answering questions she was inarticulate, trying and failing to communicate the darkness, the confusion, the helplessness and the panic as their male SS escorts ran away. She had been quite unable to cope with what seemed like two equally compelling duties, to obey orders or release the prisoners. She denied that she had written the report until the judge offered to bring in a handwriting expert, at which

---

41 Bernhard Schlink, *The Reader*, trans. Carol Brown Janeway, Phoenix: London 1988, p. 102.

point she collapsed and said, 'My handwriting? You want my handwriting?' Then she said, 'You don't have to call an expert. I admit I wrote the report.' At the end of the trial she was sentenced to life imprisonment.

By this point it is becoming obvious to the student and to the reader that Hanna's life and behaviour have been determined by the fact that she can neither read nor write and has been ashamed to admit it. She joined the SS in order to avoid the promotion she had been offered, realizing that it would expose her illiteracy; she left her job as a tram conductor and abandoned the narrator for the same reason, and she accepted responsibility for the report rather than admit that she could not write. The terror of fascism, the horrors of the Hitler regime, the academic discussions of guilt and responsibility all had passed her by as she struggled with her disability. Her love of being read to, her love of stories, was a small light illuminating her life.

The Reader is a book that challenges all our assumptions about the nature of free will and how we make judgements about our fellow human beings. In another novel, *Alias Grace* by Margaret Atwood, the character Grace experiences that same sense of disorientation when the familiar is stripped away:

> When you are in the middle of a story it isn't a story at all, but only a confusion; a dark roaring, a blindness, a wreckage of shattered glass and splintered wood; like a house in a whirlwind, or else a boat crushed by the icebergs or swept over the rapids, and all aboard powerless to stop it. It's only afterwards that it becomes anything like a story at all when you are telling it, to yourself or to someone else.[42]

Atwood's story of Grace was based on a real woman, Grace Marks, a servant in Canada who was imprisoned for life for murder in 1843, at the age of 16. She always protested her innocence. The community was divided as to whether this was a wicked woman, a femme fatale, or a weak and unwilling victim. In the author's Afterword, Atwood says that her true character remains an enigma. Grace's words in the novel have equal significance for Hanna but they also describe *The Reader*'s narrator's time with her. For quite different reasons to do with the confusion, the near-insanity of his first love and his overwhelming experience of the passionately sensual possibilities of one's body, his notions of duty, responsibility, right and wrong simply evaporated. His initial, slightly pious, belief as a student that reason can be mobilized to understand what happened in Germany and prevent its recurrence led him to say to his readers:

> We students in the camps seminar considered ourselves radical explorers. We tore open the windows and let in the air, the wind that finally whirled away the dust that society had permitted to settle over the horrors of the past. We made sure that people could breathe and see. And we placed no reliance on legal scholarship. It was evident to us that there had to be convictions. It was just as evident that conviction of this or that camp guard or enforcer was only the prelude. The generation that had been served by the guards and enforcers, or had done nothing to stop them, or had not banished them from its midst as it could have done after 1945, was in the dock, and we explored it, subjected it to trial by daylight, and condemned it to shame.[43]

---

[42] Margaret Atwood, *Alias Grace*, Bloomsbury: London 1996, p. 298.
[43] Schlink, *Reader*, p. 89.

It was while believing this that he first saw Hanna in the dock. Unable to bring the two parts of himself together while watching the trial, he realized only that a better, more experienced lawyer than the one representing her, could have cleared her. For years afterwards he struggled intellectually with the complex moral questions raised by his own knowledge of her and what he had learned during the trial:

> She was not pursuing her own interests, but fighting for her own truth, her own justice. Because she always had to dissimulate somewhat, and never could be completely candid, it was a pitiful truth and a pitiful justice, but it was hers and the struggle for it was her struggle ... She was struggling, as she had always struggled, not to show what she could do but to hide what she couldn't do. A life made up of advances that were actually frantic retreats and victories that were concealed defeats.[44]

He made no attempt to contact her, although he knew she had seen him in court, until several years later when he was facing significant emotional problems leading to long nights of sleeplessness. Presumably because his inner life was reawakening, although this is never explained, during those bleak nights he began to read into a tape recorder and send the tapes to her anonymously. He began with the *Odyssey*, the first book he had read to her. Only when she was due to leave prison did he, hesitantly, visit her and discover that she had now learned to read and write as a result of his tapes. As soon as she learned to read she began to read about the concentration camps from the books of victims like Levi, Wiesel and Amery as well as scholarly literature on the camps. He arranged work and a place for her to live when she left prison, but before she was discharged she committed suicide. She left what money she had to a woman who had survived the fire in the church and who had been a witness at the trial. The woman refused to accept the money for herself since it would imply giving absolution, but agreed that the money should go to the Jewish League Against Illiteracy in Hanna's name.

Discussion

We see here the complexity not only of who was the sinner and who was the victim, but also of the ambiguity of atonement, a complexity that was also part of the dilemma faced by Simon Wiesenthal in *The Sunflower* but is more sharply presented in this novel. The story of the boy and the older woman initially reminds us of Vizinczey's *In Praise of Older Women*, that charmingly erotic, gently amoral glimpse of the Central European bourgeoisie.[45] We want it to be like that for our narrator in *The Reader*. But fifty years after knowledge of the camps that is not possible. Just as AIDS has forced those seeking sexual partners to enquire about each other's sexual history, Germans have been forced to enquire about the moral history not only of their lovers but of their friends and their parents.

The book is particularly important as a meditation on the complexity of judgement – how would Hanna and others have been dealt with on a Day of Judgement where everything about her would have been known, rather than the

---

44 Schlink, Ibid., p. 133.
45 Stephen Vizinczey, *In Praise of Older Women*, University of Chicago Press: Chicago 1990.

partial story heard by the court? It also raises issues of the complexity of guilt. Only after she had learned to read, a skill that gave her access to books about the organization of death to which she had been recruited, could she see her life in context, could see that the SS was not just a job as Siemens had been just a job. This context enabled her to see her part in a drama she had previously seen as having nothing to do with the detail of her life.

Hanna appears to have lived in a moral vacuum, one that may be shared by more people than we are prepared to admit, people whose existence is confined to the narrow realities of 'advances that were actually frantic retreats and victories that were concealed defeats'. Learning to read led her into an understanding of her membership of the human race. The only thing she felt able to do with the awareness that opened up, the sense of her 'sinfulness', was to kill herself. Was this what happened to Judas? We are forced into questions, not only about Hanna but also about the German people. What is Schlink asking us to consider? Does Hanna represent those German people who stood aside and did nothing? Does not being able to read also mean not wanting to see what is written on the page?

Schlink has also drawn for us a disturbing portrait of the young man whose adolescence had been marked by his passionate love affair with a woman who as a concentration camp guard was a symbol of everything he was rejecting in his parents' and his country's past. How could he hold these two images together in his mind? This was and is still a dilemma for those whose loved ones, whether they be lovers, parents, family or friends, do terrible things. How far does love stretch into forgiveness? Or is the solution sometimes to distance oneself, hide behind the anonymity of the tape recorder, offer practical help but not expose the pain even to one's self?

Alice Walker's 'Goodnight, Willie Lee, I'll See You in the Morning'

In the 1990s a number of books were published with titles like *Forgiving the Unforgivable*.[46] Some are based on popular, post-Christian psychological views of the importance of claiming choice and accepting responsibility for one's life. Others, like *The Lost Art of Forgiving* and *The Art of Forgiveness*, are deeply Christian. All come into the category of self-help books. *The Lost Art of Forgiving*, published by the Bruderhof,[47] is essentially a collection of powerful stories which recount acts of forgiveness which confer peace, hope and even health to those who bring themselves to forgive. It ranges from intimate stories of personal distress to the wider issues of disputes between individuals caught in ethnic conflicts. Alice Walker communicates the first of these with great economy in her poem: 'Goodnight, Willie Lee, I'll See You in the Morning':[48]

---

[46] Beverly Flanigan, *Forgiving the Unforgivable*, Macmillan: New York 1992.

[47] Johann Christoph Arnold, *The Lost Art of Forgiving*, The Plough Publishing House: Farmington, USA, 1998. The Bruderhof is an international community dedicated to a life of simplicity, community and non-violence.

[48] Alice Walker, 'Goodnight, Willie Lee, I'll See You in the Morning', from a collection with the same title, Women's Press: London 1995, p. 53.

> Looking down into my father's
> dead face
> for the last time
> my mother said without
> tears, without smiles
> but with civility,
> 'Goodnight, Willie Lee, I'll see you
> in the morning.'
> And it was then I knew the healing
> of all our wounds
> is forgiveness
> that permits a promise
> of our return at the end.

Alice Walker tells us nothing in this poem about why forgiveness was needed and there is no reason for us to ask. It would be an intrusion even to speculate. This is a classic statement of human dignity, endurance and acceptance of the hand life has dealt you. It flies in the face of modern views of relationships between men and women, of justice or democracy where the emphasis is on the demand for equal rights. It is however at the same time deeply moving. That stoicism is what has enabled both men and women – mostly women – to survive intolerable circumstances and is entitled to be treated with respect as a way in which people cope. The country and western song 'Stand by Your Man', originally presented as a tribute to supportive wives, is now sung with affectionate irony about a lost world. The practice continues to survive in some quarters, notably in the world of politicians where there are particular rewards for this form of loyalty.

This poem reflects a more ancient response than the words of theologians, social scientists or lawyers. It is a response that is reflected in churches, temples and shrines where women continue to attend when men have given up. We see it in the faces of the women who kneel before the statues of the Virgin Mary or the Buddha or a goddess of compassion seeking comfort, in many cases wordlessly, for their unhappiness, their oppression, their poverty, their lost children. It is a mixture of faith, hope and the acceptance that there is no point in having faith or hope – yet one goes on. It does not depend on a belief in a deity or in a better life to come. It is belief in life itself and the unity of everything. This poem does not fit easily into any category of belief yet it refers us back to the great Rembrandt painting which communicates to us, without words, a fundamental human truth – that in some situations there are no limits to forgiveness – while at the same time the poem questions whether forgiveness needs even to be discussed. It just happens.

Conclusion

We have looked at six examples of responses, either of forgiveness, or denial of forgiveness, to the dilemmas created by sin. In addition we have recognized that as we have moved forward in time the question of forgiveness or denial of forgiveness has appeared less and less relevant in the stories told. The question of forgiveness is being replaced by more relevant questions which no longer simply say to understand all is to forgive all but, as in the Schlink story, recognize that, in our world, both understanding and forgiving are much more complex than we have previously realized. We are reminded that the essence of sin as seen in the Hebrew tradition is that it creates a lack of balance which requires adjustment. In that tradition, sin created a debt which had to be repaid and the powerful rituals of the Hebrew religion with its emphasis on sacrifice and atonement offered a direct pathway to God's forgiveness. He was, after all, the only one who mattered. But we are in a post-traditional world.

Rembrandt's great painting, *The Return of the Prodigal Son*, challenged the tradition of his time. It also challenged the interpretation of the Christian Church where forgiveness became a transaction involving confession of the sin to a representative of the Church and where absolution was dependent on the fulfilling of a penance set by that representative. What we read in the painting is the unquestioned, unqualified forgiveness offered in the stories told of Jesus in the Christian Bible. This unqualified forgiveness was maintained in the face of doubts expressed by his disciples and by representatives of his own faith. This was the paradigm shift to which Arendt refers when she writes of Jesus as 'the discoverer of the role of forgiveness in human affairs'.[49]

Rembrandt's work is deeply rooted in a sense of family and community. The sinner is welcomed back into both and there is a sense that he cannot exist outside that context.

Not so with the story of Hester Prynne. In writing *The Scarlet Letter*, Hawthorne was responding not only to the ideas and conversations of the Boston intelligentsia but also to his personal, uneasy reaction to his family history. His great-great-grandfather, John Hathorne, had been a leading magistrate in the infamous Salem witch trials and Hawthorne felt sufficiently soiled by this connection to adapt his name so as not to be directly associated with him. The trials had shown, among other things, the dangers as well as the strengths of community. Inevitably, one links the story of Hester with the events in Salem: the early colonists, fleeing persecution, had brought their fantasies and fears with them, particularly of women and their potentially dangerous links with Satan.

In the novel, Hawthorne uses the convention of a narrator who by accident uncovers a story he feels compelled to tell. This is an example of the novel as deception, as falsehood dressed up as truth but leaving a margin of possibility that it might turn out to be truth. The ambivalent truth Hawthorne seems to be reaching for is the notion of the free, individual woman who is not dependent on community and who can survive without it. This is a woman who does not accept the community definition of her as a sinner and therefore sees no need to ask for their forgiveness. Even if she had not 'sinned' she would have lived on the fringes of that society. She is responsible only to her God, does not seem to fear Him but rather expects Him to understand her. She neither seeks nor needs intermediaries to communicate with Him. She feels capable of defining her own codes of morality. This woman would have found common cause with some late twentieth-century theologians. Though

---

[49] Hannah Arendt, *The Human Condition*, University of Chicago Press: Chicago and London 1958, pp. 238–39.

there is no comparison in modern eyes with the gravity of their offences, we can see links with the story of Myra Hindley.

Atwood's story, *The Handmaid's Tale*, is also about a struggle between a woman and the community in which she finds herself, but here there is no ambivalence in the author or the main character. Patriarchy, religious fundamentalism and hypocrisy, all embedded in the community, are the main targets of anger. This is a novel which recognizes open anger as a valid response to 'sinful' behaviour and also offers the possibility that forgiveness is not an appropriate response. Something of the same response, this refusal to forgive, can be seen in the reactions of modern women who have been sexually abused by clergy and, on complaining, are asked by the Church for forgiveness.

Forgiveness is not always an option. For the abused women, whose forgiveness the Church too often assumes, and for Atwood's heroine it would be a submission, a loss of self rather than a discovery of, a 'return' to, the self, as was to be seen in some splendid moments in Victorian narratives such as Mrs Henry Wood's dramatic novel *East Lynne*.[50] Written in 1861, thirty years before Hardy wrote *Tess of the D'Urbervilles*, *East Lynne* offered the reader the full spectrum of sin, repentance and forgiveness. In this complex drama of passion and intrigue, each major character in the novel is touched to some degree with a sense of the religious significance of his or her behaviour. Forgiveness, which by the closing chapters becomes the central theme of the novel, is pleaded for and granted between human beings but always within the recognition that what is important is God's forgiveness since He is the ultimate Judge.

In Reed's view, what signals the collapse of the 'Victorian novel' and indeed the Victorian world-view, is the 'diminished role of forgiveness in serious literature'. He details the way in which Hardy fails to emphasize forgiveness in many episodes where earlier this would have seemed appropriate.[51] We see this clearly in *Tess of the D'Urbervilles*, when Tess, after forgiving her husband, Angel, for his sexual past, confesses her own, and asks Angel's forgiveness. His reply: 'O Tess, forgiveness does not apply to the case! You were one person; now you are another. My God – how can forgiveness meet such a grotesque prestidigitation as that!'[52] Conrad makes the same point in *Almeyer's Folly* where, rather than forgiveness restoring balance – which is its main function in the Hebrew Bible – it would reinforce the destabilization of Almeyer's view of his place in the world.[53]

Atwood is essentially saying the same thing: there are limits to forgiveness. What I am saying is that those limits are constantly being redefined. Angel's limits would now be seen by many as absurd but only in a sexual context; his was the same dilemma that affected Schlink's narrator in *The Reader* when he saw Hanna in the dock – suddenly a different person from the one he thought he knew. Atwood's

[50] Mrs Henry Wood, *East Lynne*, Collins: London 1954.

[51] John R. Reed, *Dickens and Thackeray: Punishment and Forgiveness*, Ohio University Press: Athens 1995, p. 478.

[52] Thomas Hardy, *Tess of the D'Urbervilles*, Penguin Popular Classics, Penguin Books: London 1994, p. 292.

[53] Joseph Conrad, *Almeyer's Folly: a story of an Eastern river*, Everleigh, Nash and Grayson: London 1921, p. 240.

limits are, in our own more complex multicultural and global society, very much a matter of current debate.

Along with these questions about the limits to forgiveness, we developed, in the second half of the twentieth century, a more subtle understanding of human personality and the importance of social factors than had previously been available to us. It is these which inform Schlink's novel, *The Reader*. Unlike even the clearly non-theistic stance of *The Handmaid's Tale*, it makes no reference to any form of religious belief. It is totally secular, unless one wishes to see Hanna's desire for stories as a search for transcendence. Her inability to read places her, like Hester but for different reasons, outside her community. The main difference is that she wants to belong but doesn't know how to achieve that goal. She lacks the social skills to make it possible and her sense of personal inadequacy prevents her from acquiring them. Her story is still being played out in schools in areas of social deprivation and in the Third World. She even lacks the skills to understand that she has been a victim of a sinful society. Nor does she know that she is entitled to have her forgiveness asked. It is her own community that has betrayed her.

An interesting aspect of Schlink's work is related to current post-Christian discussions which see the pursuit of justice as more important and more relevant than the pursuit of forgiveness. What he has done in this novel is to show the failure of the public justice system, of which he himself is a part, to produce justice for Hanna. It is clear in the text that a better defence lawyer or a less easily irritated or less prejudiced judge might have explored more carefully the complexity of the circumstances of her offence. While punishment might still have been appropriate, she might not have been singled out as the scapegoat, the sacrificial victim for the entire group. Even the narrator, who had once deeply loved this woman, felt, with the support of the court, able to turn his back on her. Only when his own life was falling apart was he able, if only anonymously, to renew the connection. We are left, since it is never discussed, to work out for ourselves how difficult it was for him to forgive her not only for abandoning him but for her 'grotesque prestidigitation' – to use Hardy's phrase.

Walker's poem, the final response in this grouping, takes us back to the Rembrandt painting. It is also about a family, this time of father, mother and daughter. It is a family in isolation – we know nothing of community or of what support structures might be available; we are allowed to see only the strength of the mother. It is a great strength, the essence of which lies in that word 'civility'. The feelings around the death are too deep for tears but are held within the dignity of civility. The daughter stands outside as an observer watching the interplay between her mother and her dead father and we can ask what she has learnt. She says, 'Forgiveness is the healing of all our wounds and that permits a promise of our return at the end.' Our return to what? To ourselves? But this is what our early Victorian writers were saying and we have rejected them, moving on to claim our right not to forgive. But this poem is claiming our right to forgive if we choose to, our right to forgive the person whose bed we have shared and with whom we have created new life in the form of a child no matter what else went on in the relationship. What is new, what is post-Christian, is that the choice is ours.

These responses I have described illustrate the range of responses open to us as soon as we abandon the straightforward concept that sinfulness incurs a debt to God that must be wiped out in some way in order to achieve forgiveness. This is perhaps most sharply seen in the Wiesenthal story where he seeks an answer to the apparently simple question: should he have forgiven the young soldier? His own tradition tells him that if no atonement is possible, the debt cannot be cleared, therefore there can be no forgiveness. But he is uncertain. By asking more and more people he is ultimately surrounded by voices clamouring for attention, each one being his or her own judge of what is right and what is wrong.

This is the essence of a post-traditional, post-Christian society. Increasingly we appear to reject the notion that anyone has the authority to tell us what is right and what is wrong or how to think about matters of personal morality. We may feel, exposed as we are to a multicultural range of ideas, that there is no one way of viewing a question and that we can consider and choose before responding. Rote learning of the answers offered by the catechism is no longer enough to see us through our more complex world. We define and redefine our 'sins' as circumstances change, we choose to grant or withhold forgiveness on the basis of the effect it will have not only on the perpetrator but also on ourselves for the sake of our own mental and physical health. We have moved a long way from the notions of sin and forgiveness described in the Hebrew and Christian Bibles.

We have still further to go. While increasingly we are accepting individual responses to issues of private morality, we are recognizing a clearer distinction between approaches to private and public morality. The lessons of Schlink's and Atwood's novels and the response Jean Amery made to Wiesenthal's question with its dismissal of the relevance of forgiveness in the face of more significant issues have to be addressed. Thomas Kuhn has helped us to understand that a significant point in scientific and human discourse arrives when a question has to be reformulated.[54] He describes this as part of the move to a new paradigm. I am suggesting in this work that this stage has been reached in relation to questions of sin and forgiveness. We are beginning to ask what part our understanding of sin and forgiveness can play in learning how we may live together in more humane ways.

---

[54] Kuhn, *Structure of Scientific Revolutions*.

3

The Move to a Contemporary View of Sin

Introduction

In this chapter I consider some of the main religious and social changes which have led to new definitions of sin. The first change to be discussed is what I describe as the fractured meta-narrative of Christianity in Britain, that is, the erosion of the network of assumptions that used to shape and support popular religious belief. I use the word fractured because, for many, the structures and institutions which had been built up around Christianity from the third century on to control and define the narrative continue to hold, if only precariously. I then consider some changes that have taken place in western societies, particularly developments in social policy and scientific discovery, which have been major factors causing the way we live to be described as post-Christian. As a result of this, what could be described as a post-Christian narrative of sin is emerging. A powerful aspect of this new narrative is the developed notion of structural sin, that is, sin which is embedded in the nature of some of our social structures rather than being expressed only in individual behaviour. What is new is not the existence of this sin but its emergence into public consciousness. Examples of this can be found in oppression, poverty, war, racism and sexism. Institutions of the State as well as religious institutions play a part in any analysis of structural sin.

The Fractured Meta-narrative of Christianity in Britain

We no longer live in a society that can unquestioningly be defined as Christian, that is, a society in which the overwhelming majority of its citizens accept the basic religious premises laid down by the Christian Church as relevant for membership. The core of these premises might be found in a recognition of our inherent sinfulness as members of the human race, a sinfulness which can only be repaired by faith in Jesus Christ, the Son of God, who died for our salvation. The unspoken agenda behind the premises, rarely discussed today, is that the Church has the right to define sin, that there is everlasting life after death and that our behaviour in this life determines whether we go to Heaven or Hell – or in the case of Roman Catholics perhaps experience an interim stay in Purgatory before being transferred to Heaven. Dante laid the picture out for us in the *Divine Comedy*.[1]

From the eighteenth century on we can trace the erosion of belief, not only in the Church's authority on these matters, but on the premises that underlay it. This is not

---

[1] Dante, *The Divine Comedy: The Portable Dante*, trans. Lawrence Binyon, ed. Paulo Milano, Penguin Books: London 1977.

to say that there had been no earlier questioning of the validity of seeing Jesus as divine or the Gospels as literally true. From Celsus who in the second century charged Christians with devaluing education and intelligence since they took the view, 'Do not ask questions; only believe and thy faith will save thee',[2] through to the seventeenth-century Quakers like Gerald Winstanley, and the Humanist Tom Paine in the eighteenth century, there was a constant trickle of what was seen as heretical comment.

Alasdair MacIntyre quotes Mrs Humphrey Ward's best selling novel of 1888, *Robert Elsmere*, as describing a transition from orthodox Christianity to a set of 'undogmatic religious attitudes'. In this she shows how Elsmere's loss of faith grows out of 'his encounter with some of the intellectual issues of the day'. This, MacIntyre says, 'distinguishes the debate of the nineteenth century, not only from that of the twentieth but also from earlier debates'. His argument is that earlier debates on belief had been essentially unchanged for centuries. However, 'those whose belief was put into question in the mid-nineteenth century had to cope with issues unique to their culture'. By this he meant Darwinian biology, the philosophical theories derived from Hegel 'and perhaps above all the new techniques of historical criticism, which both partly grew out of and found their most radical assumptions in the quest for the historical Jesus'.[3]

For Britain, this transition was reflected in writings like those of Thomas Hardy and Thomas Carlyle and the debates around the work of Darwin and later Huxley and was reinforced by the German theologians, particularly Strauss (translated into English by George Eliot), who concluded that while Christianity might hold deep truths and understanding, what the Gospels presented was a mythical religious view randomly based on one of a number of first-century prophets who was given the name Jesus.[4] Renan's *Life of Jesus*[5] presented him as a moral teacher rather than a divinity. Edwards describes it as 'full of praise for him as a man and a moralist but empty of any belief that he had been in any way supernatural'.[6] Nietzsche made the more interesting point that to describe Jesus, as Renan did, as a hero and a genius was an absurdity: 'As a child of God everyone is equal to everyone else … To make a *hero* of Jesus! And what a worse misunderstanding is the word "genius"! Our whole concept, our cultural concept "spirit" had no meaning whatever in the world Jesus lived in.'[7] But even with an exalted human image, before the demythologizing book was published, the scandal that his ideas invoked led to Renan's suspension from his professorial chair in Hebraic, Chaldean and Syriac

---

[2] Alasdair M. McKenzie, 'The Reaction to Christianity in Pagan Thought', Thesis 1653, University of Glasgow.

[3] Alasdair MacIntyre and Paul Ricoeur, *The Religious Significance of Atheism*, Columbia University Press: New York and London 1969, pp. 4–5.

[4] David Friedrich Strauss, *The Life of Jesus: critically examined*, 4th edn, trans. George Eliot, Swan Sonnenschein: London 1902.

[5] Ernest Renan, *The History of the Origins of Christianity. Book 1: The Life of Jesus*, translated from the 13th edn with modifications by the author, Mathieson & Company: London 1864.

[6] David L. Edwards, *Christianity: The First Two Thousand Years*, Cassell: London 1997.

[7] Friedrich Nietzsche, *Twilight of the Idols / The Anti-Christ*, Penguin Classics, Penguin Books: London 1990, p. 153.

languages.[8] At a wider level the old certainties were disappearing under the onslaught of the democratic impulse, as well as science and philosophy.

The mainstream discussion in the second half of the nineteenth century among those concerned with these issues was not about atheism or even agnosticism, although there was an active voice for both these positions.[9] The issue was a significant shift in the belief that the biblical character Jesus was divine – the Son of God – that he died for the sins of the world,[10] that his body was resurrected and ascended into Heaven. No one was questioning the significance or wisdom that people might find in the Christian Bible but they did question the divine nature of Jesus and, following the publication of Darwin's researches, the nature of God as an active participant in the affairs of the world.[11] If Jesus was simply a first-century human person – even if very wise and holy – who was crucified by the Romans for political reasons, what was the relevance of this to questions of human sin other than the good example he set? All this contributed to a loss of belief in the age-old power and authority of the Church. It was a time of intellectual uncertainty combined with political unrest.

These radical views were strongly resisted by those to whom they seemed blasphemy. Even Millais' painting *Christ in the House of His Parents*, exhibited at the Royal Academy in 1850, aroused fury because he had pictured the holy family in a working-class environment, meticulously detailing the meanness of the conditions. To present the holy family as living and working in such ordinary, human surroundings was seen as an affront to middle-class values. For some the purpose of religion and the Gospels appeared to be to support the truth of their view of themselves and their world. Hardy's novel, *Jude the Obscure*, is clearly of the view that the Church is the servant of the middle class.[12]

Working-class people, in the ugliness and squalor of the cities created by the Industrial Revolution, found little to attract them to the Church. Engels said in 1844, 'The workers are not religious and do not attend church.'[13] Henry Mayhew made the same finding.[14] This was not to say that there was no religious impulse amongst working-class people, but it was met, not by the wealthier established churches, but by lower-middle-class evangelists like the Salvation Army. In general, Roman Catholics, who came from Ireland to Britain as immigrants fleeing poverty and starvation, stoutly maintained their religious identity as an aspect of their reviled minority status.[15] Their religion's requirements of compulsory attendance at

[8] David C.J. Lee, *Ernest Renan: In the Shadow of Faith*, Duckworth: London 1996.

[9] In 1848 Marx published the *Communist Manifesto* in London with its famous, frequently abridged reference to religion as the opium of the people. In the 1880s secular and rationalist societies began to be formed.

[10] Dickens' *The Life of Our Lord*, Simon and Schuster: New York 1999, omitted from it the notion that Jesus' death was in atonement for human sin and refrained from any suggestion of his divinity.

[11] Edmund Gosse, *Father and Son*, Windmill Library, Windmill Press: Kingsmill, Surrey 1938, pp. 96ff. describes his father's desperate attempts to reconcile Darwin's theory with his belief in the 'opening chapter of Genesis'.

[12] Thomas Hardy, *Jude the Obscure*, Macmillan: London 1896.

[13] Frederick Engels, *Conditions of the Working Class*, Blackwell, Oxford 1958, p. 62.

[14] Henry Mayhew, *London Labour and the London Poor*, Griffin, Bohn: London 1851.

[15] We can see something of the same response among economic migrants of the Muslim faith.

weekly Mass and regular confession and communion were an integral part of that identity. But for the bulk of working-class men, indifference was the main response.[16] It should be remembered also that the religious impulse was being met in the new radicalism. Marxism, another great meta-narrative, trade unionism, socialism, feminism, education, democracy, were all bubbling away, inspiring idealism and the conviction of the need to create a better world here on earth rather than hope for one in the next.

It was not only the historical 'truthfulness' of the Christian Bible that was in question, or its interpretation; the Hebrew Bible to which the Christian Church had clung as its base of emotional and spiritual power was also under scrutiny. It became clear that the same questions were even more relevant here. What had been seen as a running historical narrative was, after scholastic enquiry, found to be a library of 66 books, written by different authors at different times and not at all in the order in which it was presented. It was assumed however that it could at least be regarded as having some historical value; excavations by Israeli archaeologists are now questioning even that. Professor Herzog of Tel Aviv University writing in the Israeli daily newspaper *Ha'aretz* in 1999 reported that 'the Israelites were never in Egypt, did not wander in the desert, did not conquer the land in a military campaign'. Such a statement has today, in Israel, serious political as well as theological implications.

Churches in Britain virtually ignored these debates and continued to preach the same sermons about Jesus as the (divine) Son of God and God the Father as knowing our inmost thoughts, being omnipotent, omniscient, omnipresent and interventionist. Some theologians attempted to adapt to a changing view but their message was, and still is, rarely presented in the pulpit. It was however to be found in literature. Both George Eliot and Thomas Hardy had questioned accepted church values by offering a humanist rather than theological view of sin in novels like *Middlemarch* and *Tess of the D'Urbervilles.* It became widely known that George Eliot had spurned conventional morality in her private life, but this had no effect on the sales of her books, which brought her fame, money and respectability.[17]

In the 1930s D.H. Lawrence had written a controversial novel about Christ, *The Man Who Died*,[18] which emphasized his humanity rather than his divinity, but in the post-Second World War era an even more decisive shift was experienced. Kazantzakis' publication of his novel *The Last Temptation* broke a fundamental taboo in its depiction of Jesus as a man struggling with temptation, succumbing to it and later overcoming it. His translator, Bien, claims that Kazantzakis wanted to lift Christ out of the Church altogether, to fashion a new Saviour and rescue him from a moral and spiritual void.[19] The Vatican blacklisted the novel in 1954, calling it heretical and blasphemous. When Martin Scorsese later made it into a film some cities banned its showing. Now Christ, stripped of his divinity, has been described in poetry and plays as a lover and as a homosexual – in some Christian views a

---

[16] For women, particularly Roman Catholic women, different issues were involved which are outside the scope of this chapter.

[17] Marghanita Laski, *George Eliot and her world*, Thames & Hudson, London 1973.

[18] D.H. Lawrence, *The Man Who Died*, Secker: London 1931.

[19] Nikos Kazantzakis, *The Last Temptation*, trans. P.A. Bien, Faber & Faber: London 1975, p. 517.

sinner. The poet Edwin Morgan offers us a Jesus who is a lover of both women and men.[20]

Those theologians and clergy who held on to the image of an interventionist God were faced in the depression years of the 1930s with an ancient dilemma. Previously, the debate about how a good God could allow intolerable suffering, which had arisen particularly after the slaughter of the First World War, had been confined to scholars; the faithful had been content to accept what their 'elders and betters' told them. The unstoppable tide of democratic thought in Britain led this question to be raised again during the economic and human misery of the 1930s. A new mood was abroad with the rise of political parties of the left, many of whose members were questioning all the institutions which they saw as oppressing them; the wealthy churches and their members were seen as part of that oppression. Indeed, Anglicans were described as 'the Tory Party at prayer'. The established churches, particularly in the wealthier parishes, failed to address these questions although individual clergy did so.

In Scotland, beginning in 1938, a remarkable minister, George McLeod (later Lord McLeod), was deeply affected by the poverty in his parish of Govan in Glasgow, and set up training schemes for unemployed men. Together, they rebuilt the sixth-century Columba's Abbey on the island of Iona. McLeod founded the Iona Community, centred around the Abbey, which brought together clergy and laity who had, and continue to have, a mission to work with the socially oppressed. McLeod's was one of the voices in the 1930s that reclaimed the image of Jesus as a political rebel, who if he were alive today would be standing side by side with the poor and the unemployed.

A story of a minister who preached with such a voice in the time of the 1926 miners' strike is told by Lewis Grassic Gibbon in *Grey Granite*, written in 1934, the third novel in his trilogy, *A Scots Quair*.[21] Grassic Gibbon highlights the conflict of trying to reconcile belief in the early vision of Christianity with the institutions that have grown up around it. The novel was written in the 1930s on the eve of the Second World War, which was to sharpen all these issues: young men and women would return to Britain with experience of other cultures, a sense of the vulnerability of the human body and most significantly a loss of a sense of the subservience which is an essential factor in obedience to authority. In the post-war period the public appeared to be turning to political and scientific rather than clerical solutions to human distress and suffering. This was reflected, among other factors, in ever-diminishing church attendance.

The Impact of Secular Social Policies on Perceptions of Sin

The introduction of the National Health Service, which gave free access to health care, made it possible for poor women as well as men to get medical attention. The general health of children improved and infant mortality fell largely as a result of post-war housing policies. The contraceptive pill and the new wide availability of

---

[20] Edwin Morgan, *A.D. A Trilogy of Plays on the Life of Jesus*, Carcanet Press: Manchester 2000.

[21] Lewis Grassic Gibbon, *A Scots Quair: A Trilogy of Novels*, Penguin: London 1986.

condoms which men had learned to use in the armed forces took the fear of pregnancy out of sexual activity for many and resulted in smaller, healthier families as their standard of living improved. The legalization of abortion put an end to the misery of gynaecological damage and the occasional deaths brought on by an illegal trade practised in insanitary conditions. More people felt a sense of control over the consequences of their sexual behaviour; in addition, a view of illness as a biological fact, rather than as suffering brought about by either sin or the will of God, became more widespread. Sulphonamides changed venereal disease from being God's punishment for sinful behaviour to an unfortunate interlude in one's life, and penicillin proved more reliable than prayers in healing what had been the fatal illness of tuberculosis.[22]

From the early 1960s the Houses of Parliament were increasingly engaging in secular legislation which was affecting personal human behaviour and images of sin – the Abortion Act, the Race Relations Act and the Equal Opportunities Act. The Legal Aid Act and Social Security legislation made it possible for working-class women to leave abusive marriages, to access financial aid to achieve a legal separation or divorce and know that the State would support them and their children. The rush to use these services was an indication of the distress in which many women had lived, often in collusion with pastoral advice that they should carry their cross and forgive their husband's cruelty.

In the same way unmarried mothers were given state benefits that enabled them to keep their babies rather than have them adopted. The number of babies available for adoption collapsed, and with it the stigma of illegitimacy, showing clearly how often women had been forced to give up babies they would rather have kept. We were now seeing the State actively intervening in ways that influenced the social perception of the nature of sin. There was a growing view that it was the Church which had been sinful in promoting ideas which had led to so much pain and distress – women forced to stay in abusive marriages, babies forcibly taken away from unmarried mothers, the reluctance of the churches to support services for contraception and abortion. The effects of these and other 'Christian' practices was to explode in the 1980s and 1990s with accusations of cruelty and sexual abuse perpetrated by members of the clergy, both men and women, against those children in their care in institutions which had not responded to the new sensitivity to human need.

Two significant shifts took place in the 1960s among Christians. The first was the formation of the Christian Socialist Movement in 1960, drawn from the Christian Socialist League and the Society of Socialist Clergy whose links went back to the nineteenth century.[23] The radical Methodist preacher and pacifist Donald Soper was a founder member and President until his death in 1998. The notion of Christians being socialists was not new but its most powerful association was with pacifism. The roots of political pacifism could be said to go back to Keir Hardie, the first socialist Member of Parliament and founder of the Labour Party whose aim was to

---

[22] AIDS was to reawaken the connection between sin and illness in the 1980s. It was again seen as God's punishment for sin, particularly the 'sin' of homosexuality, by religious fundamentalists.

[23] Continental European Protestant churches have played an important part in developing Christian Socialism, gaining support from distinguished theologians like Paul Tillich and Reinhold Niebuhr.

bring Christian values to bear on workers' rights. The Christian Socialist Movement had the specific intention of influencing the political parties with a mission 'to Socialise Christianity and Christianise Socialism'.[24] It remained a small organization until the election of John Smith, a committed Christian, as leader of the Labour Party in 1993, when there was a sudden explosion of interest and membership.[25]

The second shift among Christians came with the publication in 1961 of John Robinson's paperback, *Honest to God*,[26] which offered to the general reader an alternative vision of God. Robinson had questioned and rejected the traditional images of God, Jesus and the purpose of prayer as begging for favours. He offered a more transcendent image but claimed that it could be sought in the experiences of everyday lives. David Edwards described it as 'both genuinely ultimate and genuinely intimate' although in general he seemed less than enthusiastic about Robinson's approach.[27] The essential problem emerging for theologians now was how to maintain religious belief without surrendering intellectual integrity. The lasting effect of Robinson's work was that it brought the issues he discussed into the frontline of public awareness. By the end of the 1960s it was becoming increasingly clear that for the post-war generation religious teaching, particularly that using the theology of Augustine on the nature of sin, was ceasing to play any part in how most people lived their lives. What was emerging was a new secular morality, a social morality that included women claiming equality, self-respect and autonomy hand in hand with the right to take responsibility for their sexuality and reproduction.[28]

The 1960s was also the period when psychologists, influenced by Freud, and the sociologists who were developing their new discipline, were questioning the causes of crime. The idea that sinfulness was inherent had affected theories of criminality linking criminal behaviour to inheritance (the 'sins of the father' syndrome), genetically based wickedness (to be measured by the shape of the head), or just pure inborn evil. This was not so far removed from the idea of being possessed of a devil. Judges in the criminal courts were operating in a Judaeo-Christian tradition but academics were now offering theories about the effects on behaviour of poverty, parental abuse and other environmental factors; the assumption that the person committing a crime was totally responsible for that crime was losing ground. Attitudes to sin and evil had become more complex since Freud's theories of the unconscious had become more widely accepted, but now they were moving out of the private into the public domain. The Benthamite theory of nurture as more

---

[24] Taken from the manifesto called *Papers from the Lamb*, a reference to the Holborn pub where the original group discussed their faith and politics.

[25] Discussion with Graham Dale, secretary of the Christian Socialist Movement and author of *God's Politicians*, HarperCollins: London 2000.

[26] John Robinson, *Honest to God*, SCM Press: London 1963.

[27] Edwards, *Christianity*, p. 609.

[28] Nor was this was entirely new. Something of the same had been claimed by the women of the Beguine movement in the thirteenth century who were accused of harbouring the heresy of the Free Spirit which supposedly taught that a soul in union with God was freed from conventional moral restraints. See Meister Eckhart, *Selected Writings*, trans. Oliver Davies, Penguin Books: London 1994, p. xiii.

important than nature was gaining ground. This was expressed in a popular song in the American *West Side Story*, one of the new genre of dramatic musicals which were replacing musical comedy. The song 'Gee, Officer Krupke'[29] gave a satirical summary of the opposing images of the delinquent: 'Dear kindly Sergeant Krupke, You gotta understand, It's just our upbringing that gets us out of hand. Our mothers all are junkies, our fathers all are drunks, Golly Moses, nat-cher-ly we're punks.'

Every assumption of sin and virtue was opened to scrutiny and, if it seemed necessary, legislative change. Consensual sex between adult males was legalized following the Wolfenden Report,[30] transvestism was increasingly seen simply as an idiosyncrasy, sex changes became surgically available, as did knowledge about why for some people it was a psychological necessity. Living together before marriage became common practice, as did becoming pregnant without marriage. Artificial insemination for married couples, single women and lesbian couples along with surrogate mothers became part of a widely accepted pattern. The concept of illegitimacy disappeared. Divorce changed from being a scandalous minority occurrence to being a reality for one in three marriages in Britain as the law was relaxed. Laws on censorship were also relaxed and shops were allowed to open on Sundays. What was remarkable was the speed with which these changes took place. There were protests in the letters columns of some broadsheet newspapers but little attention was paid to them. From issues of significant personal morality to minor issues of daily life, the voters were rejecting previous constrictions on their personal behaviour and insisting on the legislators giving them the secular legislation they wanted.

In the introduction to his book, *Godless Morality*, Richard Holloway makes what he sees as an important distinction between sin and morality.[31] Sin he sees as essentially a religious idea which, as we have seen earlier, has been defined as disobedience to God.[32] In this understanding only blind obedience is required; there is no place for discussion or cooperation. The rules are laid down, as are the penalties for breaking them, and the rituals required for re-establishing a relationship with God. Holloway argues that we should now separate religion and ethics. He is in fact arguing for a morality that can be accepted as having validity that does not necessarily involve a belief in God.[33] Morality, which grows out of ethics, he says, tries to base itself on the observed consequences of the action: 'A wrong act is one that manifestly harms others or their interests, or violates their rights or causes injustice.'[34]

---

[29] 'Gee, Officer Krupke', from *West Side Story*, music from Leonard Bernstein, lyrics by Stephen Sondheim. Pub. by G. Schirmer Ltd/Campbell Connelly & Co. Ltd, 8/9 Frith Street, London, W1.

[30] *Report of the Committee on Homosexual Offences and Prostitution*, HMSO: London 1957 chaired by Sir John Wolfenden.

[31] Richard Holloway, *Godless Morality: Keeping religion out of ethics*, Canongate Press: Edinburgh 1999.

[32] Thomas Merton in his discussion of anti-Semitism says, 'The theology of suffering is strongly tinged with ideas of punishment, and morality becomes a morality of obedience rather than love.' *Conjectures of a Guilty Bystander*, Burns & Oates Ltd: London 1968, p. 119.

[33] Holloway, *Godless Morality*, p. 20.

[34] Ibid., p. 14.

This last thought is more complex than it appears since we live in a multicultural society which holds, among its members, different perceptions of interests, rights and injustice which have been developed over a period of time in different places with different sets of social values. The separation between religion and morality that Holloway is asking for has, as we have seen, already taken place among many Christians, particularly in the areas of marriage, divorce and reproduction. He, presumably, is asking Christians who hold to earlier attitudes or those who take what is described as a fundamentalist view of biblical teaching to take this step.

While conventional Christians could criticize Holloway for going too far by offering an uncritical acceptance of a post-modern individualist culture, a radical critique can also be offered that he didn't go far enough. The view that there is no necessary connection between religion and morality and that we need morality without religion is taken for granted already by most non-religious people. They live in that way. What he might have argued for in the section of his book which deals with what many religious people see as personal sins of the body like homosexuality is that neither Church nor State should interfere with what people choose to do with their bodies as long as they don't harm anyone else. The attitude of the Church, peering to see what goes on between the sheets rather than questioning war, poverty, torture and racism and our destruction of the planet, needs to be addressed more sharply by theologians. Holloway is in fact now raising some of these issues.[35]

The Emergence of the Concept of Structural Sin

The Second World War has been seen as a watershed in the understanding of sin.[36] The first half of the century had been seen as opening with two competing values: 'the cult of the imperial superman and the relatively new concern for human suffering'. With this had come a regular ebb and flow of permissiveness and puritanism.[37] The most significant factors after 1945 were the emergence of public knowledge of the Nazis' planned murder of communists, socialists, the mentally and physically handicapped, homosexuals, gypsies, the entire Jewish race and later in the war many Slavs, and the judgements of the Nuremberg trials. As a result the end of the Second World War brought sharply into focus not only the issue of forgiveness we saw in Wiesenthal's work but also the awareness of a new dimension of sin.

The distinction between war crimes, crimes of the State, and sin in a religious sense became blurred. The established interpretation of the Ten Commandments seemed inadequate in the face of the evidence that emerged of the depths of human depravity that had existed in the Nazi death camps. Previous centuries had seen human atrocities, many of which had the blessing of State and Church. These were

---

[35] *The Observer*, 24 December 2000.

[36] Not only of sin. In 1955, Theodor Adorno told us that 'to write poetry after the Holocaust is barbaric'. See *Prisms: Cultural Criticism and Society*, trans. Samuel and Shierry Weber, London 1967. Also quoted in Martin Jay, *Adorno*, Harvard University Press: Cambridge, MA 1984, p. 49.

[37] Oliver Thomson, *A History of Sin*, Canongate Press: Edinburgh 1993, p. 224.

not categorized as sinful because they were thought, by those taking part, to be inevitable aspects of a war, which was either just, or else in the interests of Christianity. Christian theologians in the twentieth century have been divided about the theory of the just war but the majority have continued to support the concept. The end was held to justify the means. Torture, rape, killing had been seen as inevitable accompaniments to war; it was only at the end of the twentieth century that torture and rape were beginning to be defined as war crimes. Killing in wartime is still seen as acceptable.[38]

Nations had practised genocide against other nations;[39] anti-Semitism and persecution of Jews had long been endemic across Europe but Nazism brought with it a new dimension. Just as technology had made killing with guns more effective, the Nazis harnessed technology to industrialize death. They did this with great efficiency and in the process achieved what Hannah Arendt described as 'the banality of evil'.[40] However, this vivid phrase, which expressed an important thought, particularly relevant to the bureaucratization of the procedures of the death camps, has masked another awareness. I would argue that it is cruelty, whether organized or unorganized, no matter how sanctioned by Church or State, that is intolerable. The fact that it had achieved for those acting cruelly the veneer of banality reinforces our need to identify it as iniquity, or if we maintain theological language, as sinful. Rorty quotes Judith Shklar, who argues that for liberals cruelty is the worst thing we do.[41]

Before the Second World War, information about wars had relied on newspapers or the testimony brought home by soldiers. We know from documentaries and novels that after the First World War many soldiers had found on returning home that it was too painful to describe the horrors of their experiences in the trenches. Some expressed their despair in poetry. Larkin summed it up for both the First and Second World War:

> Never such innocence,
> Never before or since,
> As changed itself to past
> Without a word – the men
> Leaving the gardens tidy,
> The thousands of marriages,
> Lasting a little while longer:
> Never such innocence again.[42]

---

[38] The Christian pacifist, Stuart Morris, said in 1937, 'War is not to be thought of as dying for what you believe in, but as killing for what you believe in', quoted in Housman's *Peace Diary* for week 32, year 2000.

[39] The classic example of this is the massacre of the Armenians by the Turks.

[40] Hannah Arendt, *Eichmann in Jerusalem: a report on the banality of evil*, Penguin Books: New York 1994, ch. 15.

[41] Richard Rorty, *Contingency, Irony and Solidarity*, Cambridge University Press: Cambridge 1989, p. xv.

[42] Philip Larkin, *MCMXIV, from The Whitsun Weddings*, Faber & Faber: London 1964, quoted in *Never Such Innocence*, ed. Martin Stephen, Buchan and Enright: London 1988.

Knowledge of the details of sin destroys our innocence.[43] In 1945 the details of the calculated killing of millions in the Nazi concentration camps came into the public domain in a different way from information of previous wars. Every cinema showed newsreels of the Allied troops entering the death camps to find hundreds of dying and emaciated prisoners. The newspapers printed photographs as well as stories which described how gas chambers and crematoria, made by respectable German firms, had been used to kill thousands each day, how their hair had been cut off to use for stuffing mattresses, their teeth extracted for gold fillings and the fat of their bodies used to make soap. Information of the details of camp life survived in spite of the determined efforts of the SS to destroy evidence of what had gone on. In his preface to *The Drowned and the Saved*, the author Primo Levi quotes Wiesenthal describing how the SS boasted to their prisoners:

> However this war may end, we have won the war against you; none of you will be left to bear witness, but even if someone were to survive, the world would not believe him. There will perhaps be suspicions, discussions, research by historians, but there will be no certainties, because we will destroy the evidence together with you.[44]

They were wrong: there was evidence left in the ruins of the gas chambers and crematoria, written testimonies buried deep in the rubble of the Warsaw ghetto, the mass graves, and the bodies, minds and hearts of the survivors. It was on the experience of the Jews who perished in the camps that attention focused after the war. The reasons for this are complex but an important factor was the powerful Jewish capacity for articulating and placing in context the suffering they had endured over many centuries. Also considerable numbers among them were formally educated professionals, people with friends in other countries and a command of several languages – unlike the victims of earlier genocidal massacres in Armenia or Australia or North America. Among those who survived there was a resolute determination to bear witness to what they had seen and endured, not only for themselves but also for those who had died. They resolved it should never be allowed to happen again.

One question that is still being explored is whether or not the people who committed these acts were or are aware that what they did was 'sinful'. I am now using that word in a non-Christian sense since many in positions of power, although they may have been brought up as Christians, had rejected that position and substituted Hitler for their God or their Christ. The question becomes one of morality (or perhaps psychology). The writer Gitta Sereny has devoted much of her life to exploring that question. For many years she interviewed significant figures in the German hierarchy without coming to a clear view. The human capacity to deny one's knowledge[45] and refuse to learn from experience seems unlimited:

---

[43] Nearly fifty years later Ian McEwan was to use the immediate post-war situation to describe the destruction of innocence of a young English man working in Germany for the Army. Ian McEwan, *The Innocent*, Picador, London 1990.

[44] Primo Levi, *The Drowned and the Saved*, trans. Raymond Rosenthal, Abacus: London 1995, p. 1.

[45] The same has been shown in the Truth Commissions that were set up in a number of African states where similar horrors have taken place in the 1990s. I will be looking at this phenomenon in a later chapter.

... personal and national immorality is not reserved to any one crime, any one place, any one ideology, any one people, any one group or any one person. The immorality of Hitler is thus equalled by the immorality of Stalin; the immorality of the Nazi torture camps in the 1930s and 1940s by the South Africa that murdered Stephen Biko and untold others in their prisons during the 1960s, 1970s and 1980s, and indeed by the increasingly emerging horrors of the past twenty five years in various South American countries. The immorality of the Lidice massacre was duplicated by Americans in Vietnam; the murder of the Jews, however uniquely awful the technique, was numerically even exceeded (though the mind recoils at such comparisons) by the Nazi slaughters of non-Jewish Russians and Poles, and all of these were more than paralleled by the even now not fully known number of Russians whom Stalin, Yagoda and Yeshov murdered no less determinedly than the Nazis murdered the Jews. Finally, with the same cynicism the West demonstrated towards those earlier crimes, nothing was done about the genocide of the Biafrans by the Nigerians, of the Kurds by Saddam Hussein (whom the West could have helped, but didn't, to remove from power), and of all educated by the Cambodians, by the Khmer Rouge, whose political ambitions the West today, to our collective shame, continues to support.[46]

This list, horrifying as it is, does not include what followed in Rwanda, Kosovo and Indonesia. The impulse to kill, to burn, to rape,[47] to loot, all the behaviours unleashed in wars, cannot be addressed in the simplistic terms of the Ten Commandments. The Seven Deadly Sins with their understanding of the power of Pride, Anger, Lust and Avarice fed by Sloth, Envy and Gluttony bring us much closer to an understanding of the human condition that makes such behaviour possible. Chaucer's Parson describes the Seven Deadly Sins as being 'all leashed together'. They are he says, the trunk of the tree from which all others branch.[48]

Even these awful (and aweful) happenings don't reflect the shock felt by observers of the human condition when the atomic bomb was exploded over the cities of Hiroshima and Nagasaki. For those who watched film of the bomb exploding and the great following mushroom cloud that billowed into the heavens it was reminiscent of Chapter 8 of the Book of Revelation. There we read of the seven angels, with their seven trumpets, the blast of each bringing a different area of destruction to humans and to the earth. It was this new capacity of the peoples of the planet to destroy themselves and the planet with them that brought many Christians, among others, to feel that they must oppose any further development of these weapons. The Campaign for Nuclear Disarmament, CND, was important in that it brought a new concept of sin to both Christians and non-believers by initiating a dialogue about the moral legitimacy of war in a nuclear age. This led to questions of the moral legitimacy of the use of weapons of war as instruments of oppression by the rulers of a State against citizens of that State and to the moral legitimacy of war itself.[49] These discussions politicized many clergy, some of

---

[46] Gitta Sereny, *Albert Speer: His Battle With Truth*, Macmillan: London 1995, p. 168.

[47] It was only after the publicity given to the rape of Moslem women in the Bosnian conflict that rape was designated as a war crime.

[48] *The Canterbury Tales*, ed. Walter W. Skeat, Clarendon Press: Oxford, 1894, 'The Parson's Tale', 10. 387–88.

[49] A member of staff of the Peace and Justice Commission of the Catholic Church offered me an unattributed but, he assured me, genuine quotation from an American bishop who said that the notion of a just war should be put in the same drawer as the notion of the flat earth.

whom, like Canon Collins, assumed leadership roles in the British movements for peace.

Another was the charismatic American, Daniel Berrigan, a radical Catholic priest who challenged his Church and the State in his actions and his writings, taking part in public demonstrations and direct action which resulted in several periods of imprisonment. Abandoning the Ten Commandments as a rule to live by, Berrigan developed a new set, which he called *Ten Commandments for the Long Haul*.[50] These are drawn from the Christian rather than the Hebrew Bible and grow out of his experiences as a peace protester.

Written from a deeply, passionately Christian perspective, the discussion around each of these 'commandments' offers a total reassessment of how to live one's life but with the warning that to do so will not be easy. Discussing the first admonition to make friends of enemies, he is moved to point out that over many years one may never succeed in making a friend of a single enemy. What one might find in the course of peace making is that one encounters 'a spiky and thorny forest of strangers and hostile folk'.[51]

In his second commandment, 'Do this in remembrance of me',[52] Berrigan discusses the alternating pressure on us to remember what vested interests want us to remember and to forget what they want us to forget. He sees in the Eucharist not only the breaking of bread and the pouring of the wine but the breaking of bones and the outpouring of blood of those who remember what is not wanted by the powerful: 'We have forgotten – it is embarrassing, discomfiting in the extreme to remember – what a true vision entails,' he says, 'the kingdom of God, the kingdom of peace, is the kingdom of the crucified'.[53] In each of the following essays written around these 'commandments' Berrigan explores the way to that kingdom. He attacks particularly what he, himself an academic theologian, sees as betrayal by his colleagues, 'whose method makes twentieth century dead-sea scrolls of the living word'.

In all of Berrigan's commandments he is challenging the established order of thinking and the establishment. He has taken the concept of sin and translated it into the sin of being an insider, of being a member of a society that creates outsiders, a society where the Church and State have joined hands to protect their mutual interests and who express their sin in murder, vindictiveness and cruelty.[54] It was this sin Jesus named in that powerful moment of silence when, in the story of the woman taken in adultery, after saying 'He that is without sin among you, let him first cast a stone at her', he turned aside, stooped down and wrote on the ground. Just as Jesus created a new paradigm by challenging the Judaic law, so Berrigan is moving to a new paradigm of the definition of sin.

---

[50] Daniel Berrigan, *Ten Commandments for the Long Haul*, ed. Robert A. Raines, Abingdon: Nashville 1981.

[51] Ibid., p. 79.

[52] 1 Cor. 11:24–5.

[53] Berrigan, *Ten Commandments*, p. 86.

[54] I would suggest that Camus' novel, *The Outsider*, offers another interpretation of the word 'outsider'. Camus is concerned not primarily with the outsider as a reject but more as the person who will not lie and who refuses to hide his feelings. See Albert Camus, *The Outsider*, trans. Joseph Laredo, Penguin Books: London 1982, p. 118.

It is in Asian Christianity however that we find one of the sharpest challenges to a European, mainstream Christian interpretation of sin. As part of his own attempt to analyse the nature of sin, the theologian Andrew Sung Park questions how the reality of sin is understood in the world today.[55] He looks at the work of a number of European theologians, Niebuhr,[56] Barth,[57] Tillich and Bultmann,[58] to support his view that liberal theologians have understated the gravity of sin,[59] while neo-orthodox theologians stress its seriousness. Park describes Niebuhr's view that the concept of sin is crucial to Christian theology. Niebuhr sees pride as the primary sin, since pride is a denial of our finite nature, and sensuality as only secondary, centring his discussion of anthropology in the doctrine of sin, so depicting 'man as sinner'. Park sees Karl Barth's doctrine of sin as being unique since it placed sin within the doctrine of redemption: 'For him, only through Jesus Christ do sinners become aware of their sinful nature.'[60] Barth sees rebellion against God's grace in Jesus Christ as the fundamental sin and that sin as being expressed in pride, sloth and falsehood. In pride one exalts oneself to be like God, in sloth we succumb to stupidity, inhumanity and anxiety, in falsehood we oppose the truth of Jesus Christ and ultimately fall into the idolatry of false religions.

Park describes Tillich as seeing the heart of sin as estrangement from God and the story of the Fall as the symbolic portrayal of that estranged state. The marks of this estrangement are set out as unbelief, hubris and concupiscence, all of which grow out of self-centredness. In unbelief, Tillich claims, we withdraw our own centre from the divine centre, in hubris we see ourselves as the centre of ourselves and of the world, and in concupiscence we draw everything into our own centre. Moving on, Park sees Bultmann, influenced by Heidegger's discussion of authentic and inauthentic existence, as finding the root of sin in existence without faith which expresses itself in ingratitude, unbelief, surrender to the world and bondage to death.

All these theologians stress the personal, existential aspects of sin in idiosyncratic ways that refer more to the Seven Deadly Sins than to the Ten Commandments. As with the Seven Deadly Sins the underlying imperative of individual sin as involving the community, an aspect of sin which was so much a feature of the Judaic tradition, is hardly to be seen. The main emphasis is on the private self in relationship to God in Christ. In contrast a new generation of theologians has emerged, many of whom, like Park himself and like Berrigan, reject the view that sin is simply a private matter to be explored within the family or within relationships but urgently requires to be understood within a political and

---

[55] Andrew Sung Park, *The Wounded Heart of God: The Asian Concept of Han and the Christian Doctrine of Sin*, Abingdon Press: Nashville 1993, p. 70.

[56] Reinhold Niebuhr, *The Nature and Destiny of Man*, Nisbet: London 1941, pp. 178–240.

[57] Karl Barth, *Church Dogmatics*, ed. G.W. Bromiley and T.F. Torrance, 13 vols, Edinburgh: T&T Clark, 1969, 4:403.

[58] Rudolph Bultmann, *Primitive Christianity*, trans. R.H. Fuller, New York: Living Age Books 1989, p. 55.

[59] Park gives Frederick R. Tennant (1866–1957) as a classic exponent of liberal theology at the turn of the twentieth century who treats sin as 'an evolutionary residue of our animal origin, reducing it to sensuality'.

[60] Park, *Wounded Heart*, p. 71.

social context. This is not to deny individual responsibility for sin. It is rather to redefine the boundaries of acceptable human behaviour.

Park pushes these issues further by introducing the Asian concept of 'han' into the discussion. He argues that throughout its history the Christian Church has been concerned with sin but has ignored the importance of the pain of the victims of sin. These victims, he writes, 'express the ineffable experience of deep bitterness and helplessness'.[61] This experience of pain is what in the Far East is called 'han'. Park sees it as a critical wound of the heart, rooted in the hearts of the victims of sin and violence. It expresses itself in feelings of sadness, helplessness, hopelessness, resentment, hatred and the will to revenge. We can use this concept of 'han' as a way of recognizing the feelings of the survivors of the Holocaust, the Palestinians in the occupied territories, the Kosovo Albanians, the Kosovan Serbs, abused women and children, the unemployed and the exploited.[62] Park believes that sin and 'han' must be considered together if we are to develop comprehensive understanding and describes the present form of the doctrine of sin as 'inadequate to diagnose and address the world's problems'.[63] He recognizes however that in some recent theological developments a less one-sided notion of sin may be developing – particularly in liberation and feminist theology.

Sins Identified by Liberation Theology

This response to what could be called societal or structural, rather than individual, sin was most dramatically seen in the development of liberation theology in the Third World. This movement of the late twentieth century saw theology as a form of critical reflection on the struggle for liberation from social, political and economic oppression. It was principally, but not entirely, supported by Roman Catholic clergy, mostly Jesuits, but these priests encountered severe criticism from the Vatican. One of the most prominent liberation theologians, Gustavo Gutierrez,[64] expresses his commitment as interpreting the Bible and the Christian tradition from the specific perspective of the poor and marginalized.

Some western Christians are moving in the same direction. Towards the end of the twentieth century the most active issue to engage them has been that of the Jubilee 2000 Campaign, which has pressed for Third World debt to be cancelled. Members of this group believe that it is sinful for rich governments like Britain's to take interest payments from countries which are unable to provide health and education services for their people. As an ecumenical group, Jubilee 2000 campaigned for the waiving of Third World debt in accordance with God's instructions to Moses that after seven times seven years debts and slavery should be cancelled.[65] Demonstrations, led by church members, in Europe and North America

---

[61] Park, Ibid., p. 10.

[62] These thoughts are relevant to the discussion in Chapter 1 about the mobs seeking vengeance on paedophiles.

[63] Park, *Wounded Heart*, p. 73.

[64] Gustavo Gutierrez, *Essential Writings*, SCM: London 1996.

[65] Lev. 25:8–10.

have influenced governments to consider this question and, directly influenced by this, the UK government in 1999 made the unilateral decision to begin cutting the debt. It is clear however that these movements and ideas represent only a minority of those who identify themselves as Christians.

The liberation theologians in particular have revolted against the individualistic views of sin. Gustavo Gutierrez confronts what he sees as the threefold nature of sin: economic and socio-political oppression, historical determinism and spiritual sin. An individual view of sin is helpless in the face of the injustice and oppression that has been part of human history. In a city like Bristol, where great fortunes were based on the slave trade, a television programme which brought the descendants of slaves into a dialogue with the descendants of slave owners highlighted a new sensitivity to that history.

This new response has been demonstrated perhaps most vividly in the reaction to oppression of the indigenous black community in South Africa and the support given to that oppression by some groups of Christians who claimed biblical authority for their position.[66] These groups were challenged, not by academic theologians but by practising priests in a range of churches, particularly the Anglican and Methodist, who rejected apartheid as sinful and un-Christian. Other theologians like Dorothée Soelle, Jürgen Moltmann and Frederick Herzog have stressed the social dimension of sin over a range of issues like feminism and ecology. Soelle makes the point that 'The Protestant consciousness of sin is innocuous and distresses no one in its indiscriminate universality, for it identifies sin, not theoretically but *de facto*, with a universal human fate comparable perhaps to smallpox, against which we are protected by vaccination.'[67]

Sins Identified by Feminist Theology

Feminist theologians have made it clear that most concepts of sin are based on a male-centred understanding. Berrigan related his sixth commandment, 'Let him who is without sin', to the position of women in the Church. He sees the Church, uneasy and guilt-ridden, as the circle of accusers before the community of women, like the accusers of the woman taken in adultery.[68] Here too he sees a place for the ironic imagination of Jesus who sees that reality is other than the law, other than convention. The Church, he says, regards this community of women as 'suspect, under judgement from birth, denied access to altar and pulpit, consigned to lowest places – pariahs whose only crime is their biology'. Jesus stands with them, Berrigan believes, as He stood with 'the outcast, the lepers, the rag-tag elements of street, market, hovel'.[69]

Two women who see themselves working as feminist activists and scholars within the Christian tradition are Rita Nakashima Brock and Susan Brooks

---

[66] This is discussed by Michael Lapsley in Michael Worsnip, *Priest and Partisan*, Ocean Press: Melbourne 1996.

[67] Dorothée Soelle, *Political Theology*, trans. John Shelley, Fortress: Philadelphia 1974, p. 89.

[68] John 8:3–11.

[69] Berrigan, *Ten Commandments*, p. 108.

Thistlethwaite. They illustrate this in their research into prostitution.[70] The woman
working in prostitution[71] has traditionally been seen as an archetypal sinner while at
the same time exerting fascination for both men and women. In the Christian view
she can only be saved by grace, as was Magdalene, and we see the use of this name
in the various institutions that have been set up for 'fallen women'. Brock and
Thistlethwaite take a more practical view of the possibilities of helping women
escape from their economic dependency on the sex industry.

There has been a significant shift in some Christian women's understanding of
sin which has forced them to question their place within the Christian tradition.[72]
The beginning of the wave of feminist theological writing can be identified in an
article written in 1960 by Valerie Saiving:

> It is clear that many of the characteristic emphases of contemporary theology ... its
> identification of sin with pride, will to power, exploitation, self assertiveness, and the
> treating of others as objects rather than persons ... it is clear that such an analysis of
> man's dilemma was profoundly responsive and relevant to the concrete facts of modern
> man's existence ... As a matter of fact, however, this theology is not adequate to the
> universal situation ... For the temptations of woman *as woman* are not the same as the
> temptations of man *as man*, and the specifically feminine forms of sin ... have a quality
> that can never be encompassed by such terms as 'pride' and 'will to power'. They are
> better suggested by such items as triviality, distractibility and diffuseness; lack of an
> organizing centre or focus; dependence on others for one's own self definitions ... In short
> underdevelopment or negation of the self.[73]

This was the first clear statement that definitions of sin, including the Seven Deadly
Sins, have been written by men for men although used against women. Women
theologians like Noddings,[74] Plaskow[75] and Hampson[76] responded to this with
powerful statements of the need for women, who have accepted a role as sinful
daughters of Eve who by her disobedience brought shame on all women, to abandon
their taught roles of self-effacement and self-sacrifice. A main target of feminist
attack is the theologian Niebuhr (also under attack from Park), who is seen as
holding 'an essentially isolated model of the human self'.[77] Hampson offers the

---

[70] Rita Nakashima Brock and Susan Brooks Thistlethwaite, *Casting Stones*, Fortress Press:
Minneapolis 1996.

[71] I am using the phrase woman or women working in prostitution in an attempt to avoid the
depersonalization associated with the word prostitute. At the same time I recognize that men also work in
prostitution but they do not seem to incur the same opprobrium as women.

[72] Because we are in the middle of a paradigm shift it is impossible to make any unqualified
statement about a Christian view of any group within the Church. Christian women range from the angry
and resentful to the secure and content, with many shades between.

[73] Valerie Saiving, 'The Human Situation: A Feminine View', *Journal of Religion*, 40 (April 1960),
pp. 100–112, reprinted in C.P. Christ and J. Plaiskow, eds, *Womanspirit Rising: a Feminist Reader in
Religion*, Harper and Row: New York and San Francisco 1979.

[74] Nel Noddings, *Women and Evil*, University of California Press: Berkeley, Los Angeles and London
1989.

[75] Judith Plaskow, *Sex, Sin and Grace*, University Press of America: Washington, DC 1980.

[76] Daphne Hampson, *Theology and Feminism*, Basil Blackwell: Oxford 1990.

[77] Ibid., p. 124.

work of Judith Vaughan as an example of an excellent critique of Niebuhr's view: she sees the self as only having meaning in relation with others. It is the view that the individual is essentially free and autonomous that makes it possible for Niebuhr to define sin as pride, rather than Saiving's view that women's sin may be, to pick out only one phrase, 'dependence on others for one's own self definition', that is, possibly, lack of pride.

This discussion, important and disruptive of conventional Christian attitudes at the time it was being presented, has largely been overtaken by social and political change in the position of women both within and outside the Church. The concessions made to equality may have taken the edge off some of the passion that went into the earlier discussions leaving women theologians with a seemingly unending task of reinterpreting biblical text. From the 1960s on, feminism has taken a number of forms. The Dutch theologian Riet Bons-Storm focuses on three: liberal, romantic and political. She sees the liberal feminist as being concerned with issues like equality with men in civil rights, access to education and professional opportunities and pay. Romantic feminism celebrates the female body and its psychological and spiritual potential, while political feminism focuses on an analysis of power structures in society, mainly the imbalance of power between men and women.[78]

Some people might argue that significant changes in male/female power relationships since the 1960s have resulted in more women taking on male characteristics which lead them into male temptations. But discussion of sin or of forgiveness has taken a back seat to the discussion of justice. Some women, of whom Daphne Hampson is one,[79] have abandoned the concept of sin as an aspect of a relationship with a Christian God whose representatives on earth rule a patriarchal and hierarchical Church. These women have not abandoned an idea of God or of the Divine but they have anticipated Holloway's view of a morality which does not require belief in a God to sustain it.

The range of feminist exploration is perhaps best represented in an issue of *Concilium* edited by Elisabeth Schussler Fiorenza. In her introduction she says, 'it is no longer appropriate to speak of feminist theology in the singular'.[80] The issue celebrates 'feminist theological struggles and intellectual achievements' over the ten-year period from 1986 to 1996 and claims to chart future directions in a range of cultural and religious contexts. The *Concilium* contribution to feminist theology over this period has taken the form of challenging traditional theology 'in such a way that the experience of multiply oppressed women can move into the centre of theological reflection'. Fiorenza sees this work taking place in the context of an increasing 'fundamentalist–nationalist' backlash against women.

The voices of the women taking part come from different geographical, religious and theoretical positions. The geographical contributions weave through Latin America, Australia, Africa and Europe: again we find new ideas coming from the non-European world, reflecting the experience of women who have known

---

[78] Riet Bons-Storm, *The Incredible Woman*, Abingdon Press: Nashville 1996.

[79] Daphne Hampson, *After Christianity*, SCM: London 1996.

[80] *Feminist Theology in Different Contexts*, ed. Elisabeth Schussler Fiorenza and M. Shawn Copeland, SCM: London 1996.

oppression and its consequences directly. The process is summed up in an early Australian contribution to the international dialogue on the nature of feminist theology.

Feminist theology for women in Australia is not something one can find primarily in books. It occurs, rather, in the daily, urgent, sometimes desperate exploration, reassessment and re-creation of meaning which women are continually making in their lives. In this sense, feminist theology is the collective and individual pool of women's experience which is continually growing and changing as we act it out in our lives and interpret it for ourselves and each other in our conversation.[81]

The theologian Marcella Althaus-Reid reinforces this view in her essay in the same volume. She describes how, while working in a poor council estate in Dundee, Scotland, she learned that:

> ... the corporeality of feminist theology comes into life and 'leaves the books' when we observe the queues of women with children waiting for the local post office to open to cash their giros. This is the body language of the poor women, living at the geographical margins of the cities. They are women of suffering, but also have a great capacity for solidarity, resilience in the struggle against violence and deprivation, and an immense talent for organizing themselves for their children's welfare or whatever they feel could give them a more dignified life. With some of these women we 'read the Scriptures' while walking in the little shopping centre in the afternoon, when the wind swept along the empty beer cans and discarded bags of French fries and the graffiti seemed to be the only thing alive in the area. The gigantic poster of a washing powder brand helped us to talk about cleansing, and guilt, and what could be the meaning of 'redemption' and 'cleansing from sin', in a context of the patriarchal fear of menstruation.[82]

These voices reflect the process of change. We are, as Kuhn recounts, constantly reformulating questions which once served us as assumptions. Most of the people doing this are those whom we have previously seen as marginal. One such marginal theologian who is trying to save a Christian position is Don Cupitt. The decline in church attendance, begun in the mid-nineteenth century, led him to say in his Lenten message for the year 2000 that this decline is now running at 25 per cent per decade and that a survey of 500 18-year-olds showed 77 per cent as having no religious beliefs.[83] He considered first what this means for the future of religious belief and second, why the churches do not respond to this situation. On the first point he suggested that people will either have a religion to which they have been converted or one which they have worked out for themselves. We see the first response in the number of charismatic religions or cults that have grown up and the second in the numbers of people who develop a structure of private morality, such as humanism.

It had widely been assumed that older people continued to have a firm investment in a religious belief, turning to it more actively as they approached

---

[81] Marie Tulip, 'Women Church', *Australian Journal of Feminist Studies in Religion*, August 1987, quoted in *Concilium* 1996/1, p. 17.

[82] Marcella Althaus-Reid, 'The Indecency of Her Teaching', *Concilium* 1996/1, p. 139.

[83] Don Cupitt, Radio 4, 12 March 2000.

death.[84] Research presented to the annual conference of the British Society of Gerontology in the year 2000 questions this assumption.[85] The responses indicated that as people aged there was a general questioning of authority, a diminishing belief in the idea of a personal God who can alter action as a result of prayer, lack of belief in a future life and a sense of disappointment with both the churches and the clergy.[86]

Cupitt believes the churches do not respond to the changes because they have a fundamental fear of reform. He traces their dilemma back to the abandonment of the early Church's belief in the coming of the Kingdom promised by Christ. When this failed to materialize, a church religion developed which concentrated on personal sin and personal salvation. He believes that the solution for the Church lies in rediscovering the Kingdom tradition but applying it to the world as we live in it, a world in which personal sin has gone and there is no concept of salvation after death. He sees the continuation of the Kingdom tradition to have been expressed within anarchism, socialism and the teachings of Martin Luther King. Current European religion he sees simply as heritage. The previous year Cupitt had written:

> Orthodox religion served well in pre-modern times, but with the rise of modern science and critical thinking, and with the rise also of democratic politics and humanitarianism, it has become hopelessly out of date. We now need to make the move away from the old cruelly-authoritarian Church Christianity to a new this-worldly and democratic Christian humanism.[87]

This sums up both the problems and possibilities of the new wave of thinking. In that sense we live in a post-Christian society which continues nevertheless to involve in its rituals the institutions of a form of Christendom in which it no longer believes and wants to change while continuing to see itself as Christian.

Conclusion

We appear to be living today on the residue of a Judaeo-Christian inheritance that has been diminishing most rapidly over the last 150 years. In the nineteenth century, Matthew Arnold (1822–88) was already writing of how:

> The sea of faith
> Was once, too, at the full, and round earth's shore
> Lay like the folds of a bright girdle furl'd;

---

[84] This is the view expressed by Evelyn Waugh in his description of Lord Marchmain's return to religion in *Brideshead Revisited: the sacred and profane memories of Captain Charles Ryder*, Chapman & Hall: London 1960.

[85] Professor Peter Coleman, Southampton University, presented the views of 340 people over the age of 65 who were interviewed between 1978 and 1998.

[86] It should be said that as yet none of these factors appear relevant to the evangelical churches which serve ethnic groups like the Afro-Caribbean community.

[87] *SoF* (Sea of Faith) No. 30, Autumn 1999.

But now I only hear
Its melancholy, long, withdrawing roar ...[88]

After the Second World War the secular institution of Parliament[89] increasingly filled whatever moral vacuum existed by passing legislation which gave citizens healthier and more autonomous lives and in doing so released them from the constraints, particularly sexual and reproductive constraints, imposed by the Church. This went hand in hand with a sustained leakage of church attendance.

There seems, however, to have been no diminishing of the human drive to seek meaning and purpose in life, a meaning which had previously been offered to many through a connection with the Church, even if that contact was marginal. There is a consistent, if diminishing, appetite for institutional involvement in the great ritual passages of life: baptisms, marriages and funerals. But the star footballer David Beckham felt able to say 'I want to have my child baptized but I haven't yet decided into what faith.' It is as if the ritual itself rather than the meaning of the ritual is what is important. This may be a factor in a continuing religious impulse which finds new ways of expressing itself in contemporary life. The decoration of the body with tattoos and penetrative jewellery has its own religious antecedents; we create new temples in shopping malls. It may also reflect MacIntyre's comment that in some circumstances, 'religious belief tends to become not so much belief in God as belief in belief', demonstrated by President Eisenhower's assertion that everybody should have a religious faith, 'and I don't care what it is'.[90] The American Anthropological Association has concluded that e-business has become a faith in its own right, complete with adherents, rituals and a communal sense of spiritual progress.[91]

The fractured meta-narratives of Christianity mean that we are faced with the question of how any activities in our communities can be legitimized or for that matter criminalized in any way other than through the justice system. How do we tell right from wrong? Who other than ourselves is to tell us what is sin and what is virtue? For those of us who have no wish to accept the answers offered in *The Sun* or an agony aunt page in a magazine, this is a question that lies behind every decision we make, either privately or publicly. To some extent we are muddling along in matters of personal morality. If we are to accept the Kuhn thesis of how we move from the old paradigm to a new, we must recognize that before we leave one paradigm behind we must find a convincing alternative to which we can move. In other words we have to mend a leaky ship while we are still at sea. Post-Christianity, or for that matter post-modernism, are not ports, they are simply sea passages to be

---

[88] Matthew Arnold, 'Dover Beach', *The Penguin Book of English Verse*, ed. John Hayward, Penguin Books: Harmondsworth 1956, p. 344.

[89] The secular Parliament holds on to the ritual of starting the day with Christian prayer. This is an example of the contradictions so often encountered in the post-Christian world. When the Scottish Parliament was inaugurated, after much discussion, it was decided to open proceedings with contributions from a range of faiths.

[90] MacIntyre, Alasdair and Ricoeur, Paul, *The Religious Significance of Atheism*, Columbia University Press, New York and London 1969.

[91] *The Times*, 27 December 2000.

crossed before again reaching a temporary harbour which we will again one day find no longer serves our needs.

Some church leaders have also changed their views. A repetition of high levels of poverty and unemployment in the 1980s was responded to in Britain by demands from many religious groupings for government intervention to ease the suffering. The Church of Scotland Assembly and Glasgow's Archbishop (later Cardinal) Winning were among those who spoke out; the Church of England wrote what was for them a radical report, *Faith in the City*.[92] All of these reactions involved condemnation of the government of the day, which responded by declaring that government policies were no concern of the Churches and that they should stick to religious matters. The Church leaders were, whether or not they were explicitly stating it, tacitly acknowledging the existence of structural sin. This awareness is a much greater threat to the establishment than any amount of individual sin.

Sin, we now know, is not only a personal matter. Sinful thinking and behaviour can be woven into the attitudes and assumptions of our institutions and our economies. In this chapter we saw how in the second half of the twentieth century we have been forced to confront not only our own human capacity for destructiveness, but the fact that whether we want to or not we cannot avoid responsibility as individuals for what we do as a nation. This was a central lesson of the Nuremberg trials although it has never been fully recognized.

Changes in social policy and scientific knowledge have taught us that what we call individual sin depends to a large extent on the social circumstances in which we live. The legalization of abortion wiped out the profession of illegal abortionists who often mutilated the reproductive systems of young women terrified of being branded as sinners. Some religious groups may still choose to see abortion as a sin but abortion is now a matter of individual moral choice for the majority of women.

New individual sins have been created as a result of a more refined understanding of the effects of behaviour, for example, drunk driving, or buying furniture from non-sustainable forests. The first is dealt with by the justice system, the second by community disapproval. Marital abuse is now seen as intolerable and sinful in the eyes of both the law and the community, whereas previously a blind eye was turned. Other sins, like sexual activity between consenting adults, have been decriminalized. In some cases the balance of blame has shifted. But if, as a society, we allow a significant decline in unemployment and job opportunities for young males and as a result crimes against property rise, we have to ask where does the responsibility for sin lie? Is it coincidence that a high proportion of young people in our prisons is illiterate, not from lack of intelligence but from lack of good teaching? These observations call for a socially embedded, reflexive morality which cannot be derived from first principles or an authority – divine or otherwise – 'out there' beyond our understanding or control. It must be socially and collectively shaped in each society and in each generation.

The emergence of a global economy and a global communication system has forced us into areas of knowledge about the nature of structural sin we would sometimes prefer not to have. Life would be simpler if we couldn't read. It is also

---

[92] *Faith in the City: A Call for Action by Church and Nation*, The Report of the Archbishop of Canterbury's Commission on Urban Priority Areas 1985.

simpler if we have less international news on television and more game shows and comedies. It is disturbing to learn about our responsibility for global warming, to see mutilated African children, hear of women sold into sexual slavery, to read statistics of national and world poverty, to see refugees begging on the streets of our towns. Worst of all, the collapse of our meta-narratives of Christianity and of Marxism may leave us feeling we have no one to blame. Most of us no longer believe in the devil, many appear to have bonded with capitalism. Is anyone to blame and, we must ask, where in all this is the relevance of forgiveness to this new perception of sin?

4

Contemporary Perspectives on Forgiveness

Introduction

In this chapter I consider a range of post-Christian attitudes to forgiveness. This is not to say that these attitudes have no connection with Christianity; the first three case studies grow directly out of the Christian tradition. But in each there is a person who challenges the interpretation of that tradition in the communities in which they lived. The second half of the chapter describes how some Christians are now attempting to take on board the new 'scientific' understanding of human processes, initially explored by Freud, and to link this to the Christian tradition in a variety of ways. These attempts are reflected in the remarkable growth of psychological self-help books and in the setting up of 'Institutes of Forgiveness' in the English-speaking world. This post-Christian emphasis on forgiveness rather than on sinfulness may be a reflection of uncertainties about the definition of sin and of a franker capacity to assert our own emotional needs. We may also have a powerful sense that as a global community we are behaving in ways that require some form of forgiveness.

From the early 1960s a clearer understanding began to emerge that the significant changes taking place in attitudes to authority, to politics and to the family were not temporary but part of a transition to a new order of social values. The Protestant ethic, which had served an industrial society well, reinforcing values of achievement, self-control, independence and endurance, was no longer relevant to young people in a post-industrial society. Traditional values were being replaced by notions of self-actualization, self-expression, interdependence and the capacity for joy.[1] An unchanging, absolute view of sin of the kind defined by the earlier values was replaced by a view that behaviour had to be assessed in relation to its context. The idea that a new age was emerging became commonplace and was translated into a culture expressed in the ways in which people dressed, the kind of music they listened to and the way they related to each other.

A New Order of Social Values

The core view of people who shared these beliefs, attitudes and practices was that our global civilization had reached a stage where a new social and cultural paradigm was emerging. The institutions which had served us were considered to

---

[1] Eric Trist first presented this construct at an Edinburgh seminar in 1964. It was later incorporated in: F.E. Emery and E.L. Trist, *Towards a Social Ecology: contextual appreciation of the future in the present*, Plenum Press: London 1972.

be no longer relevant to new needs or to the new society which was thought to be emerging. New ideas, attitudes and practices would have to be developed to meet the new situation. Particular emphasis was placed on the relationship between human beings and the planet we share and on which we depend. The main paradigm shift was seen to be from a Cartesian world-view to a post-Cartesian holistic approach in all the disciplines, particularly science and medicine. Religion was seen as embodying a broader concept than that embraced by any of the existing faiths.

These ideas were reflected in cultural changes and practices in the economically advanced countries of North America and Europe. Two centres which were seen as contributing most to the new thinking were the Esalen Institute at Big Sur in California and the Findhorn Foundation in Scotland. Both these groups placed particular emphasis on the importance in human relationships of having love for all living things and for the planet. They saw the central message of the universe as love, a message into which anyone could tap and from which anyone could draw strength.[2] Later in this chapter I describe the development and the work of the Findhorn Foundation.

New Age ideas are best known to the general public through what is described as alternative therapies. Its practitioners often draw heavily on eastern spiritual and therapeutic traditions. Many of their therapies and practices stem from cultures and philosophies which challenge the Platonic, Pauline and, most recently, the Cartesian notion of duality of mind and body, a view which informed orthodox western science and medicine from the Enlightenment until the second half of the twentieth century.

What is relevant to this work is that these alternative therapies have in common a belief in the effect of emotions on health and the self-healing potential of the human body. The ability to forgive wrongs done to us is seen as central to good health. For the radical Shelley, 'to forgive wrongs' was included in those virtues which led one to be 'Good, great and joyous, beautiful and free',[3] surely a superb description of the pleasures of good health. The dark side of these beliefs is their assumption that negative thinking causes illness, so humans are responsible for creating their own illnesses. Ill health may then be seen as sinful. Sickness as a moral fault is implicit in a miracle where healing takes place as a result of the forgiveness of sin.[4] Since some believe that the 'negative' behaviour which accounts for misfortunes may have occurred in previous existences, long before the victim was born, this suggests some very dark implications when it comes to explaining disasters like the Holocaust.

Many New Age therapists see physical illness as a reflection of emotional or spiritual malaise and its cure in spiritual development. One New Age guru, Caroline Myss, uses as a model to achieve health three spiritual traditions: the Hindu

---

[2] It was perhaps inevitable that in some cultic communities there were individuals who used similar powerful ideas in corrupted ways. There was often confusion between the physical and spiritual expressions of love.

[3] Percy Bysshe Shelley, *Prometheus Unbound*, act 4, 1. 570 in *The Complete Poetical Works of Percy Bysshe Shelley*, eds Thomas Hutchinson and Humphrey Milford, Oxford University Press: London 1940.

[4] Mark 2:5.

Fig. 1   The Pope holding up the Gospel during a ceremony at St Peter's Basilica.
Photo: Vincenzo Pinto. Reproduced by courtesy of Paul Popper Ltd.

Fig. 2   Marcus Harvey, *Myra*, 13 × 10.5ft., acrylic on canvas, 1995. Photo: Stephen
White. Reproduced by courtesy of Jay Jopling/White Cube, London.

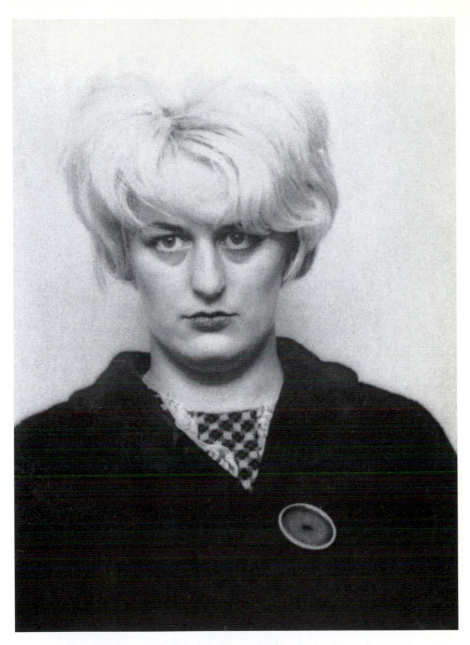

Fig. 3   Myra Hyndley as a 'brassy blonde', a photo taken during her trial.
Reproduced by courtesy of PA Photos Ltd.

Fig. 4   James Bulger's headstone. Reproduced by courtesy of PA Photos Ltd.

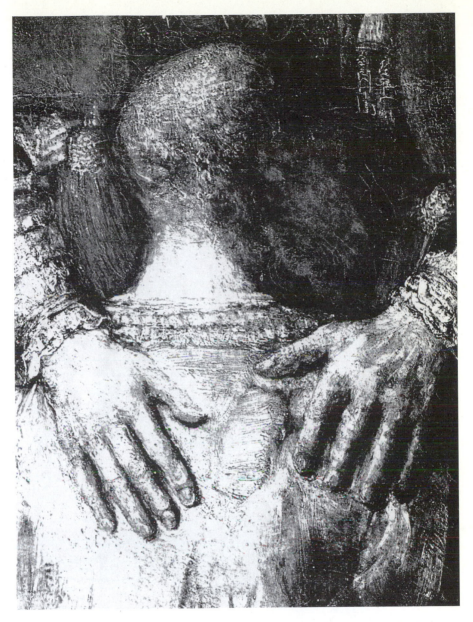

Fig. 5   Rembrant van Rijn (1606–1669), *The Return of the Prodigal Son* (detail),
265 × 205cm., oil on canvas, 1668–1669, Hermitage, St Petersburg, Russia.
© Scala/Art Resource, New York.

What about the children?

UN sanctions are slowly sapping the lifeblood from the Iraqi people, while Saddam rules on. **Elinor Wakefield** and **Seb Wills** report on a student campaign to end the embargo

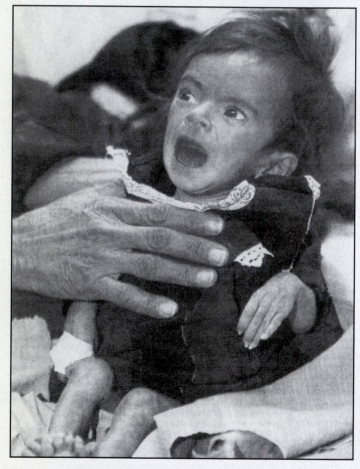

A child in pain: dehydrated and malnourished, this Iraqi baby is among thousands of youngsters suffering the effects of UN sanctions

PHOTOGRAPH: RAMZI HAIDAR

Fig. 6   A child in pain: dehydrated and malnourished, this Iraqi baby is among thousands of youngsters suffering the effects of UN sanctions.
Photo: Ramzi Haidar. Reproduced by courtesy of Agence France Press.

Fig. 7   Peace banner, hand painted by a women's peace group.

chakras, the Christian sacraments and the Kabbalah's Tree of Life.[5] Each of these she sees as having seven elements[6] which represent different levels of spiritual energy: the seven chakras of the human body as defined in Hinduism, the seven sacraments of Christianity and seven of the ten levels of the sefirot, the Tree of Life of the Kabbalah. The chakra system is an archetypal depiction of spiritual growth through seven distinct stages in which we move from the material and physical world to a more refined understanding of personal and spiritual power. Each ascending chakra offers a spiritual lesson or challenge common to all human beings. The early Christian Church identified seven sacraments which were, and still are, seen by many Christians as endowing the recipients with a means of grace. Symbolically each sacrament can be seen as a stage of empowerment that invites the Divine directly into a person's spirit. The ten sefirot are the qualities of the Divine that also form the archetypal human being. Our task as human beings is to ascend to our divine source by evolving these ten qualities within ourselves.[7] We can see the archetypal meanings of these three systems as having powerful similarities. The three traditions appear to be addressing the same human realities.

Myss considers that the strongest poison to the human spirit and therefore to the human body is the inability to forgive oneself or another person. Exploring these three systems she found that each offers a quality which addresses specifically the capacity to forgive. In the Hindu chakras it is level four, where the spiritual life-lesson is related to love, forgiveness and compassion. In the Christian sacraments Myss chooses the sacrament of marriage as symbolizing the sacredness of loving and caring for oneself in order that one can fully love and have compassion for another. In the sefirot, the Tree of Life, we find Tif'eret, whose qualities are compassion, harmony and beauty. This sefirah is considered the trunk of the tree. The underlying theory is that not only our minds and spirits but also our physical bodies require love to survive and thrive[8] and we violate this energy when we act towards others in unloving ways. Her view is that the holding of negative emotions towards others or towards ourselves, or intentionally causing pain to another, poisons our own physical and spiritual systems.[9]

The emphasis in New Age communities like those at Big Sur and Findhorn is not on sin but on love, healing and forgiveness. While some individuals speak of God, more speak of the Universe, but whichever form is chosen is seen as a source of positive and loving energy. This means that any failure on the part of the individual is their own fault, for which they have to take responsibility. Sin is hurting another person or creature or damaging oneself or the planet. Every form of existence is considered to be linked. Each of us is part of the whole. But most of all sin would be seen as blocking the possibility of communion with the spirit – in other words an

---

[5] Caroline Myss, *Anatomy of the Spirit*, Penguin Books: Harmondsworth 1998.

[6] We are reminded here of the pagan significance of the number 7.

[7] Myss, *Anatomy of the Spirit*, p. 74.

[8] Ibid., p. 84.

[9] This is sometimes hard to believe when we see the blooming health and good fortune of some of the world's greatest rascals. See Ps. 37:35, 'I have seen the wicked in great power, and spreading himself like a green bay tree.'

experience that could be described as the Ultimate Reality. It is to clear the way to such an experience that forgiveness of the self and others is necessary because only by clearing the blocked channels and releasing one's capacity for love can peak experiences, religious experiences or mystical experiences become possible. These are the goals which could be described as essentially egoistic.

A New Age Community

The community I have chosen to describe is the Findhorn Community. Founded in 1962 by Eileen and Peter Caddy on a bleak caravan park at Findhorn Bay on the north-east coast of Scotland, the community is an important phenomenon and is best understood if we recognize the Gnostic roots in which it is based. Both these people had left partners and children to be together but believed that in doing so they were serving a higher spiritual purpose. Eileen was the vehicle for spiritual guidance. Overwhelmed with guilt and anxiety at the thought of leaving her family, she surrendered herself to God and experienced for the first time the inner voice which was to guide both their lives and lead to the creation of an international spiritual community.

While Peter had a background in esoteric theory and the western mystery tradition, Eileen had none; yet in their partnership it was she who took on the role of spiritual leader while he followed. She began daily meditations but struggled hard against what she saw as surrender to divine will. They endured many financial and emotional difficulties before settling, now with three children, on the present site. Every step of their path was guided by messages from Eileen's voice and visions. Their essence can be summed up in one of these messages: 'To achieve absolute freedom, you must live fully those words, "Let go, let God". When you do, all strain and resistance goes and you are no longer clinging on to anything of the self . . . .'

Clearly these messages are in the direct tradition of western Christian mysticism but perhaps Eileen Caddy herself fits most closely into the Beguine tradition of the early thirteenth century, with its aura of domesticity and poverty.[10] What is significant is that the spiritual leadership was embodied in a woman while her husband had to create a role for himself in the practical affairs of community life. Another similarity lay in the fact that there has been in Findhorn, as with the Beguines, no single rule and no agreed way of life. The only unity is the desire to lead a life within which one's spirituality can be developed and the increasing materialism of the society challenged. This was as real an issue during the rise of urbanization in the thirteenth century as in the second half of the twentieth, and was reflected in the writing of St Francis of Assisi and Thomas à Kempis.

Findhorn is now a thriving, internationally recognized community showing many of the aspects of a traditional religious community. The daily routines are designed to help in the development of one's spiritual life. The work of the community, whether it is cooking, cleaning, gardening, running conferences or publishing

---

[10] Saskia Murk-Jansen, *Brides in the Desert: The Spirituality of the Beguines*, Darton, Longman & Todd: London 1998.

books, is seen as a spiritual contribution to the general well-being. The thought that 'to work is to pray' has been adapted from the Benedictine spiritual tradition. Group work is usually begun and ended with a moment of silent thought, and meditation rooms are as central to daily life as dining rooms or sleeping areas. The ability to love each other and to forgive each other is seen as central not only to the life of the community but to the future of the planet. Riddell's book on its history is subtitled 'Creating a Human Identity for the 21st Century'.[11] To outsiders this may seem a rather grandiose aspiration but it is based on the assumption that human beings have the capacity to be better than they are. A more worrying aspect is that an underlying community agenda implies that human beings can become perfect. Joseph Campbell saw the aspiration to perfection as inhuman. He said, 'That is why some people have a hard time loving God, because there's no imperfection there. You can be in awe but that's not real love. It's Christ on the cross that becomes lovable.'[12] Christ either on or off the cross is not, in my experience, much talked about in Findhorn.

The use of candles, music and other traditional methods is seen as an aid to spiritual awareness. The daily practice of ritual is seen as both a catalyst and a vehicle for community and exploration into earlier forms of ritual. Ritual is seen as a way of drawing on other religious traditions, which may be helpful to those contending with modern problems. Richard Olivier, a theatre director who offers courses at Findhorn and other centres of New Age thinking, came to this interest through a personal search[13] which brought him into contact with people like the American writers Robert Bly and James Hillman, both of whom have used ritual as part of a therapeutic process. Olivier, while engaging with western traditions, has also worked with African Dagara cosmology (Fire, Earth, Water, Nature and Mineral), a tradition in which the expressed principal task of a community is to maintain balance, which is an aspiration we have also seen in the covenantal tradition. In Dagara this is a state in which all the elements are functioning smoothly and any disturbance in the community would be diagnosed and healed through ritual. We see again the blending of disparate traditions in a way which underlines the conviction of a common, basic, human experience.

In the Findhorn Community, discussion of relationships between members of the community occurs regularly in small groups normally based on work activities, giving formal opportunities for resolution of current difficulties. The reader will recognize that these are patterns which have been developed over hundreds of years in religious communities and in this century in the medical/psychiatric context of therapeutic communities. What is different is that religious and medical/psychiatric communities have learned the necessity of tougher disciplines than those so far observed by the mainstream New Age adherents.[14] In the latter the assumption is

---

[11] Carol Riddell, *The Findhorn Community: Creating a Human Identity for the 21st Century*, Findhorn Press: Forres 1990.

[12] Joseph Campbell with Bill Moyers, *The Power of Myth*, ed. Betty Sue Flowers, Doubleday: New York 1988.

[13] Richard Olivier, *Shadow of the Stone Heart: a search for manhood*, Pan: London 1995.

[14] I am not here dealing with the smaller more tightly organized cults, which may have highly disciplined, punitive techniques, which ensure conformity and 'balance' in their communities.

often that love is the answer to all relationship difficulties, and while this may indeed be the case, what is not taken into account is that anger can be an equally important factor in human relationships. Anger is often seen as 'sinful'. There seems to be no recognition that if anger is suppressed and not acknowledged it does not disappear. It is liable to leak out in destructive ways.

What is new is the plurality of sexual freedom between consenting adults alongside stable nuclear families. Other members may choose celibacy but, unlike the Christian tradition, this is not seen to convey status. There is no association between sin and sexuality. While inevitably there are tensions when relationships may change, develop or die, the central doctrine of taking responsibility for one's own life and accepting how other people choose to live theirs seems to come into play most effectively. Hearts will be broken, but there will be support networks, which will help to ease the pain. Tolerance is seen as an essential virtue, forgiveness an obligation. An important factor may be that entry to the community has to be preceded by a year of in-service training. This can be seen as the equivalent of the monastic practice of the noviciate. The year gives people an opportunity to find out their ability to tolerate the life-style of the community and also gives the community an opportunity to assess whether the candidate can be accepted. It is in the nature of a community like this that it will attract a proportion of people with a range of mental health problems, some of which may be intransigent. Such a person would be asked to leave. There is however available among community members a wide range of therapeutic skills, to which members have access either by paying for them or using some form of exchange of skills.

A Conference on Forgiveness

In October 1999 the Findhorn Community organized a conference on forgiveness. Visitors from Europe, Africa, the Middle East and both the Americas attended, demonstrating both the international importance of current enquiries into the nature of forgiveness and the way in which Findhorn has established itself as a New Age centre for discussion of such an issue. I attended the conference, met many of the speakers and in the following sequence have selected only those points which seem most relevant to understanding the main interpretations of forgiveness offered.

Those attending were united by two beliefs: one was the importance of acknowledging a spiritual dimension to their lives, though that could be expressed within a variety of beliefs which ranged from New Age convictions through conventional Christianity to humanism and atheism. The other was a recognition of the importance of the capacity for forgiveness as an aspect of the human personality. What divided them was a difference of opinion in the role forgiveness could play in human affairs. For some participants forgiveness should be unconditional even in the most harrowing circumstances; to refuse forgiveness is to damage oneself and deny the divine in the other. The alternative view was that forgiveness was not always possible, not always appropriate, that forgiveness cannot be conceived of in isolation from the circumstances which have created its need, and that anger aroused by the offence which required forgiveness must be treated with respect. This difference could be seen as a clear fault line in the composition of the conference, cutting across gender, ethnicity and religious or non-religious belief. It was also a fault line dividing those with a collective, 'social' context for their assessment of behaviour – and often some practical experience of the politics of persecution, violence and forgiveness – from those concerned with individual, personal, emotional life and spiritual well-being.

Aba Gayle: North America   The first view that forgiveness should be unconditional was put forward in the opening address by Carolyn Myss, whose views I have already discussed. It was followed up in the next session by a powerful statement from an American woman, Aba Gayle, who spoke movingly of her experiences following the brutal murder of her teenage daughter. She had, she said, spent eight years in a rage of anger and hate against the man responsible. Her lawyer had promised her that he would be executed but although he had been found guilty, he had been kept waiting on death row. After these eight years Aba Gayle moved house and found in her new neighbourhood a small friendly church, which she began to attend. From the church's library, she began to borrow and read a range of books on spirituality. Discussing these with a group in the church confronted her with a new set of questions about how she was living. She started to feel that she should find out from the man who had killed her daughter why he had done this terrible thing. It took her a long time but ultimately she found the courage to write, and his response gave her the courage to do something even more difficult: she visited him.

She described how she drove to the prison, tears streaming down her face, terrified of what was ahead of her – not only in meeting the man, but also because, for this very ordinary American woman, a prison was a fearful place. But she faced the horror and listened to the man's story of his appallingly damaged childhood, his later life and his drug habit that led him to kill her daughter. She came away shaken but continued to write and visit him. She now campaigns for his release and has developed a ministry for inmates on death row in San Quentin State Prison. Since then she has gone on to speak through the Southern United States for Murder Victims' Families for Reconciliation and engage with the Alternatives to Violence campaign. She speaks about forgiveness as the alternative to hate and violence and is currently running a campaign to have the first Sunday of every August declared an International Forgiveness Day in 148 countries by the year 2005. Aba Gayle summed up what she had learned:

- There is no death.
- We are all one – divine children of God.
- You can choose to be right or to be happy.
- Hate, anger and rage affect your health.
- Only the present exists.
- You choose to be a victim or not to be a victim.
- Forgiveness is a gift you give yourself.

This can be seen as a fair summary of a New Age testimony. She has developed her own theology, taking from Christianity and other traditions what she finds helpful. She exemplifies the view of the future presented by Don Cupitt, as discussed in

Chapter 3. She finds within herself authority for what she believes and seeks no other. She puts her conviction of the validity of her own experience into practice but does not ask questions about the wider social circumstances that create or encourage the behaviour that has to be forgiven.

I would offer the example of Aba Gayle as the purest form I have encountered of the view that forgiveness should be unconditional – with the reservation that forgiveness may not necessarily be instantaneous, but the culmination of a long and painful process. This woman sweated her way through eight years of rage, anger and hatred. She made a journey through a private hell and emerged, with the support of her fellow religionists, into a different world. That support should not be underestimated since through it she was given the dignity of her feelings. They created for her a sacred space in which she was free to be herself and to be valued in all her aspects, including the period she has spent in rage and hate. The journey she made stripped her of attitudes and ideas and images of herself she had previously taken for granted. In her rage, anger and hatred, her soul, essence, psyche – whatever one chooses to call it – was stripped naked. This nakedness made it possible for her to be open to a new vision of herself. Comparisons could be made with an intensive psychoanalysis where, having gone through the hell of confronting your shadow self, you emerge feeling like a different person looking at the world in a different way. Similar descriptions have been given by mystics like St John of the Cross and St Theresa of Avila of their 'dark night of the soul'. For Aba Gayle it was a slow transformation, not the dramatic 'turning' Augustine describes but no less effective.

Michael Lapsley: South Africa   Father Michael Lapsley, an Anglican priest and member of the religious community, the Society of the Sacred Mission, put an alternative view with equal cogency. He is a big, rather beautiful man who disconcerts on first view by having metal claws instead of hands. As an Anglican priest he moved from New Zealand to South Africa with strong, long-held, pacifist views. He said that Anglicans come from a long tradition of sitting on the fence but in South Africa he couldn't find one. Everyone in this apartheid regime was either an oppressor or the oppressed. He found himself defined not by his humanity but by the colour of his skin: he couldn't wash off the white. His pacifism crumbled, he joined the ANC, becoming an activist supporter. Expelled by the regime, he travelled round the world telling the story of the struggle against what he had come to see as one of the greatest crimes against humanity – the apartheid system. In 1990, with Mandela released and the regime on its last legs, he relaxed his guard. He was sent a letter bomb by the South African security force inside a religious magazine. It blew off his hands and left him blind in one eye.

He believed that he had become the focus of evil but that God accompanied him on the journey he was then forced to take. In the compassion and care shown to him he began to recognize the beautiful aspects of humanity and to see the bombing as redemptive – good coming out of evil, life coming out of death. He realized that if he were filled with bitterness and revenge the regime would have won. His path could be described as a move from victim to survivor to victor, as he moved from being an object of history to being a subject of history. He is clear that he could not have made that journey alone, that God was with him. In his belief he gave his journey a moral content and filled it with a sense of reverence. Now he feels himself, with no hands, to be more of a priest than he was with hands. In his brokenness and incompleteness he is simply reflecting a condition central to the human race. In surviving his brokenness he has become important to others, particularly since now he cannot attain the western illusion of complete independence.

He says, 'I am no longer a victim, nor even simply a survivor. I am a victor over evil, hatred and death. The apartheid regime and all who supported it carry the responsibility for the loss of millions of lives throughout Southern Africa.'

But for Michael Lapsley, 'forgiveness is not on the table'. He holds F.W. de Klerk politically and morally responsible for outrages like the one he suffered, yet de Klerk has disclaimed responsibility. Twenty-four thousand people came to tell their stories to the Truth and Justice Commission and of these seven thousand asked for amnesty. No one, says Michael Lapsley, has said 'I did it' to him. Who, then, he asks, is he supposed to forgive and what does forgiveness mean? He finds that some churches use discourse about forgiveness as a glib, cheap and easy ploy; some preachers even use it as a weapon. Forgiveness, he believes, is costly, painful and difficult, and is a choice. If someone is unable to forgive, perhaps it is because no one has listened, acknowledged and reverenced what their experience has meant to them. In South Africa people have been damaged in their humanity in a wide variety of ways – not only by what they did or had done to them, but also by what they didn't do. He has had to come to terms with the role played in the apartheid struggle by Christian theology. He concludes that the Christian Gospel was the main tool of oppression.

Lapsley now explores these questions of faith and forgiveness in workshops with victims of violence and torture and also with the perpetrators of these crimes. He includes among the latter those who simply stood by and did nothing, seeing them sometimes as the same perpetrators. He asks everyone to answer the same questions: 'What did I do? What was done to me? What did I fail to do?' He insists that we are all involved. If we accept this we might do well to consider how we might answer these questions in our own communities. Centrally he sees reparation and restitution as integral parts of forgiveness.

Both these people, Gayle and Lapsley, come from a Christian tradition although this has been interpreted in different ways. Both have moved out from a personal trauma to extend the significance of what happened to them to the wider community. Aba Gayle would appear to have first sought personal redemption, putting herself into balance with God, before being able to move forward. In his experience of being a victim of apartheid, Michael Lapsley never seems to have had any sense of being thrown out of balance in his relationship with God. Throughout he has felt himself at one with God's teaching and God's wishes for His creation – that was his lodestone. As far as Lapsley was concerned, it was the apartheid regime that was out of balance. He joined the struggle in order to save his humanity and his relationship with God. He believed that the Christianity which supported, or even turned a blind eye to, apartheid was a doctrine of death masquerading as a doctrine of love. Lapsley seems to me to have reached both into history and into the future to shape his shift from the Christian pacifism which informed his earlier years. His claim for justice and reparation has all the poetic and religious power of the Hebrew Bible but it also reflects the modern secular argument of restorative justice which, while it has much in common with Hebrew theology, is not turning to God as a source of authority for its views.

He describes what he calls, in South Africa, 'bicycle theology'. A young person will steal a bicycle and six months later come back asking forgiveness. The bicycle however does not come back. Lapsley finds this unacceptable. For him repentance requires not only repentance but also restitution and more. His link to the Hebrew Bible can be found in Leviticus 6:5: 'he shall even restore it in the principal, and shall add the fifth part more thereto'. He also quotes the Christian Bible where Luke mentions only repentance as the precondition for forgiveness[15] but later tells the story of Zacchaeus. This describes what happened when Jesus passed through Jericho: Zacchaeus, a rich publican, but not very tall, was so desperate to see Jesus that he climbed a tree. Jesus, seeing him, said 'Zacchaeus, make haste, and come down; for today I must abide at thy house.' Zacchaeus was delighted but the others gathered round were shocked that Jesus had chosen to be the guest of a sinner. To display his virtue Zacchaeus said, 'Behold Lord, the half of my goods I give to the poor; and if I have taken anything from any man by false accusation, I restore him fourfold.'[16] Jesus' reply was a reassurance that Zacchaeus was a good Jew, 'a son of Abraham'.

Helen Bamber: London   Views on forgiveness not grounded in a Christian view nor in New Age thinking were also put forward at the Findhorn conference. Helen Bamber, whose background is Jewish, founded the Medical Foundation for the Care of Victims of Torture and sees forgiveness as playing a very small part in the rehabilitation process. At the age of 19, in 1945, Bamber entered Bergen-Belsen with the Allies and stayed for two-and-a-half years with those who were 'liberated' but had nowhere to go. It was in Belsen that she learned the importance of allowing people to tell what had been done to them, the power of listening to their testimony and recognizing their experiences. She has continued the work ever since in the face of the global epidemic of torture, which we now, thanks to the work of the human rights organization Amnesty International, admit exists but as a nation do little about. She sees torture as an attempt to kill a human being without their actually dying, and as a form of bondage which holds people for ever. One of the central components of torture is uncertainty, and defences must be built against that uncertainty. The mind must also be separated from the body. But this means abandoning trust and abandoning love; it also means abandoning the vital connection between mind and body. Jean Amery, the Austrian philosopher whose response to Wiesenthal's question was quoted earlier, was tortured by the Gestapo because he was active in the Belgian resistance and then deported to Auschwitz because he was Jewish. He wrote:

Anyone who was tortured remains tortured ... Anyone who has suffered torture never again will be able to be at ease in the world, the abomination of the annihilation is never

---

[15] Luke 6:32.
[16] Luke 19:8.

extinguished. Faith in humanity, already cracked by the first slap in the face, then demolished by torture, is never acquired again.[17]

Essential though they are for survival, these defences against feeling are not helpful on release from imprisonment. Often people are not able to speak about what has happened to them. Ways have to be found to make that possible – if not verbally then symbolically. Those who have suffered deeply need recognition of what has happened to them, validation of their right to speak and claim justice before they can even think about forgiveness. They need the 'other' to reflect back to them the reality of their experience. The terror we experience in reading about and entering into the world Kafka creates is precisely the lack of this reification. The role of the Medical Foundation is to contain and accept anguish, shame and anger. In addition it accepts a role of political intervention on behalf of asylum seekers and advocated the need for an international criminal court where torturers can be brought to justice. This was eventually established in 2003. The foundation also works with perpetrators of torture and it is in this work that forgiveness has more status. The perpetrators need to ask for forgiveness; but how do we relate this to Michael Lapsley's view of the demands that have to be made on those asking forgiveness?

The main difference between the conditions for forgiveness laid down in the Hebrew Bible or in the Christian Bible and the situations that confront us today may be those of scale. In small communities one knows who is one's aggressor or victim – as is the case in Northern Ireland. Some negotiation may be possible. Reconciliation is indeed essential if they are to go on living together in the same community, within sight of each other and each other's family. Exile and imprisonment have traditionally been one way of removing the irreconcilable other; the use of modern weapons of war has now made it possible for this solution to be escalated into what we call ethnic cleansing. The movement of asylum seekers across continents can now separate the torturer from the tortured so that *rapprochement* is never a possibility. Forgiveness, Bamber concluded, is something more needed by the perpetrators to receive than by the victims to give.

In Britain, the demonstrations of asylum seekers from Chile against General Pinochet offered one of the few opportunities his victims would ever have of seeing the man they considered responsible for their inhumane treatment and calling for justice. These Chileans were not in Helen Bamber's view asking for revenge; they were asking for justice. Again, as with Michael Lapsley, forgiveness was not on the table. The Bamber position is that we have first to listen to the voices of ordinary people asking for justice.[18] She sees the establishment of an International

---

[17] Quoted in Primo Levi, *The Drowned and the Saved*, trans. R. Rosenthal Abacus: London, 1995, p. 12.

[18] There is a large body of literature on justice which has emerged in the last twenty years. It is seen as possibly the first of the social virtues. One of the most influential figures has been John Rawls, *A Theory of Justice*, Harvard University Press: Cambridge, Mass. 1971. Modern views of justice tend to be based on ideas of human rationality, human intuition and community rather than ideas of 'cosmic justice' or the will of God.

Criminal Court as a first step, perhaps crude but one which will ultimately bring change.

Freud and the New Therapies

The Secular Rabbi: The Influence of Freud on Forgiveness

Another effect of the Second World War or, more precisely, of the events leading up to it was the influence of Jewish Freudian and neo-Freudian psychotherapists who escaped the Nazi death camps by emigration to Europe and North America. Their theories were greeted in some circles as the answer to all of life's problems. The notion that by exploring our unconscious motivations and bringing our sinful natures (that our natures were sinful was assumed) into the light of day, we could become purer, healthier, nicer and happier human beings was deeply attractive to those seeking to replace superstition with reason. The link with the Platonic view that 'the life that is unexamined is not worth living' and the injunction to 'Know thyself' added to the frisson of recognition and approval. Central to this was the thought that examining and knowing oneself achieved forgiveness both of the 'other' and of oneself.

What has been less recognized is the link between Freudian thought and the Judaeo-Christian tradition.[19] Both Erik Erikson in his *Young Man Luther*[20] and Norman O. Brown in his *Life Against Death* have drawn attention to the connections between Freudian doctrines of sin and redemption and a Lutheran view of the human condition.[21] Freud may have shed the theism, but he retained much of the religious ambience. His messianic conviction of having brought a great truth to the world, the role of his disciples, the rituals, the sacred writings, the sense of mystery, the aura of a cult are all in the religious tradition. Perhaps the most religious concept of all is to be found in the analytic setting itself – a sacred space where the most private and terrible secrets of the human heart can be safely shared and redemption found. And this could be undertaken with the confidence that there was a rational, scientific basis to the giving up of oneself in this way – which at the same time honoured fantasy and imagination. This made it possible for Harold Bloom to write that 'no twentieth-century writer – not even Proust or Kafka – rivals Freud's position as the central imagination of our age'.[22]

---

[19] It has also been argued that the roots of psychoanalysis lie in the Jewish mystical tradition with which Freud was familiar and that Freud, consciously or unconsciously, secularized Jewish mysticism. See David Bakan, *Sigmund Freud and the Jewish Mystical Tradition*, Beacon Press: Boston 1975.

[20] Erik H. Erikson, *Young Man Luther: a study in psychoanalysis and history*, Faber & Faber: London 1958. Erikson makes the slightly tongue-in-cheek comment that Luther could be thought to have saved theology from philosophy only to have it exploited by psychology, p. 200.

[21] Norman O. Brown, *Life Against Death*, Sphere Books Ltd: London 1970, pp. 182ff.

[22] Harold Bloom, 'Freud, the Greatest Modern Writer', *New York Times Book Review*, 23 March 1968, quoted in Richard Webster, *Why Freud was Wrong*, HarperCollins: London 1995.

Freud himself was under no illusion about the contribution he had made. He claimed that there had been three blows to human narcissism. One was given by Copernicus to cosmology, one by Darwin to biology, and psychoanalysis delivered the psychological blow.[23] In the early days he was ambivalent about the fact that his converts – the most appropriate word – were almost exclusively Jewish. This is seen as a factor in his welcome of the Protestant, gentile Jung as a disciple. Later he felt free to say, 'I don't know whether you're right in thinking that psychoanalysis is a direct product of the Jewish spirit but if it were I wouldn't feel ashamed.'[24]

Edmund Wilson suggested that there was a natural reason why such a disturbing new movement should have a Jewish origin. He described how the Jewish Marx fought so uncompromisingly for the dispossessed classes and how Proust transferred from a persecuted race to the artist and the homosexual both that race's tragic faith in society and the inner conviction of moral superiority. Freud, Wilson thought, was 'one of these great Jewish minds of the first generation that had been liberated from the closed Judaic world, still remembered the medieval captivity and ... were likely to present themselves as champions of other social groups which had not been freed or vindicated yet'.[25] By acknowledging the validity of sexual drives, the 'sexual impulses that civilization had outlawed or that puritanism had tried to suppress', Freud offered an avenue of escape from guilt through a form of forgiveness.

What is even more rarely discussed is the link between Freud's thought and Jewish mysticism. It has been argued that the roots of psychoanalysis lie in the Jewish mystical tradition with which Freud was familiar and that Freud, consciously or unconsciously, secularized Jewish mysticism. Bakan offers an interesting if rather complex suggestion that Freud was deeply, possibly sometimes unconsciously, influenced by mystical traditions found in books such as the Zohar and the Kabbala. He says that progress had taken place, from the Enlightenment on, in exploring human concerns, and by the end of the nineteenth century the West was ready to consider human sexuality. Freud's approach however was not part of the western tradition. His was to be found in the Kabbalistic tradition which, mixed with superstitious ideas, would have made it seem nonsensical to the modern enlightened mind. Bakan argues that Freud's use of sexuality as the basic idiom for the expression of all the deeper and more profound problems of mankind is 'entirely in the spirit of the Kabbala': 'In contrast with other ascetic forms of mysticism, the Jewish mystics ascribed sexuality to God himself ... And drawing from the fact that the Bible uses the same word for both knowledge and sexual relations, knowledge itself is viewed as having a deeply erotic character.'[26] We are in a world that would have been understood by D.H. Lawrence, a world that treats

---

[23] Sigmund Freud, *Collected Papers*, ed. James Strachey, 5 vols, Hogarth Press: London 1950–52, V, p. 173.

[24] Quoted in Ronald W. Clark, *Freud: The Man and the Cause*, Jonathan Cape and Weidenfeld & Nicolson: London 1980, p. 242.

[25] Edmund Wilson, *To The Finland Station: A Study in the Writing and Acting of History*, Secker & Warburg: London 1941, p. 306.

[26] Bakan, *Sigmund Freud*, pp. 271ff.

sexuality with reverence and refuses to see it as a sin in its own right. Only its abuse is sinful.

Freud's 'talking cure' has now spawned more than four hundred variations and, in Britain, six times that number of practitioners of the art. The traditional one-to-one sacred space has been expanded to include working in triads or even in groups, but the same conditions of privacy and confidentiality are expected to apply. While research studies have failed to show significant benefits from the various schools of these therapies, the popularity of each is undiminished, as is the enthusiasm and conviction of the therapists. Several large-scale studies have shown that patients recover at about the same rate whether they are given psychotherapy, drugs or a placebo.[27]

Horgan quotes the belief of Jerome Frank, a former professor of psychiatry, that psychotherapy should really be considered as a form of literary criticism. A patient's clinical history 'resembles a text, and psychotherapy a collaborative effort of patient and therapist to discern its meaning'.[28] Horgan continues, 'There is no single, correct way to treat a patient, just as there is no single way to read a book. Different readers will find different meanings in the same text, and different psychotherapists will interpret the same patient's remarks and clinical history in different ways.' He also claims that evidence shows religious belief offers the best cure of all and relates the success of Alcoholics Anonymous to this factor.[29] I would suggest that the unstated religious component of psychotherapy may be a major factor in its effectiveness and makes it so deeply satisfying to most of those who engage in it either as priests or communicants. Horgan's basic view is that the reason Freud's ideas have survived so successfully is because the neurosciences have so far not come up with anything better – although they keep trying.

What does recovery mean in this context? To take one example: those seeking therapy do so out of a sense of unease and imbalance in their lives. Again we see the concept of 'balance' as representing some central human aspiration. Depression is the most common expression of this failure to achieve a sense of balance. It is thought to be reaching epidemic proportions and said to be costing the UK economy two billion pounds a year.[30] Depression is recognized to be a symptom of either a personal sense of failure or of repressed anger, either of 'sin' or having been 'sinned' against. What therapy has to offer in this context is either an acceptance of oneself, that is, forgiveness of oneself, or else forgiveness of the other. Both of these responses can be seen as redemptive, just as the therapist can be seen as the Redeemer.[31] What is more religious than that?

Oliver James argues that as societies in the developed world satisfy ever more material and biological needs and desires, their inhabitants become more rather

---

[27] John Horgan, *The Undiscovered Mind: How the brain defies explanation*, Weidenfeld & Nicolson: London 1999.

[28] Ibid., p. 90.

[29] Ibid., p. 121.

[30] *The Guardian*, 7 December 1999.

[31] I am deliberately using theological language in order to emphasize that I see the therapist adopting the role previously taken by the priest as a representative of God.

than less dissatisfied.[32] He sees this as related to the growth in individualism and the way in which the rise of liberal individualism in English-speaking nations represented a significant break with a medieval world-view of collective welfare and harmony. The liberal view, he argues, insists upon the individual's right to choose and engage freely in a search for personal gratification.[33] This search is most acutely focused in one or other of the therapies which have grown out of the original Freudian adventure and can be seen as a secular search for spiritual ease. This drive to individuality deprives the person of the comforts of the collective, which in every community appears to have organized rituals which ensure a degree of order and regularity in daily life.[34]

The quality of the therapies offered varies widely. Few people can afford the cost in time or money for those psychoanalysts most faithful to Freud's original concept. Counselling services, however, which are cheaper and some would argue less demanding, have become widely available and are offered by the State for almost every human experience of distress. In public disasters like the Lockerbie plane crash, the Dunblane massacre or the Paddington train crash, they are offered free as a social service. One of the most common reactions to a disaster is to feel guilty, to feel that one is somehow responsible. Where previously the support of one's family, friends or one's religious faith gave some sense of meaning to bereavement or distress, their unavailability for many means that counselling has come to be offered as a way of strengthening the individual's ability to cope and to forgive. What is clear is that every form of therapy shares something of the methods that human beings have in the past found powerfully reassuring. The sacred space of the confessional is replicated in the sacred space of the therapist's office, the confidentiality is assured in both settings, there are opening and closing rituals and once the process is under way the therapist assumes a god-like power. It is a spiritual journey into the shadows of one's inner life, often into repressed pain and suffering, a journey which in fact it can feel dangerous to take alone no matter how strongly one wishes for autonomy. Like a child going into a dark forest, one needs a hand to hold.[35]

Self-help Books

J.C. Arnold's book, *The Lost Art of Forgiveness*,[36] is a classic example of the explosion in the publication of easily read books which can be used as a personal aid to find forgiveness by offering compelling examples of that possibility. The

---

[32] Oliver James, *Britain on the Couch*, Century: London 1997.

[33] Ibid., p. 322.

[34] For a more detailed discussion of the neutralization of disorder in communities see Simon Roberts, *Order and Dispute*, Martin Robertson: Oxford 1979, Chapter 3.

[35] This journey into inner space is also recognized as dangerous and in a wide range of mystical tradition as requiring a guide. The image of a guide taking one into sacred spaces is also seen in Dante's journey, accompanied by Virgil, into the world of the dead in the *Divine Comedy*.

[36] J.C. Arnold, *The Lost Art of Forgiving*, The Plough Publishing House: Farmington, PA 1998, see Chapter 2.

emphasis tends to be entirely on the power of individual response even in situations which clearly involve corporate responsibility. The book's cover shows a photograph of a naked 9-year-old Vietnamese girl, burned by napalm, crying, arms outstretched, running towards the camera with plumes of black smoke billowing in the sky behind her. Arnold tells how, 24 years later, the girl, Phan Thi Kim Phuc, visits Washington DC to lay a wreath for peace, and briefly meets the helicopter pilot, John Plummer, who had helped in the napalm raid in which she had been burned. He had spent the following years in an agony of conscience. In their short time together, 'Kim saw my grief, my pain, my sorrow ... She held out her hands to me and embraced me. All I could say was "I'm sorry; I'm sorry" – over and over again. And at the same time she was saying, "It's all right. I forgive you."'[37]

This is presented as a solution, which it may have been for this man, but offers no comment on the morality of governments continuing to have military forces which napalm small girls.

The book ends with a chapter on forgiving God – the same issue as that facing devout Jews in the death camps. For the orthodox Jewish community this had been essentially a religious question: where had God been when they were in the camps? The underlying question for some was: could they forgive God? Fifty-five years later, at a service in Hamburg for more than a hundred German victims of a Concorde air crash in Paris, the Roman Catholic Bishop of Hildesheim, Josef Hemeyer, 'his voice cracking with emotion', asked similar questions: 'God, where were you in Paris? Why have you deserted us?'

Arnold argues that it is easier to blame God and then forgive him than to face the possibility that there really might be no one to blame – no focus for our anger. He sees the solution lying in our 'developing a willingness to learn from our experiences, to grow from them and produce something positive out of what can otherwise seem like an entirely negative time of our lives. Where there appears to be no reason for our suffering, we need to give it one.'[38] Part of the human condition seems to be the need to give some meaning to our lives, to make sense of the forces that would otherwise overwhelm us.

The stories in Arnold's book are told with great compassion and without judgement. They are also told without any direct reference to Christian belief, although that is implicit. In this sense the book differs little from Flanigan's *Forgiving the Unforgivable*, which is described on its cover as 'a comforting guide to recovery and healing'. Both differ significantly from other books published in the same period, which have a frankly theological approach.

Institutes of Forgiveness

Many of the self-help books read as if the authors are embarrassed about making a clear religious statement and are trying to make what they are saying acceptable to an audience which may not share their basic Christian beliefs. It

[37] Arnold, Ibid., p. 118.
[38] Ibid., p. 132.

may be that it is the publishers, concerned with the number they sell, who determine the tone of the text. All include a strong emphasis on the effects of non-forgiveness on physical health as well as on emotional health. A wider understanding of these particular traumatic effects has led to a range of Institutes of Forgiveness being set up in the United States in the 1990s. Some bring together academic work and field work. Others, like the most recent, also the first in the United Kingdom, set up in the new University of Coventry under the title of The Centre for the Study of Forgiveness and Reconciliation, are at this stage purely academic.

The International Forgiveness Institute, based at the University of Wisconsin at Madison, most clearly illustrates the range of activity that can be undertaken. It claims no particular religious position but rejects what it describes as 'relativism'[39] in favour of centring itself in a moral position rather than primarily in psychology or self-help. It does this by claiming, 'all of the ancient traditions that discuss forgiveness (Hebrew, Christian, Islamic, Confucian and Buddhist traditions among others) and the vast majority of modern philosophical writings place forgiveness within morality or the quest for good'.

Robert D. Enright, the Institute's president, in defining forgiveness sees it as being moral in two senses. The first of these is that in forgiving, we give up the resentment to which we are entitled. Giving up resentment in this context is moral (and paradoxical) precisely because we are giving a gift to the one who injured us.[40] The gift is that we no longer resent the injurer even though we have a right to resentment. The second is that forgiveness is moral in that the forgiver reaches out to the other who injured him or her with at least one of three moral principles: merciful restraint, generosity, and/or moral love (*ahab* or *hesed* in Hebrew, *agape* in the ancient Greek). By merciful restraint is meant that the forgiver refrains from deserved resentment or revenge. By generosity is meant that the forgiver actually begins to give good things to the injurer, such as attention, time, favourable judgements and so forth. By moral love is meant that the forgivers give of themselves toward the rehabilitation and betterment of the injurer. The language used is very reminiscent of what we hear in the New Age communities. It picks and mixes from a range of religious sources.

The field work with clients is based on the assumption that the one who forgives may not at first be aware that they are using a moral principle but, at some stage in the proceedings, it will become clear in their language or behaviour that such is the case. The speed at which resentment is abandoned will vary, some being slower than others to move towards a merciful, generous and/or loving response. Some may say they are forgiving without in fact having met the criteria of the above definition, but if so, they may be condoning, excusing or forgetting rather than forgiving. One may condone without any moral response, as is required in forgiveness. Nor is forgiveness the same as reconciliation, which includes at least two parties coming together in mutual respect. Forgiveness is one person's moral

---

[39] There is an implication that a 'relative' interpretation or evaluation is not a 'moral' one. I reject that view, believing that precisely because the behaviour is related to the social context that moral judgement of a serious kind becomes possible.

[40] Cf. Aba Gayle's basic beliefs quoted above (p. 77).

response to another's injustice. One can forgive and not reconcile, as in an abusive marriage.

The Institute has formulated a process of forgiveness which involves a prescribed number of stages through which the forgiver has to pass and a prescribed number of stages for receiving forgiveness from another. These processes, they claim, have been shown to be effective in a number of projects. One was with a group of elderly women who tested positively for depression and anxiety. The goal was for each member to forgive one person who had in their opinion inflicted considerable psychological hurt on them. The women were divided randomly between a forgiveness group who followed a treatment model based on Enright's process and a control group who met in a structured way but who were given no guidelines for forgiveness. At the end of the eight-week period during which they met, on re-testing, both groups significantly decreased in depression and anxiety but the 'treatment' group showed significantly higher forgiveness profiles.[41] Other studies giving successful results included forgiveness intervention with men hurt by a partner's decision to abort their child,[42] and forgiveness as an intervention goal with incest survivors.[43]

The most comprehensive account of psychological research and theological perspectives is to be found in a collection of studies edited by Everett L. Worthington for the John Templeton Foundation in Philadelphia.[44] In his introduction, Worthington makes the point that while forgiveness has been a matter of religious, philosophical and personal concern for many centuries, scientific study began only recently. Before 1985 only five studies investigating forgiveness had been identified. In the following 13 years more than 55 had been conducted, both to study forgiveness and to help people learn to forgive. In an attempt to explain this he cites the fall of communism, increased racial tensions in communities and violent conflicts within nations. Other possibilities he suggests include the growth of a communitarian movement as well as what he describes as 'a growing post-modern philosophy', combined with the publication of the first popular quasi-theological self-help book.[45]

---

[41] John H. Hebl and Robert D. Enright, 'Forgiveness as a Therapeutic Goal with Elderly Females', *Psychotherapy*, Vol. 30, Winter 1993, No. 4, pp. 658–66.

[42] Catherine T. Coyle and Robert D. Enright, 'Forgiveness Intervention with Postabortion Men', *Journal of Consulting and Clinical Psychology*, Vol. 65, 1997, No. 6, pp. 1042–46.

[43] Suzanne R. Freedman and Robert D. Enright, 'Forgiveness as an Intervention Goal with Incest Survivors', *Journal of Consulting and Clinical Psychology*, Vol. 64, 1996, No. 8, pp. 983–94.

I have failed to find any objective criteria for success that might not have been brought about by the simple opportunity to talk about their concerns, but this is an issue that affects all attempts to assess the value of therapeutic methods. Enright has developed the Enright Forgiveness Inventory (EFI) which is widely used and correlates significantly and negatively with anxiety using standard statistical techniques.

[44] Everett L. Worthington, Jr, *Dimensions of Forgiveness: Psychological Research and Theological Perspectives*, Templeton Foundation Press: Philadelphia and London 1998.

[45] This is rather a ragbag of explanations for a very complex question. It is clear however that forgiveness has moved rapidly up the agenda of significant social and religious issues. The book referred to is *Forgive and Forget* by Lewis B. Smedes, HarperCollins Paperback: San Francisco 1996.

Worthington's *Dimensions of Forgiveness* looks at forgiveness in religion, basic social processes, the effects of scientific intervention in interpersonal needs for forgiveness and, most helpfully, an annotated bibliography on forgiveness and related concepts. He also gives suggestions for future research. Unsurprisingly, since the work is firmly based in the American culture where 90 per cent of the population are assumed to attend church, a religious dimension to forgiveness is a recurring subject of interest throughout. One study taking a random sample of 1,030 adult men and women explored the association of religious variables and prayer with forgiveness. They reported that 'people involved in their religious traditions, particularly traditions that give forgiveness a central theological emphasis, tend to report a greater willingness to forgive others than those who are less involved in religious faiths that place such emphasis on forgiveness'.[46] But although in the study the vast majority (94 per cent) of respondents said that it was fairly, or very, important for religious people to forgive, only 48 per cent said that they usually tried to forgive. Eighty-three per cent said that they would only be able to forgive if God helped them, while only 15 per cent believed they could use their own resources. The use of prayer seemed to be an important factor in helping people to forgive. It is as if anger and hurt can be so powerful that some individuals feel unable, without some external support or encouragement, to let go of their negative feelings.

What emerges clearly from the scientific approach is that no consensus on forgiveness has yet been developed by researchers. Indeed, some of the researchers argue against creating one in the belief that a multiplicity of definitions would result in healthy competition. A follow-up conference to the studies considered that a useful field for future research might be the study of forgiveness as a personality trait which might result in the discovery of a characteristic of 'forgivingness'. There may even be hope of a gene for forgiveness, as was proposed for altruism. Other areas to examine were forgiveness of self, forgiveness of God, and 'the distinguishing of forgiveness from related processes like reconciliation, exoneration, condoning, pardoning, confessing'. Perhaps most important was the realization, to my knowledge the first scientific acceptance, of the importance of unforgivingness.

To conclude this section I want to include the clearest presentation of unforgivingness that has come my way. In Holland in 1989 a woman spoke out about her experience of asking for help from a pastor of the Dutch Reformed Church and being sexually abused by him. It quickly became clear that this was a widespread issue. Two years later a meeting was called of ten churches and a programme to help victims was established. Two telephone help lines, one Catholic, one Protestant, were set up. Among the first callers was an 82-year-old man who had been abused as a boy of nine. Another was of a woman in her sixties, who went to a priest after her daughter committed suicide, asking 'where was God in this situation?' He kissed, touched and caressed her, telling her that this was therapeutic. When she complained, his colleagues denied that what she said was possible and the priest continued his duties.

---

[46] M.M. Poloma and G.H. Gallup (1991) in Worthington, *Dimensions of Forgiveness*, p. 276.

Some of these women set up a travelling theatre group to spread an educational message. One of the songs they sing is called 'Forgiveness'. This is an uneasy translation:

No churchly product is so in demand
As forgiving, forgiving, forgiving.
You swallow the injustice as Our Lord has meant
Forgiving, forgiving, forgiving.
So the violator goes ahead, the molestation doesn't end
Forgiving, forgiving, forgiving.

Chorus:
Forgiving, forgiving, forgiving is the word.
Forgiving is for centuries in churches always heard.
The victims bow their heads, full of forgiveness,
So the one who lays his hands on you demands another kiss.
Forgiving is the highest virtue, especially for women
And all male misconduct we dust aside, for ever Amen.

What did you learn as a little girl of four?
Forgiving, forgiving, forgiving.
Even though your opponent was so obviously wrong,
Forgiving, forgiving, forgiving,
Even though you were hurt, deep into your core,
Forgiving, forgiving, forgiving.

These verses were written by women whose loyalty to a self-defined interpretation of Christianity is clear but who reject the institutions that require women's forgiveness to be automatic, unquestioning and non-reparative. In this process they have redefined for themselves the nature of sin and the process of forgiveness, a process which we have consistently seen as a reflection of a post-Christian position. That does not mean that these women would recognize themselves in that description.

Conclusion

The Findhorn Community was set up by people seeking to put into practice a new way of life as an alternative to the orthodox Christian tradition. In a sense, they can be seen as carrying on the Gnostic tradition, in which by learning to know oneself one is learning to know God: the self and the divine are identical. Elaine Pagels quotes a Gnostic teacher, Monoimus: 'Abandon the search for God and the creation and other matters of a similar sort. Look for him by taking yourself as the starting point ... Learn the sources of sorrow, joy, love, hate ... If you carefully investigate these matters you will find him in yourself.'[47]

Findhorn may be seen in a number of different ways, ranging from scorn at a bunch of middle-class 'hippies' to a new view of community which is part of the

---

[47] Elaine Pagels, *The Gnostic Gospels*, Penguin Books: London 1979, p. 19.

return of the prophetic voice. The latter is how they see themselves – leading the people of this planet to a new relationship with the divine. What is impressive is how they combine the grand scheme, like bringing together several hundred people from all over the world to talk about forgiveness, with an attention to detail that provides a warm welcome, superb, wholesome food, good accommodation and sessions that start on time. Also important is the lack of rigidity of belief or attempts at proselytization. All faiths and none are accepted, but a sense of the divine in all things is assumed. From my point of view, the serpent in the Findhorn garden is the belief that perfection of spirit can be achieved and that this can be found through love and forgiveness for oneself and between individuals. Their conviction is that failure to forgive – and the use of the word 'failure' is relevant – damages both one's health and one's spirit.

This can sometimes be true. It was this sense of damage that led Aba Gayle to take the journey of forgiveness to her daughter's murderer. One can only applaud the spiritual freedom it brought not only her but also the man involved. She deserves even more applause for her campaign to abolish the death penalty. It would be difficult however to see Michael Lapsley as a spiritually damaged man. What he is asking for is a social and theological recognition of the concept of restorative justice and a recognition that we are all involved: he 'takes no prisoners', that is, he allows no one to opt out of the discussion. This raises the most important questions which relate not only to Lapsley's own injury but also to the whole process of repairing the damage done by the apartheid system. Is forgiveness always relevant and if so to whom – the perpetrator or the victim? Is it possible to forgive and not forget?

Helen Bamber might well reject these questions as being irrelevant to the healing of those who have been tortured. She is concerned to help first the body and then the mind to forget its memories of pain and helplessness. Once this is done, primarily through a caring and listening process, if people choose, they can turn their attention to more esoteric issues. Both she and Lapsley see the opportunity to have one's experiences and feelings listened to as the most important component of being healed.

Issues at the conference ranged from the importance of concern for the individual and the individual process of healing at both a physical and spiritual level, to the importance of community as a place of healing. Some speakers dealt with one, some with the other. Lapsley was the only one who addressed both issues together, combining personal and political passion, not only for individual healing but also for social justice. But even he posed his discussion in the context of apartheid and its effects. He did not ask his audience to consider whether their own societies suffered from 'sinful' action and inaction, posing the same problems of inhumanity which called for a response. When one member of the audience raised this question it was not reacted to by Lapsley or anyone else. His narrow focus may be understandable but his message fails if his audiences do not draw wider conclusions which relate to their own responsibilities.

What is perhaps puzzling is why forgiveness has become such a dominating issue in western popular culture. There are not only the areas I have described of self-help and therapy but a range of, often sensational, programmes on television and articles in magazines that deal with the subject. An obvious possibility is that withdrawal from formal church connection deprives people of the structures within which problems of conscience and guilt could be examined and discussed. This is particularly important during a period when rapid changes are taking place in attitudes to personal morality. Another is the ubiquity within a global communication system of the presentation of the horrors of human behaviour and the sense of helplessness that goes with that overwhelming sense of pity and terror. We have to face our responsibility as a nation either for playing a part in those horrors or to intervene to mitigate them both within the nation or internationally. Thirdly, we have, in our examination of our own history of racism, lost some traditional scapegoats. Those brought up in the tradition of Bulldog Drummond and a range of children's magazines could always rely on a sinister foreigner, often yellow in colour, whom we could hold responsible for a variety of insults to our way of life. In spite of the attempts of some to keep these prejudices alive, in general they are no longer effective. We are being forced to grow up and take responsibility for ourselves as individuals and citizens. Learning to understand the nature and place of forgiveness is a central part of this process.

But there is also a rapidly expanding interest in forgiveness in the United States, where there seems less evidence of these three factors than in Europe. This is reflected in the most sensational television programmes where participants accuse each other of appalling acts of insensitivity, then collapse in mutual forgiveness in each other's arms. The United States is also the source of the majority of self-help books.

Leaving the conference and turning to the more 'scientific' attempts to study forgiveness, we find ourselves in a very different world. Interest has exploded in the field of psychology. Forgiveness, particularly of the self, has always been a major component of the work of individual psychotherapy. Those psychologists newly engaged in the exploration of the processes of forgiveness appear to see the inability to forgive oneself or others as primarily a technical problem and their task is to relieve the symptoms of anxiety and depression that can accompany it. They attempt this using, primarily, group work. Their conviction of the importance of their calling is clear. The areas they see as causing failure to forgive are concentrated on direct interaction between human beings and this is the focus of the work undertaken. There has been a tendency to see the failure to forgive as an inability to forgive rather than a choice not to forgive, but the nature of unforgivingness is now slowly beginning to be considered.

The rational choice not to forgive is emerging as one of the most important shifts in a post-Christian view of the world. In this sense, it must be distinguished from the blind urge for revenge we have seen in the parents of murdered children, or what I see as the politically calculated decision to keep Myra Hindley in prison. It had previously been a basic assumption in Christendom that forgiveness was a duty and a necessity if one was to seek forgiveness for oneself.[48] This view has been eroded, particularly in relation to what we describe as structural sin or iniquity, where forgiveness is likely simply to ensure that the iniquity continues. This raises the fundamental question expressed by the song of the Dutch women victims of pastoral abuse. In whose interest does forgiveness operate?

---

[48] Matt. 6:12.

The power holders and dominant groups will always see forgiveness as a 'good' since it maintains order, prevents disruption and protects regimes. It is only by questioning whether or not forgiveness is justified, appropriate or creative that we will be able to recognize its true value.

5

The Persistence and Intensification
of Structural Sin

Introduction

In this chapter I shall be looking at aspects of human behaviour about which there has been moral ambivalence. For some people they have been clearly 'sinful', for others they have simply reflected the realities of life. Perhaps the most basic defining characteristic of acts seen as truly 'sinful' is that they provoke a sense of shock. What causes the shock will vary over time and place. I have searched for a word with which to replace the comparative clarity of the word 'sin'. The words 'sin' and 'sinner' are rarely used in ordinary conversation in their original sense. The phrase 'it's a sin' has evolved into a colloquial expression meaning 'it's a shame'. Another trivial use of the word is found in the phrase, 'For my sins', implying a judgement passed on the person using the phrase by themselves. Our language is full of this verbal archaeology. Because of this I use the word iniquity[1] as an alternative to the word sin and transgressor as an alternative to sinner, simply to remind myself and the reader that we are now moving out of a Christian, theological world into a secular world. We are also moving away from concentration on sin as an individual act perpetrated by an individual person and turning attention to what can be described as collective, corporate or structural sin, in which individuals participate but none of them is easily described as solely responsible. Each person involved carries some responsibility. Collective or structural sin is in fact a breeding ground within which individual sin can flourish.[2]

Our New Confusion

We have seen that we are living today on the residue of a Judaeo-Christian inheritance. The meta-narratives of Christianity and Marxism have fractured so we are faced with a new question: how is anything in a post-Christian, post-Marxist world legitimized or criminalized? How do we tell right from wrong? In this work we have now to abandon the word sin along with its theological implications in order to apply ourselves to understanding how, in contemporary society, new issues

---

[1] Iniquity, described in *The Shorter Oxford English Dictionary on Historical Principles*, Oxford University Press: Oxford 1973, as the 'quality of being unrighteous or (more often) unrighteous action or conduct: wickedness, sin. Injurious or wrongful action towards another; now generally connoting gross injustice or public wrong. Want of equity, injustice, unfairness. The name of a comic character in the old morality plays, also called the Vice, representing some particular vice or vice in general, p. 1074.

[2] One example is the global industry of sadistic pornography, which offers images of sadism against women and children.

94

of behaviour evolve and are classified, issues which would previously have been described as sinful, or not recognized as sinful, with all the religious implications of that word intact. Taking an interventionist God out of the equation means that we, as humans, have to take on the responsibility for attitudes and decisions that were previously projected onto an omniscient and omnipotent deity. What is important is that these attitudes and decisions have to be arrived at with humility. In rejecting the role of a deity in determining our moral life we are also rejecting the idea of omniscience and omnipotence.

There will be an inevitable overlap and reference back at some points in this story. The word iniquity can also be taken to mean sin and a transgressor can also mean a sinner. Transgression is essentially the act of passing over or beyond due bounds.[3] It is the setting of these bounds or boundaries, without the insistence of referring back to a Hebrew or Christian text, that becomes the task of the post-Christian society. The philosopher Elizabeth Anscombe, herself a devout Christian, argued that 'notions like "moral obligation", "moral duty", "morally right" and "morally wrong" are now vacuous hangovers from the Judaeo-Christian idea of a law giving God'.[4] The fact that there is no longer a single word we can comfortably use reflects the complexity of judgements we are now making and the often contradictory attitudes to them. The words we use frequently require a story round them to explain why the behaviour we are describing seems wrong since there can be so many interpretations of meaning involved. We tend to use adjectives rather than nouns; we describe behaviour we reject as brutal, inhuman, unacceptable, wicked, evil, humiliating, cruel, irresponsible. We can be talking about behaviour *to* adults, children, or animals; or about the behaviour *of* adults, children or institutions. We can be talking about the behaviour of one country to another as easily as of one individual to another. We can challenge each of these judgements and have only a few friends who agree with us. We can equally be part of a huge majority opinion, side by side with those who disagree with us on other issues.[5]

It is this amoeba-like quality that distinguishes post-Christian attitudes to behaviour we used to describe as sinful. Human nature has shown a fairly limited capacity to invent new wicked acts; what happened in Nazi Germany, and what could happen in a nuclear holocaust, are simply quantitative rather than qualitative leaps – burning one person at the stake and one hundred thousand with a bomb requires a similar lack of empathetic imagination, though the invention of the atomic bomb was a qualitative leap in our potential as humans to be destructive. The Seven Deadly Sins identified by Pope Gregory VI and described in such detail in medieval literature continue to be essential motivating factors in human iniquity with one essential addition, which was not at that time seen as relevant. There is now a considered view that some of the most intolerable behaviour in our society

---

[3] This is also based on the definition in the *Shorter Oxford English Dictionary on Historical Principles*.

[4] See her seminal paper 'Modern Moral Philosophy', 1958. Quoted in her obituary, *The Guardian* 11 January 2001: G.E.M. Anscombe, 'Modern Moral Philosophy', in *Ethics, Religion and Politics*, volume 3 of her *Collected Papers*, University of Minnesota Press: Minneapolis 1981.

[5] This was the case with those people who massed at the English ports to protest against the live export of calves and sheep. Their only shared conviction appeared to be rejection of cruelty to animals.

derives from an unmet need for love and approval.[6] For the human being in the grip of this compulsion there is almost nothing they will not do to satisfy it.[7] One of the most dangerous human responses to this need is the ability to obey orders without question, a response which derives from that need. This is why Eve is such a brilliant role model for the human race and the ability to choose to disobey so important. She has been rescued by feminist theorists like Pamela Norris from her role as the first and original 'sinner':

> Eve had excellent reasons for eating the forbidden fruit: it looked good and was nourishing, and it promised her the priceless gift of wisdom. She took and ate, and was rewarded with the ability to pass on her knowledge to future generations ... Perhaps what is most important is Eve's recognition of the need to challenge boundaries, to make the imaginative leap, however difficult, unpredictable and even dangerous into a new phase of existence.[8]

In this chapter I have chosen to look at some issues which I believe to be serious iniquities, iniquities which the formal institutions of Christianity have failed to address, though many individuals and small Christian groups have done so. Both philosophy and literature have produced a vast literature on the issues I want to discuss but my questions grow out of a sociological, psychological and political background. The three issues on which I concentrate are poverty, slavery and violence as it is expressed in war. I describe these as structural sin since they are woven into our social structures, structures of the State and of the Churches. Challenging them involves challenging those structures and requiring them to redefine the boundaries of sinful and moral behaviour.

Poverty

Simone Weil suggested that if you want to become invisible there is nothing easier: become poor. Poverty is not a popular subject. At best it arouses embarrassment in individuals and in the power holders, embarrassment too often handled by turning aside. At worst the poor are blamed for their own misfortune rather than regarded as victims of an unjust and oppressive social system. I want to look at the effects of poverty on the lives of the poor in Britain. In numerical terms, poverty in Britain may appear to bear little relation to the crushing poverty in the Third World which results in illiteracy, severe malnutrition and high rates of infant mortality. But all these effects do exist in Britain. Here I concentrate on what is known as the Fourth World, that is, the world of the poor in affluent societies. There is a solution to this poverty, but it is a solution blocked by vested interests and greed. Poverty in the

---

[6] Alice Miller, *The Untouched Key: Tracing Childhood Trauma in Creativity and Destructiveness*, Virago Press Ltd: London 1990, p. 160.

[7] Consider the story of Dennis Nilsen, the young Scottish civil servant, living in London, who killed, had sex with and then cut up youngsters he picked up in pubs. This is told in the study *Killing For Company* by Brian Masters, Coronet Books: London 1986.

[8] See Pamela Norris, *The Story of Eve*, Picador: London 1998, pp. 403–4.

Fourth World can lead to poor education, illness and early death, as well as the equally important factor of destructive spiritual poverty. I have chosen to use Lynne Ramsey's film, *Ratcatcher*, to illustrate the damaging spiritual effects of poverty, rather than focus on the many statistics which emphasize the physical effects.[9]

Poverty is a form of violence. Life for a child living in a poverty-stricken community can be as destructive for a child's soul or personality as an experience in a concentration camp. It may even be more so since the child emerging from the camp has his or her experiences put into a context which gives meaning to that experience. The child brought up on a neglected and desolate housing estate is offered no such context. The film *Ratcatcher* tells the story of a Glasgow family living in a deprived, peripheral area of the city. The normally desolate and bleak environment is made even more unattractive by a strike in the cleansing department of the local authority; the streets and back courts are littered with black bags filled with rubbish. These bags become infested with rats – the local youngsters kill them with sticks. The rats and the killing become a metaphor for the lives of the human inhabitants of the area and how their lives are destroyed by the setting in which they live.

We see the effects on children of the broken lives of the adults who are supposed to protect them – adults who have lost the capacity to care for themselves, living in a society that offers them no opportunities for work, self-respect or choice. In the family round whom the film is based, the mother is trying to maintain some kind of order in a house that is too small and run down; she is also struggling to make financial ends meet on an inadequate income. Her goal is simply to survive. She cares for her children but is drained of the energy it would take to give them the emotional support they need. The irregularly employed father behaves like an irresponsible son, always meeting his own needs to drink and watch football before considering the needs of his family. There are three children: two girls, the elder of whom is trying to escape her mother's fate and is already experimenting with city-centre prostitution, the younger seeking love and attention, and a middle child, a boy, caught between childhood and adolescence. Through the experiences of this boy, James, we see the struggle of the human spirit to survive despair and to respond to any glimpse of hope.

The film opens with the drowning in the local canal of a boy with whom James was playing, a death for which he feels in part responsible. This drowning symbolizes the lack of parental supervision and the lack of local authority care for the community. The canal is a clear hazard for children, but equally an attraction for them in an area which offers no safe opportunities for adventures or fun. James drifts through the film, dreaming about the drowning, watching in a detached way his parents' erratic relationship, his sisters, his younger friend with learning difficulties who loves animals – even the rats – and an older gang. He sees and hears round him constant anger, casual cruelty, and ugliness of the spirit and of the environment. He begins to experiment with drinking his father's beer, smoking a cigarette and joining in the gang bang of an older girl who out of her own needs lies back passively and lets herself be used.

---

[9] *Ratcatcher*, dir. by Lynne Ramsey: 1998.

The viewer's heart sinks as it appears that James is drifting into an acceptance of this way of life but is lifted again in a glorious episode where, having formed a tentative relationship with the older girl, whom he met again on the banks of the canal, he helps her, borrowing the fine comb and powerful soap his mother uses for her children, to clean the lice from her hair. She ends up washing her hair in the bath. Taking his clothes off, James joins her and they share a delightful childlike game, washing and splashing each other. In this episode they both recover their innocence – a kind of baptism – and end up sitting side by side on the sofa, wrapped in towels, eating sandwiches and watching television ... a modern sacrament. We see the potential childhood these two might have enjoyed.

Running away from a particularly unpleasant fight between his parents, James takes a bus ride as far as it can go and finds himself in the countryside where new houses are being built beside a wheat field. Here he finds a new joy, a transcendent experience of running and rolling in the wheat. He returns home reluctantly when darkness falls. Finally the army moves in to clear the rubbish bags and a riot of rat killing ensues. Even James' friend who loves animals is caught up in the hysteria of killing. Yet another of James' fragile beliefs in goodness is destroyed. He is sinking into a drowning, suicidal despair when we see in the closing sequences the family carrying their few household goods through the now-harvested wheat field to one of the new houses being built there. They have, in spite of all the odds against them, been rehoused. The film ends with a close-up of James' face. For the first and only time in the film he is smiling.

No one in this film appears to be aware of the injustices under which they are living. The men and boys take refuge in alcohol, sex, football and violence; the women comfort each other and try to survive. The children move restlessly from place to place with wild hearts, seeking love. No one in the film offers explanations of what is happening; there is no coherence in people's lives, no sense of anyone interpreting the nature of the society in which they live, no belief in anything or anyone. They swim and sometimes drown in a sea of indifference. The structures of work groups, trades unions, local or central government, which could hear what these people have to say or would give them a voice, are absent. For James' family, even the process of rehousing them was a matter of inexplicable fate over which they had no control. Although the film ended in that moment of hope, it leaves us unconvinced that, without job opportunities and the back-up services of health and education, the problems the family bring with them will not destroy even that. We fear that the glory of James' smile may fade.

Discussion

James lives in Glasgow, a city which boasts three universities – places of higher learning – and skyscapes that are dominated by church spires. The city shops are glittering temples of consumerism where a woman's dress can cost more than a month's income for a family; houses exchange hands for three-quarters of a million pounds. There are also high levels of unemployment and so many families unable, because of their poverty, to pay taxes that the local authority struggles to find money to pay teachers, social workers and cleansing workers. Of all the households which include dependent children in the city, 27 per cent have only one adult in them and 37 per cent have no one in a paid job. On Glasgow's periphery are large areas of public housing, in one of which this film was made, whose families are most vulnerable to these shortages since they are the powerless; they are as powerless as those for whom Gutierrez claimed freedom and justice in order that they might achieve a 'human' life.[10]

The Christian Bible reserves its most powerful condemnation for those who abuse children. Poverty, endemic in British society, condemns a third of British children. It is from communities such as James' that homeless children, are drawn – children often unwilling to stay and be brutalized by parents from whom they once expected love. They are the ones with sufficient courage and energy to move out even if that means for some begging and prostitution. The world of the poor is another country. This world still exists in Britain and the stories that were told by Charles Booth and Henry Mayhew in the Victorian era are in this decade being retold by writers like Beatrix Campbell[11] and Nick Davies.[12] Davies in particular tells us what is happening among the people most damaged and degraded by hopelessness and poverty. They in turn find it harder not to become brutal, corrupted and degraded, doing unto others what was done to them. Our precarious skin of civilization cracks, as it did for some in the concentration camps. As humans we are all vulnerable to the dark forces. Those who benefit from poverty and those who turn their eyes away from it are all complicit in this structural sin.

But this is not a problem of individual sin. A large part of the reason for the growth of poverty in Britain has been deliberate government policies on taxes and benefits.[13] Voters who gave the government the majority of votes endorsed these policies. Other European countries took a different path. The British have chosen to construct and live in a society which has made a communal decision that some people – and their children – are more entitled to respect, dignity, choice and freedom than others. These people have access to good education and good jobs; flowing from that come the other benefits of an income which makes possible good housing, healthy food, the maximum health related to one's genetic inheritance, holidays, newspapers, but most of all a low level of anxiety about the issues of daily survival. This in turn leads to better opportunities for kindly, personal interaction within families. The dark forces within them are less likely to overwhelm happy, confident people.

Poverty has also become a weapon used by nations to impose their will on other nations through the use of sanctions. These create poverty and hunger for the common people rather than damaging the rulers. In fact, the anger this arouses can prop up and reinforce dictatorial regimes. Children, in particular, suffer the effects of these measures.

---

[10] Gustavo Gutierrez, *Essential Writings*, ed. James B. Nickoloff, SCM Press: London 1996, p. 3.

[11] Beatrix Campbell, *Goliath: Britain's Dangerous Places*, Methuen: London 1993.

[12] Nick Davies, *Dark Heart*, Chatto & Windus: London 1997.

[13] Joseph Rowntree Foundation, *Inquiry into Income and Wealth, vols 1 and 2*, Joseph Rowntree Foundation: York 1995.

Slavery

In this section I discuss the iniquity of slavery, an iniquity which continues to exist in individual countries and is growing within the global market. It is widely believed in the West that slavery ended after the American Civil War, when it was abolished in the southern United States. This is not the case. Slavery takes many forms in today's world: a traditional, biblical form which continues to exist in Mauritania, bonded slavery which is endemic in Asia, wage slavery in the forests and mines of Brazil, and international slavery which specializes in bringing women and children into prostitution. All of these bring economic rewards to those engaged in this trade. These forms of slavery destroy and degrade the humanity of those enslaved and corrupt the humanity of the slavers, since in order to make money they must deny any capacity for empathy and compassion they may have had and learn to see their fellow humans as objects to be bought and sold. I then look briefly at the practice of slavery in which women and children are bought and sold as objects to be used sexually before showing how poverty can destroy the human spirit.

Mauritania

If it were possible to be sentimental about slavery, it would be in Mauritania. Here slavery is carried on, as it has been from biblical times, in the biblical pattern of the slave being part of the owner's family and the family feeling a sense of responsibility for the slave and his family. All of the slave's family are of course also slaves and work for the owner's family from early childhood on. The system reflects the best practice of American southern plantation life when slavery was practised there. Slaves in Mauritania feel loyalty and responsibility to the families they serve, are frequently given considerable responsibility which involves travel, have regular responsibilities outside the home – like selling water in the street, an activity that earns significant income for their master. Others' work may alternate between the urban world and the master's farm in the countryside. A slave and his owner can develop a relationship of mutual respect and some affection. They can even be seen walking hand in hand. Slaves know that they will be cared for in old age. So what's wrong with that? Is it not reminiscent of the Garden of Eden?

These practices breach the United Nations mandate that no one can own another human being. They also totally ignore the human right to have some degree of choice in how you live your life. The women in the slave family are used in the work of the household and the children are added to the work roster as soon as they can make a physical contribution. Any children born are born into slavery. There is no question of them being given any education; they are simply trained to play their part in the household economy. The economy is the key to this system. For minimum input in the cost of food and shelter, slave owners can run their farms in the country and their businesses in the town for maximum profit. But even in this comparatively remote area of West Africa, the Serpent has raised his head to ask the age-old question about freedom from oppression.[14] Two Mauritanian organizations,

---

[14] See Luke 4:18: 'he hath sent me to preach deliverance to the captives ... to set at liberty them that are bruised'.

SOS Slaves and El Hor, work to help free slaves in spite of their leaders, many of whom are themselves ex-slaves, being arrested and imprisoned. Kevin Bales argues that the rulers of Mauritania will fight as hard as the slave owners of the American South did to retain their privileges. He also maintains that 'were the western countries to link their remission of Mauritania's staggering foreign debt to a government programme to give land to slaves, thousands more could achieve a sustainable freedom'.[15]

The New Slavery

Bales describes for us the new forms of slavery which have emerged since the Second World War and the reasons for this emergence. The first is the dramatic increase in population. Since 1945 the world population has almost trebled from about 2 billion to more than 5.7 billion. Across Southeast Asia and the Indian subcontinent the countries are flooded with children, more than half the population being under 15. In countries already poor, what resources they have are overwhelmed. Without work, people become desperate and life becomes cheap. The second factor is the rapid rate of social and economic change, which has meant that with modernization the ruling group, along with their family and friends, have become immensely wealthy while the poverty of the poor has increased disastrously. Enormous sums have been paid for weapons to keep dissidents under control, draining the countries still further of resources. Meanwhile, traditional ways of coping have been lost as the globalization of the world economy has damaged the small-scale subsistence farming on which families relied. Government policies have converted land to produce cash crops for export. Millions of peasants have been bankrupted and driven from their land – sometimes into slavery: 'For the first time in human history there is an absolute glut of human slaves. A modest estimate is 27 million of which perhaps 15 to 20 million are to be found in bonded labour in India, Pakistan, Bangladesh and Nepal.'[16] Those of us living in North America and Europe benefit from their work because of the cheap imports of grains, rugs, jewellery and other artefacts.

Bonded Labour

The practice of bonded labour, widely applied in Pakistan, brings misery to millions of families. The procedure is as follows: a man is given a job and a loan by an employer, normally a landowner, to buy food and clothing in order to start work. In theory the money will be repaid from his wages but in practice the loan has to be constantly topped up for him to feed himself and his family. He ends up owing much more than he originally borrowed and he has to keep working in the usually forlorn hope that some day he will be able to pay this off. His wife and children are considered to be included in the bondage and all other members of his family are seen as responsible for the debt. If he dies, they are expected to take

---

[15] Kevin Bales, *Disposable People: New Slavery in the Global Economy*, University of California Press: Berkeley, Los Angeles, London 1999.

[16] Ibid., pp. 9–14.

on the debt. Any attempt on the part of him or his family to escape is dealt with by brutal repression. The families live in extreme poverty without access to educational or health services. While officially this is not slavery, it takes the same form. The landowner considers that he owns his employees body and soul. This is seen to be particularly the case at election time, when the bonded labourers are lined up and sent in wagons to vote for the candidate of the landlord's choice. Needless to say his candidate will be the one least likely to question the system of bonded labour.

Contract Slavery

In the mining areas and in the jungles of Brazil, forms of industrial practice are employed that bear only the most marginal similarity to what we understand as normal. The photographs of Sebastian Salgado have shown us something of the brutal working conditions in the gold mines, where armed guards stand over the workers.[17] What goes on in the camps in the jungle where the forests are being destroyed is less widely known because of the precautions taken by the contractors to prevent access.

One American film crew which managed to get images of the appalling conditions in one camp showed their film on the evening before the Mayor of Matte Grosso was asking Congress for additional funding. The funding application was refused until improvements were introduced, particularly for the care of children. The Brazilian government then ruled that children should not be allowed to work in the camps. Two results came of this. The first was that one camp was built which included a school and a health clinic. This became a show camp to which visitors could be taken. The second result – deriving from the ruling about children not being allowed to work – was that 30,000 women and children, on their own, were simply dumped at a road side without money or transport. This does not mean that children are no longer employed, simply that a gesture had to be made.[18] Nevertheless we can see what an important part vivid mass communication could play in developing a new morality.

The men are attracted to the camps by offers of work. Recruited in the towns, they are taken by lorries into the jungle, given a loan to buy food and accommodation for themselves and their families. With no history of industry they lack the experience and sophistication which would protect them from the exploitation to which they are subjected. The camps are usually many miles from main roads and become virtual prisons – guards pursue men if they attempt to escape and beat them mercilessly when they are caught. They are trapped in a spiralling circle of debt since their wages are not sufficient to live on.

---

[17] Sebastian Salgado, *Photo Poche*, intro. Christian Caujolle, Centre National de la Photographie: France 1993.

[18] In spite of its minimal effects this is an interesting example of how vivid mass communication can play a significant part in educating a wider public and giving them some responsibility in what is going on even in distant countries.

War Slavery

In Burma today, tens of thousands of men, women and children have been captured by the army and used as labourers on government construction projects or as aides to the army in military campaigns against indigenous people. While they are not technically slaves, violence is used to keep these humans in bondage. The motive is economic – the saving of labour costs either for the army or construction projects. International companies who invest in Burma are complicit in this iniquity since both the US State Department and many human rights organizations have confirmed this situation. In the African wars children are kidnapped, taught how to shoot and kill, often with the aid of drugs, and the girls are used to sexually service the soldiers.

Sexual Slavery

I view sexual slavery as a separate form of slavery because of its international ramifications and the complexity of its structure. It does however have certain factors in common with those previously described. The sexual slavery of women, like other forms of slavery, carries with it the weight of generations. The bodies of women share the economic value of the bodies of men. They can be put to work, either in the fields or in the household and can produce children to continue the work, just as a herd of cows does. But they have an additional value – as objects of sexual desire – and for this reason if for no other they have been stolen, bought, sold and even married so that their possession is secure. In this section I will look at one form of sexual slavery associated with war, then at the form of sexual slavery which has developed to meet the global market of prostitution.

One of the best-documented studies of sexual slavery in wartime is contained in the testimonies compiled by the Korean Council for Women Drafted for Military Sexual Slavery and the Research Association on the Women Drafted for Military Sexual Slavery by Japan.[19] There was a fifty-year silence over the estimated 200,000 Asian – mainly Korean – women, euphemistically named 'comfort women', who were forced into sexual service for Japanese troops in the Second World War. The delay in sharing knowledge of what had happened to these women was more related to their shame than the guilt of the men who had planned and carried out this outrage. The 'comfort women' policy was planned, established and managed, and the women recruited, by the chiefs of the army and navy general staff.

The extensive deployment of 'comfort stations' for the exclusive use of the military began in 1937, after the Nanking Massacre when an estimated 115,000 Chinese were killed. Japanese soldiers referred to the comfort stations as *nigyuichi* ('29 to one'), a reference to the number of men each woman was expected to service each day. Evidence of comfort stations has been confirmed in China, Hong Kong, the Philippines, Singapore and every other occupied area of the Far East. It has long been assumed that soldiers were entitled to see the women of conquered

---

[19] See Keith Howard, ed., *True stories of the Korean Comfort Women*, Cassell: London 1995.

territories as available to relieve their sexual needs either by paying for their services or raping them. In the West the use of local brothels has been seen by the officer class as helpful in keeping their men under control and since the First World War prophylactics have been issued to help avoid infection. There is however a qualitative difference when, as happened with the Japanese, women in occupied countries were forced to leave their homes to service occupying soldiers. These women, as I have said mostly Korean, were drawn from a powerfully patriarchal culture where respectability and chastity were seen as essential to a woman's self-respect and her family's honour.

When, after the war, these women were released, their shame was such that neither they nor their families spoke of their experiences. Silence and forgetting were their techniques of survival. Ultimately a number of former Korean 'comfort women' found the courage to break their collaborative silence. Making their story public 'turned them from individual survivors into collectives of resistance'; North and South Korean 'comfort women' met together for the first time in 1992.[20] For these women to break their silence and redefine themselves, from sinners, to survivors, to resisters, involved great pain and courage, since their families and community viewed them as shameful. Some 'comfort women' who have since died have been buried in a sacred space (The Hill of Missing Home) where people who died for the nation are buried. This gesture has had great significance in challenging the stigma of national dishonour and transforms the 'defiled prostitute' into a 'national heroine'.

Some aspects of organized sexual slavery for economic purposes are to be found now in every country in the world. A recent investigation in Britain found young girls held in slavery and forced to be prostitutes in Birmingham and Manchester.[21] Most women and children[22] are drawn from countries where they are living in abject poverty. Usually they are promised jobs in their own or another country so leave their homes willingly; subsequently they are imprisoned, raped and beaten until they accept their fate as sex workers. Those who are taken to countries other than their own have their passports taken away and are even more helpless. Thailand is frequently used as a case study for a society where the bodies of young women are cheap. Sometimes sold to agents by their own families on the understanding that they are going to work in factories, these young women are supplied to brothels in Japan, Europe and North America, where they are brutalized and enslaved. Kevin Bales describes how criminal gangs, usually Chinese or Vietnamese, are known to control brothels in the United States that enslave Thai women. Women are rotated round brothels to escape the attention of law enforcement officers.[23] The world in which sexual slaves live, whether in Thailand,

---

[20] Anon., 'Comfort Women', *Trouble and Strife: The radical feminist magazine*, No. 41, p. 59.

[21] *The Game's Up*, Children's Society, 1996 and Maggie O'Kane, 'Death of Innocence', *Guardian* G2 pp. 2–3, 12 February 1996.

[22] An investigation undertaken by *The Observer*, 14 January 2001, states that there is a growing demand from British paedophiles for foreign children as young as six who can be ordered from abroad through pimps, then imprisoned in private West End flats. As they grow too old for the paedophiles they are sold on into adult prostitution.

[23] Bales, *Disposable People*, p. 70.

New York or London, is like the world of the concentration camp: there are only those who have power and those who have no power. Each must find a way of adjusting to their enslavement and find 'strategies invented to enable them to live in an unliveable situation'.[24]

Discussion

These kinds of slavery are related to the use and abuse of power for economic ends. The powerful use the bodies of slaves as if they are machines with no human identity. This was how the pyramids were built and it is how some food, cloth, carpets, furniture, jewellery, and many other goods come to the West today. They come more cheaply than would otherwise be possible, and 'respectable' firms enmeshed in global capitalism tolerate many of these practices. In some countries where these practices flourish, the culture of human rights is poorly developed particularly in respect of women. In some Far Eastern countries, for example, it may be thought that to be born a woman may be a punishment for misdeeds in a former life. Western ideas of human rights are largely products of Renaissance humanism and the Enlightenment, and even with that it took more than a century of industrial struggle before the West had a clear view of workers' rights. Even now in the twenty-first century they can be threatened. We should not be patronizing but we should be concerned with enabling change to take place. Anger is an appropriate response, as is compassion for the victims: there is no appropriate forum for forgiveness in the iniquities described. Within the larger iniquity of slavery we find a network of transgressions in which humans destroy their fellow humans with beatings, rape, starvation and a variety of tortures. Perhaps the worst transgression lies within those of us in the West who collude with these practices by continuing, even when we are aware of the source, to buy from firms who accept these practices in order to increase their profits and the value of their share holdings, and to close our eyes to the exploitation of women and children in prostitution.

Bales tells us that 'Slaveholders, business people, even governments hide slavery behind smoke screens of words and definitions. We have to penetrate this smoke and know slavery for what it is, recognizing that it is not a "third world" issue but a global reality – a reality in which we are already involved and implicated.' He goes on to point out that churches were at the core of the original abolitionist movement out of the religious tradition of the need of freedom from captivity of both the body and the spirit. The fact that slavery is an abomination that denies the sanctity of life and crushes the young and vulnerable requires their current involvement.[25]

Violence and War

Both poverty and slavery are forms of violence in that they represent the oppression of groups of people. Wherever we look we find conflicting interests and divergent

---

[24] R.D. Laing, *The Politics of Experience*, Penguin: Harmondsworth 1967, p. 95.

[25] Bales, *Disposable People*, p. 261.

ways of finding resolution to conflict, but from the second half of the twentieth
century we have seen the most serious attempts to formulate new responses to
mediate conflicting interests. These attempts are themselves responses to the need
to reformulate ideas of right and wrong, sin, iniquity and transgression in the light
of new knowledge and understanding of the human potential for self-destruction.
These new approaches are essentially non-violent, since those involved in new
mediation processes increasingly see violence as more likely to escalate conflict
rather than resolve or diminish it. This is not to say that they are pacifists – the view
they hold can best be described as pragmatic.

Violence has been an accepted response to individual and group conflict over
many millennia. It has both positive and negative aspects, in a sense related to our
capacities for passion, energy and courage. We can have a violent response to
seeing or experiencing cruelty or injustice if rejection of these is part of our cultural
response. We can use it creatively in many forms of art. Some people we designate
as criminals see violence as an art form and in some cultures the violent man is seen
as a hero.[26] On the other hand it can result in cruelty and injustice, forms of
violence like rape or the physical and sexual abuse of one's partner and children. In
advanced industrial societies, many aspects of the previously assumed entitlement
to this violence have now been questioned, but we would be foolish not to recognize
the power, excitement and pleasure that the infliction of cruelty can create in the
most average person.

The State, by creating police forces, has taken upon itself the responsibility to use
violence to maintain order and prevent random violence in the community.[27] This
can be a positive use of organized violence, although we are given regular glimpses
on television of how it can also be abused. In theory certain groups, like women and
children, are now protected from domestic violence; rape within marriage is now a
criminal offence in Britain, as is the rape of men by men. However, these practices
are proving difficult to control.[28] Legislation against violence among football fans
has been tightened up. The State can also organize violence in less acceptable ways,
as we saw in Germany under Nazism and in Britain in the 1980s during the miners'
strike. Clearly the impulse to violence is deeply embedded in the human creature
and, while women are not immune, it appears to be most powerfully demonstrated
in the young male of the species, a capacity the State seems both to wish to dispel
but also to utilize, particularly in wartime.

---

[26] See Jimmy Boyle, *A Sense of Freedom*, Canongate Press: Edinburgh 1977.

[27] In turn the community has taken on the task of controlling unnecessary violence by the police
through a complaints process.

[28] Between February 1998 and February 2000, Strathclyde Police statistics show that they were called
to a total of 22,400 domestic disputes, of which over 9,000 involved physical violence. The Glasgow
Women's Support Group Survey (1990) showed that of the 1,503 women responders to a questionnaire,
52 per cent had been frightened of the men they lived with because of their behaviour, such as being
slapped, kicked, hit, constantly shouted at or accused of things they hadn't done. For most of these
women this was a regular or frequent event. The University of Manchester Wife Rape, Marriage and the
Law Survey (1991) showed that one in seven of the 1,007 women whose cases were looked at (14 per
cent) had been raped by their husbands; in almost half of the rapes violence was used or threatened. One
in three women of those raped with violence were pregnant. Source for these figures is the Glasgow
Women's Support Project.

War as an Aspect of Violence

One area, rarely questioned, is the legitimacy of the use of organized violence in war. The assumption that organized violence between nations should take over when diplomacy fails to resolve conflict – or even before it has been tried – is held by the vast majority of the citizens of this planet. This arises, not necessarily from a reasoned conviction, but because people may not have been offered an opportunity to discuss it or influence the decisions involved in resolving conflict. This happened even in Britain in relation to entering the war in Kosovo. Parliament, representing the people of this country, was totally bypassed; the war was undertaken without it being officially declared. The decision had been made by a handful of people in the Cabinet. There was no democratic outcry because people had by that time been persuaded by the media that war was the only solution to the conflict. In contrast, the build-up to the second Gulf War in 2003 was marked by massive political protests in Britain and around the world. In spite of these, the Prime Minister eventually secured a majority vote in Parliament to support his personal determination to enter the war. Some are left questioning whether simple majorities are sufficient to settle such grave issues.

The images presented by the media during the Kosovo conflict were of brave young men from the Allied Forces bombing from aeroplanes and equally brave young men from Serbia and Kosovo energetically trying to kill each other on the ground to gain territory – that most ancient of goals. In the 2003 Iraq conflict, the emphasis was on the 'shock and awe' to be created in the common people by massive bombing. What we also saw were harrowing pictures of women and children suffering and in despair, the most recent being the image of an Iraqi child whose arms had been blown off, an image which was met with revulsion world-wide. We see these images repeated in every conflict in every country. There is no evidence that the women suffering in these conflicts are given any opportunity to consider whether organized violence as a way of resolving conflict is desirable or inevitable. The decisions to react with violence are made by their husbands and sons or by their rulers. The makers and sellers of armaments must welcome and encourage the idea of violent responses to conflict since this ensures continuous profits for their shareholders.

The basic iniquity of modern war as waged by nations of the First World is that because of advances in technology those who suffer most in modern war are civilians. Not only are they killed but their homes and their economies are destroyed.[29] Many recent wars reflect the failure of the economically advanced nations, which have united themselves in the West, to recognize their responsibility to the poorer nations of the world. They continue to manufacture and sell armaments which Third World governments buy as status symbols, but inevitably use against their neighbours or to subdue what they describe as dissidents in their own countries.[30]

---

[29] This destruction offers economic opportunities for firms in the West to come in after the war and rebuild the destroyed infrastructures.

[30] Money used for armaments if spent on health and education would naturally lead to more democratic regimes, which the leaders of these countries do not usually want.

Judging by the last three major wars in which Britain was engaged, the two Gulf Wars and Kosovo, there appears to be an increasing tendency to engage in war which totally subjugates the enemy rather than seeking a break into which diplomacy can be reinserted. When conventional weapons fail or are thought inappropriate, the use of sanctions as a method of subjugation brings suffering, not to the powerful but to the powerless. Lurking always in the background is the threat of the use of nuclear weapons by Britain and the United States, instruments of mass destruction which not only have the capacity to destroy cities and their civilian populations but have the possibility to destroy the planet itself. Both these countries have shameful numbers of their citizens living in poverty, which could be relieved by the money used to create and maintain these weapons. The alternatives to war are never addressed.

The History of Christian Opposition to War

Canon Stuart Morris described war as 'not to be thought of as dying for what you believe in, but as killing for what you believe in'.[31] This reflects a view that has been held since the early years of Christianity and is a story perhaps best told in Nuttall's history of Christian pacifism. He takes four historical points between the first and twentieth centuries which illustrate a conscientious repudiation of war. By following his pattern we can see also how the roots of secular rejection of war developed. The periods taken are the early Church, the pacifism of the medieval sects, the Reformation groups of Anabaptists and Mennonites on the Continent and the Quakers in England. Nuttall deliberately limits his discussion to 'organized and conscious groups of Christian pacifists, not isolated, prophetic figures' and points out that, while the position of the early Christians may seem the least relevant, each group to some extent 'made its own the witness of those who had gone before'.[32] Nuttall also points out that the principles underlying Christian pacifism have differed at different times. The view that God is a God of love is, he says, a comparatively recent inclusion in the pacifist argument; certainly he finds no trace of it in the pacifist discussions before the beginning of the nineteenth century.

Any discussion of war forces us to acknowledge the ambivalence of Christian views of virtue. Matt Ridley tells us that the anthropologist and historian John Hartung 'has taken the much loved Judaeo-Christian phrase "Love thy neighbour as thyself" and subjected it to searching scrutiny'.[33] According to Hartung it was devised by Moses to soothe the dissension and internecine violence among the Israelites, but referred directly to 'the children of thy people' and was not an encouragement to 'general benevolence'.[34] He also quotes Richard Alexander: 'the

---

[31] He added, 'and there is no surer method of destroying your ideals than by trying to protect them by a method which inevitably destroys them'. In Stuart Morris, *Conscripting Christianity*, Peace Pledge Union pamphlet, 1937. The pamphlet was the text of a sermon broadcast by the BBC on 1 August 1937. Morris later resigned Holy Orders.

[32] Geoffrey Nuttall, *Christian Pacifism in History*, World Without War Council, Basil Blackwell & Mott: Berkeley, CA 1971.

[33] Matt Ridley, *The Origins of Virtue*, Penguin Books: London 1997, pp. 191–92.

[34] J. Hartung, 'Love thy neighbour', *The Skeptic*, Vol. 3, 1995, No. 4. Hartung ends his essay with the bleak view that only an extra-terrestrial enemy could create a universal morality.

rules of morality and law alike seem not to be designed specifically to allow people to live in harmony within societies but to enable societies to be sufficiently united to deter their enemies'. We have continued to laud the classical virtues of manliness and bravery which are essential components of warfare, while paying lip service to the Christian virtues of love, modesty, acceptance and humility – the alternatives to the Seven Deadly Sins. It could be argued that in the main we have encouraged women to take responsibility for maintaining the Christian virtues while men have been given the freedom to choose the classical virtues.

Turning to the early Church, Nuttall sees the defining point as the year 313, when Constantine made Christianity the official religion of the Roman Empire. As a consequence of this, he says, 'everything was altered for the Christians and has remained different ever since'.[35] Since 313, the Church has officially accepted war. Nuttall quotes W.E. Orchard: 'Christianity has accepted the State, and ... this carries with it the necessity for ... the waging of war.'[36] By the fourth century, the Church had authorized the *forcible* suppression of pagan rites – a precedent for the later violence against heretics – and by 416 non-Christians were actually forbidden to serve in the army; the army and the Church were now indissolubly linked with the authority of St Augustine that war may be 'just' for Christians. The gradual reversal of the anti-war teachings of the early fathers was intensified in the seventh century by the need for large-scale armed defence against Islam.

Before this the relationship had been very different. Refusal among Christians to take part in military service was mainly, but not only, due to their fear of idolatry, since a requirement was to take the oath as part of pagan rites. It must be remembered that the early Christians came mainly from Jewish stock and that the First Commandment, 'Thou shalt have no other Gods before me',[37] was powerfully imprinted. The other factor, reflecting their relationship with the State, was their reluctance to take part in the life of the world which they saw as the product of an evil system which had to be rejected. This led Celsus, the second-century critic of Christianity, to make the accusation that while being willing to enjoy the advantages of the Empire, they would do nothing to ensure its preservation: 'If all did as the Christians, there would be nothing to prevent things from getting into the hands of the barbarians.'[38] This is still the strongest argument used against pacifists today.

In linking itself to the State, the Christian Church moved inevitably from being a Christian sect in the Roman Empire to becoming the Holy Roman Empire in which the Emperor was a Christian emperor and the Pope an imperial bishop, working together in a common purpose to establish total control of the known world. Any opposition or criticism was not to be tolerated and, where heard, was quickly driven underground. War and oppression led Milman to use the phrase, 'the military Christianity of the Middle Ages'.[39] The earlier case for pacifism was no

---

[35] Nuttall, *Christian Pacifism*, p. 4.

[36] W.E. Orchard, intro. to C.J. Cadoux, *The Early Christian Attitude to War: a contribution to the history of Christian ethics*, Headley: London 1919.

[37] Exodus 20:3.

[38] Nuttall, *Christian Pacifism*, p. 9.

[39] H.H. Milman, *History of Christianity: from the birth of Christ to the abolition of paganism in the Roman Empire*, John Murray: London 1963, p. 288.

longer relevant so a new foundation had to be laid: this was found in the Christian Bible which at this time was still forbidden to lay readers. In that sense, the dissidents were precursors of the Reformation but the point with which we are concerned is that they appear to have taken the Sermon on the Mount literally and saw it as a repudiation of war.[40]

In the seventeenth century, it was the Quakers who founded an anti-war movement which still, in the twenty-first century, holds to its earliest beliefs. For George Fox, Nuttall writes, 'it was not war in itself which was out of the question, so much as the attitudes of mind and spirit which dispose men to war and without which war would not be possible'. Nuttall sees the Society of Friends, as the Quakers are called, as having been influenced by the humanism of the Renaissance with its new respect for personality and new faith in human capacities. The Friends' repudiation of war as an affront to the human soul was in part a response to this new humanism. The sixteenth-century Christian humanist Erasmus had written, 'Who will give to this manifest madness [*manifestariam insaniam*] the names of zeal, piety and fortitude, devising a way whereby it is possible for a man to whip out his sword, stick it into the guts of his brother, and nonetheless dwell in that supreme charity which, according to Christ's precept, a Christian owes to his neighbour?'[41] This was expressed even more directly in Erasmus' tract, the *Complaint of Peace*: 'How can you say "Our Father" while you are thrusting the sharp steel into the body of your brother?'[42]

Erasmus and his circle, the 'London Reformers', leaders of the English Renaissance,[43] aspired to create a radically new social order and in doing so addressed the question of war and peace. They saw that unless wars could largely be prevented, the social reconstruction they sought would be impossible. They were drawing on the rich heritage of antiquity, not accepting the view that war is an action of a divine Providence but a man-made evil which could be lessened if not entirely eliminated in a just and rational society. Rival visions of the origin and function of war, according to Robert Adams, are to be found in two enduring and contradictory myths. The first is of the Golden Age of peace and bliss to which we can never return and which we betrayed with our brutish nature in the Fall; the second is the myth of Prometheus who challenged the gods of Olympus in order to bring fire to humans. The Prometheus myth celebrates our ability to challenge the status quo, to move out of brutishness, to develop art and technology, constantly to improve.

Poets, historians and philosophers in history, captivated by the idea of the Golden Age, saw the history of wars as representing the degeneration of that idea. Adams tells us that Pythagoras, Lucretius, Ovid, Seneca and Plutarch all gave

---

[40] There were three main heretical groups – the Waldenses of France and Italy, the Lollards in England and the Moravian Brethren of what is now the Czech Republic, all of whom were violently oppressed.

[41] Nuttall, *Christian Pacifism*, p. 52.

[42] See Robert P. Adams, *The Better Part of Valor: More, Erasmus, Colet and Vives, on Humanism, War and Peace*, University of Washington Press: Seattle 1962, p. 49; from Erasmus, *The Praise of Folly*, trans. H.H. Hudson, Princeton University Press: Princeton, NJ 1941, p. 101.

[43] Quoted in Adams, *Better Part of Valor.*

vivid descriptions of how this degeneration had taken place. Starting with killing animals, humans progressively became brutalized until they even began to enjoy the manslaughter that went with war and glorify the leaders who led them into it. The Roman Stoics thought 'just' wars virtually impossible and denounced martial 'glory' as false: 'Pliny concluded that man, the only animal addicted to perpetual war upon its own kind, is not only ethically inferior to the most frightful beasts but indeed lives more in disorder and violence than any known animal.'[44] With such a depressing view of human development it would be difficult to plan as Erasmus and the Reformers did for social reform and a new order of peace and justice.

Erasmus' anti-war satire, *The Praise of Folly*, written in 1509, is based on a cheerfully optimistic, Promethean view that tried to clear away the idiocies of war and create more humane structures, 'a flowering of what Erasmus called the peaceful "genius of this island"'. Shakespeare reflected this in Gaunt's speech:

> This other Eden, demi-paradise,
> This fortress built by Nature for herself
> Against infection and the hand of war,
> This happy breed of men.[45]

Living in a society which described war as glorious, glamorous and deeply Christian, Erasmus offered an alternative view. Using the personification of Folly as a mouthpiece, he presented a Christian–Humanist vision of war and war-makers as 'beastly, hellish, corruptive of human society, unjust and unchristian'. He did not see war as inevitable and necessary, but as something created by corrupt men. On the other hand he does not offer the standard view that the bestiality man shows in war is related to the Fall and man's sin. His humanism leads him to examine the human capacity for irrational and anti-human behaviour. In describing it as hellish, Adams claims that Erasmus is drawing our attention to the barbarity of unreason which leads to frenzy. The notion that war is corruptive of human society is implicit in the phrase he uses: it is 'so pestilential that it brings with it a general blight upon morals'.[46] Finally in describing it as unjust and unchristian he is questioning the use and abuse of power, both of the papacy and the monarchy.

Erasmus was writing in the period of the fading medieval dream of a unified ideal society of Christendom, a Pax Ecclesiae within which all humans could be part of a single society ruled by one Natural Law. Corruption and decadence destroyed that dream and the Reformation finally closed the door on it. Hobbes in the seventeenth century was able to say, 'the natural relation of any two states is war'. Since the Renaissance, peace has been a temporary condition but the messages Erasmus has left with us are still relevant.

---

[44] *Erasmus on War*, ed. D. Gibb, p. 15 and quoted in Nuttall, *Christian Pacifism*, p. 58. In practice however Erasmus was prepared to permit a defensive war or any just war. His pacifism was primarily humanitarian and not theological and biblical according to H.A. Bender in his biography of Conrad Grebel, p. 201, as quoted in Nuttall, p. 78.

[45] *Richard II*, II.i.42–45.

[46] Adams, *Better Part of Valor*, p. 53.

By the eighteenth century, Kant, who it seems had a 'peculiar hatred of war', called it 'the scourge of mankind'. In his essay *Concerning Perpetual Peace*, he wrote, 'So act, that you treat humanity, whether in your own person or in the person of everyone else, always as an end, never merely as a means.' In the same century, in England, Blake was writing as radically:

> And all must love the human form
> In heathen, turk or jew.
> Where Mercy, Love & Pity dwell
> There God is dwelling too.[47]

But it was in the late nineteenth and early twentieth centuries that this humanist message was put into the political context of international socialism and an avowedly secular anti-war, but non-pacifist, movement was created. The case made here was that in war workers were fighting fellow workers and that they should join together over national boundaries to create a new and better international society. Conscientious objection, expressed in the refusal to bear arms, was disallowed for both religious and political objectors in the First World War – they were sent to prison – but was reluctantly recognized in the Second World War when objectors were allocated by tribunals to ambulance or agricultural work or the mines.

The horrors of the First (and subsequently, the Second) World War galvanized a wide range of people to reopen the question of the validity of war as a method of solving conflict. Keir Hardie, the first socialist to be elected to Parliament, had opposed Britain's entry into the First World War in Parliament but his was a lone voice. Eight million Europeans were killed and it was felt that those mainly responsible were ignorant generals locked into a past culture where men could be thrown at the enemy without consideration of the cost. The nature of the soldiery had changed, as had the technology of the weapons.[48] This was the first conscript army in Britain, drawn from all strata of society; in some cases all the sons in a family were killed. Children were left fatherless and a generation of young women were faced with spinsterhood because of the shortage of young men. Never before in modern times had there been such social devastation. The Black Death was the most recent equivalent. Gradually news leaked out of the horror of the trenches in which the men had lived and from which the battles had been waged. Drowning in mud, living with the unburied dead and rats, men were sometimes driven out of their minds as well as losing an arm, a leg or their sight, if they survived. Arriving home as heroes they had to face the economic depression of the post-war years.

Poetry and novels had attempted to describe what had happened during the First World War and now a spate of novels reflected the despair of the economic depression that followed. It was the production of armaments for the Second World War that turned the economic tide – the armaments were seen as a solution, not as

---

[47] William Blake, 'The Divine Image' in *Songs of Innocence and Experience*, Orion Books Ltd: London 1994, p. 10.

[48] Eric Hobsbawm, *Age of Extremes: The Short Twentieth Century 1914–1991*, Michael Joseph: London 1994 points out that 1914 opened the age of massacre, p. 24.

the seeds of a new problem. The horrors of the Second World War in which it is thought 54 millions were killed,[49] including many civilians, combined with new fears of the potential use of the atom bombs which had been dropped on Hiroshima and Nagasaki. This led to the establishment of the Campaign for Nuclear Disarmament, initiated by the philosopher Bertrand Russell. While it had some Christian connections (the chair for many years being held by the Methodist, Canon Collins), CND, as it became known, was overtly secular and political. The arguments used were secularly humanist and pragmatic although the practice of public processions and annual Easter pilgrimages to Aldermaston had all the atmosphere of pre-Christian religious ceremonies. This is the point at which the anti-war case began to be presented – except for those theistic members who gave their own personal view – without reference to a Christian position or to the sinful nature of war. The secular case against war began to be formulated.

The Role of Women

A defining moment in the history of the British anti-war movement was the setting up of a women's peace camp in 1982 at Greenham Common, 30 miles west of London, where NATO had decided to base one-quarter of the United States Cruise and Pershing nuclear weapons in Europe. The lack of any national debate about this decision had led to outbreaks of civil disobedience all over the country and a conscious link was now made between feminism, pacifism, gender and war. The iniquities that were part of gender issues for women and the iniquities of war in its brutalities were seen as the consequences of systems rather than as the problems of individuals. These same issues had been earlier addressed by Virginia Woolf in her book *Three Guineas*.[50]

Responding to men who were asking women how to prevent war, 'with the sound of guns in our ears', Woolf replied:

> We can best prevent war not by repeating your words and following your methods but by finding new words and creating new methods. We can best help you to prevent war not by joining your society but by remaining outside your society but in cooperation with its aim. That aim is the same for us both. It is to assert the rights of all – all men and women – to respect in their persons the great principles of Justice and Equality and Liberty.[51]

This is an early assertion of the Kuhnian view that in times of change important questions are not answered but reformulated.

In the same response Woolf writes, 'As a woman I have no country, as a woman I want no country. As a woman my country is the whole world.' This was the view that the Greenham women attempted to live out in their day-to-day lives. Many women, in Britain, northern Europe and North America, began to see themselves as the custodians of the moral argument against the nuclear weapons which had grown out of the first atom bomb. Non-violent direct action groups were set up in various

---

49 Hobsbawm, ibid., estimates that in addition four and a half million Europeans were uprooted, p. 49.

50 Virginia Woolf, *Three Guineas*, Hogarth Press: London 1952, p. 206.

51 Quoted in Michael True, *To Construct a Peace*, Twenty-Third Publications: Mystic, CT 1996, p. 46.

countries where nuclear weapons were based. For the first time in their lives, women had become politicized by the realization that their countries were being transformed into launch pads for weapons of mass destruction. They were willing to suffer imprisonment and ridicule for their beliefs, experiences not new to religious women but, like the suffragettes, these women were seeking the Kingdom on earth, not in an afterlife. One of the more interesting aspects of the women's campaign was their feminist and humanist nature. They hung the wire fences surrounding the nuclear bases with the clothing of small children, they wove webs to represent the web of life and hung them on the gates of defence institutions, and they broke into military bases and planted flower bulbs. One women's group called themselves the Gareloch Horticulturalists. These actions were metaphors to combat what they saw as the destructive, evil behaviour of governments – the iniquity I am trying to describe.

Vietnam as a Turning-point

The war which had most sharply questioned conventional attitudes to war was the United States' campaign in Vietnam, both while it was being waged and after the soldiers were brought home. The word 'Vietnam' has entered the language as a metaphor for a battle that cannot be won. The United States already had a low-key history of conscientious objection on pacifist grounds, but during the Vietnam War this swelled to a deluge – not of pacifism as such but of revulsion against this particular war because of what was seen as the barbarity and injustice of the manner in which the war was being waged. Young men due for conscription voted with their feet, leaving the US for Canada and Europe in spite of the threats made against them that they would lose citizenship and never be able to return.

The US government had made the decision, which they later realized was a mistake, to allow camera and film crews to record the action of the war. While people, both in the US and Europe, were eating their supper they were also watching villages being napalmed and the inhabitants running, screaming and dying in flames on the evening television news. The newspapers reproduced haunting pictures of women and children dead and dying, especially the unforgettable picture of a small Vietnamese girl running along the road naked and on fire, fleeing from the bombs. To an extent never before witnessed, all over the US – particularly in universities – and in Europe, anti-Vietnam War demonstrations took place. People were reacting, not out of an intellectual belief, but from their feelings of revulsion at the real meaning of war, as distinct from the official propaganda and justification. This is the sense of shock which I referred to earlier that helps us to identify iniquity.

The United States, unable to cope with the criticism at home and their failure to defeat the jungle-based Vietcong, retreated from the conflict, badly damaged in its self-esteem. The after-effects of the war were almost as damaging for the country which believed itself not only virtuous but also impregnable. Every small town had lost someone. Evidence showed that American soldiers could behave savagely and brutally and kill indiscriminately.[52] A high proportion of them had taken drugs to

---

[52] Part of the argument against French colonial wars, particularly in Algeria, was that a whole generation of young men was being corrupted there.

dull the awfulness of the tasks they were expected to perform and had become addicted. Treatment centres had to be set up for those returning with post-traumatic stress, which too often led to physical abuse of their families and alcoholism.

In their involvement in the Gulf War, twenty years later, the United States put into practice the lessons learned in Vietnam. Not only was public information strictly controlled but modern technology was used to inflict casualties on the enemy from high-flying planes piloted by young men using computers. Thus distanced, they could not themselves be emotionally involved or attacked. The industrial nations had sanitized modern warfare for their own soldiers in order to enable them to bomb, kill and destroy without any sense of guilt. Also, nations now chose interventions in wars which could be won quickly. General Colin Powell, who led the US forces in the Gulf War, was reported as saying, 'We do deserts, not jungles.'

However, it was not modern war that was waged in the Balkans or in Africa in the last decades of the twentieth century. Here war was fought as it has been for centuries, using whatever weapons came to hand – guns, machetes, or matches which set fire to and destroyed homes, buildings and schools. The rape of women and the killing of children belonging to the enemy have always been part of the warrior's repertoire but this, because of modern communications, became international rather than only local knowledge. In the Balkans, Christian Serbs raped Muslim women, not just to dishonour them in the eyes of their husbands but to implant Serbian seed in their wombs. The older practice of ripping out the foetus of a pregnant woman continued. The agony of these women is impossible to describe. In Africa, soldiers with AIDS raped women with the intention of passing on the virus, but also sought out girl children in the hope that by having sex with a virgin their own condition would be cured. The lower arms of enemy children were cut off, so that in future they would not be able to hold a gun. It also meant, of course, that they were unable to work. Aid agencies tried to cope with impossible situations with limited resources in poverty-stricken countries while millions of pounds were being channelled by western countries into the making, selling and buying of arms so that people can kill each other. Sadly, this situation has not ended with the close of the twentieth century, but continues into the twenty-first in Sierra Leone, Congo, Colombia and many other countries.

Discussion

In any group we will find conflicting interests and divergent ways of finding resolution to conflict, but from the second half of the twentieth century we have seen the most serious attempts to formulate new responses to mediate conflicting interests. These attempts are themselves responses to the need to reformulate ideas of right and wrong, sin, iniquity and transgression in the light of new knowledge and understanding of the human potential for self-destruction. The new approaches are essentially non-violent since those involved in new mediation processes increasingly see violence as more likely to escalate conflict rather than resolve or diminish it. This is not to say that they are pacifists – the view they hold can best be described as pragmatic.

Conclusion

In this chapter I have explored three of those iniquities which I see as being most likely to destroy the essence of being human – poverty, slavery and violence, particularly the violence that explodes into war. Clearly these three are closely linked. I am suggesting that these iniquities are caused not so much by the traditional Christian sins – perhaps with the exception of greed – as by the way the structures within which we live and which we have helped to create destroy the human capacity to respect and empathize with another human being either in their joy or in their pain. Human beings are turned into objects that can be used and abused, bought and sold, hired and fired and manipulated by governments whose agenda is linked to power and commerce.[53] Such practices are of course not new. Such lack of empathy for others, particularly for outsiders, has always been present in the human race. But its effects have become qualitatively more destructive in our time, thanks to advances in modern and military technology, communication techniques and cheaper international travel and trade. We have always to ask the question – who benefits?

The Evangelical Christian argument presented by William Wilberforce and others against the worst excesses of human cruelty was based on the belief that any action that was capable of destroying the essence of the divine in humans, that is to say, the human quality which reflected humans in their aspect of *imitatio Dei*, or their belief in the imitation of Christ as described by Thomas à Kempis,[54] was intolerable. If slavery was to degrade humans to that extent, then, no matter the economic cost, slavery must be abolished. Christianity had not previously appeared to find any contradiction between its teaching and the practice of slavery, and continued that tradition – that some people are less human than others – in South Africa, among devout Christians under the guise of the policy of apartheid, and in the tribalism of Northern Ireland and the former Yugoslavia. It may be that what we were seeing in the campaign against slavery was a reaction that owed more to Enlightenment humanism being grafted on to an Evangelical view than Christianity itself. While the Renaissance had been the breeding-ground of these ideas, by the end of the eighteenth century the writings of Thomas Paine had begun to bring issues of human rights to the forefront of cultural thought.[55] A post-Christian view focused on these issues might substitute the phrase human dignity or human rights for the phrase *imitatio Dei*, but would hold to the principle that degrading that which is the essence of a human being cannot be tolerated.

I have only touched on the fringes of the practice of iniquity. The question I am left with is this: is the notion of forgiveness with its hangover from the Judaeo-Christian tradition in any way relevant to these iniquities or do we have to find some other lens for looking at these issues – perhaps the lens of justice or the lens

---

[53] These issues have been powerfully presented from a deeply Christian perspective by George Newlands in *Generosity and the Christian Future*, SPCK Press: London 1997.

[54] Thomas à Kempis, *The Imitation of Christ*, trans. Leo Sherley-Price, Penguin Books Ltd: London 1959.

[55] Thomas Paine, *The Basic Writings of Thomas Paine: Common Sense, The Rights of Man, The Age of Reason*, Wiley Book Co.: New York 1942.

of human equality? When a child is brutally tortured and killed by her parents or guardians in a modern, wealthy city like London, the immediate response is to find a scapegoat. We imprison the people directly responsible, then seek out the individual social worker or doctor to punish rather than ask the more difficult questions that are to do, not with individual failings, but with underfunded and overworked institutions, with government lack of care for immigrant children, with poor coordination of services. These are the structures of governments which fail in their duty of protecting their citizens, linked to a lack of strong 'community' sense among neighbours. This same failure is to be found in the toleration of poverty in the interests of the wealthy.

Before moving on in this discussion it is important to accept that the issues in this chapter, and others issues we have not discussed here, like patriarchy, racism, or the iniquities practised against the environment we all share, highlight a new awareness of our interdependence and mutual responsibility. A major shift is taking place in the former notion that there is an easy distinction to be made between the sinner and the righteous. This is as relevant for Myra Hindley and the other actors we considered in Chapter 1 as for our shared responsibility for war, slavery and poverty. Recognition of this is part of the new paradigm. From now on our global world will always contain, in every country, different cultures, traditions and interests as a result of the movement of peoples across the planet. Some degree of conflict of values is inevitable and currently it appears to have exploded beyond tolerable limits. Living in a world of immediate, vivid global communication, we can no longer plead ignorance of the iniquities I have described or deny our complicity in them.

The covenantal traditions of Judaism, which maintained balance in the lives and in the wars of the people of Israel, wither in the face of new military technology and the nuclear threat. The powerfully held myth of a pure early Christian vision of forgiveness allied to grace falters as we struggle in our more complex understanding of sin and iniquity. The role of sin appears more complex than we had been led to believe, the role of forgiveness more limited. The failure of the institutions of Christianity to confront these issues, or even to withdraw from collusion with them, has led to a moral vacuum which is being met by secular attempts both within the legislative process and through community action to find ways of managing our affairs more effectively, humanely and peacefully: wealth without poverty, cheap goods without slavery, sexuality without exploitation, conflict without war.[56] In attempting this we may be forced to remember Emily Dickinson's warning:

> Much Madness is divinest Sense –
> To a discerning Eye –
> Much Sense – the starkest Madness –
> … 'Tis the Majority

---

[56] One example of this is the growing movement called Global Resistance. The books which have most strongly influenced its actions are: Naomi Klein, *No Logo: no space, no choice, no jobs*, Flamingo: London 2001 and George Monbiot, *Captive State: the corporate takeover of Britain*, Macmillan: London 2000.

In this, as All, prevail –
Assent – and you are sane –
Demur – you're straightway dangerous –
And handled with a chain –[57]

---

[57] *The Complete Poems of Emily Dickinson*, ed. Thomas H. Johnson, Faber & Faber Ltd: London 1977, No. 435, p. 208.

6

How Do We Live Together?: Final Conclusions

Introduction

In previous chapters I have attempted to show the ways in which moral principles are created, not discovered, by people working collectively. They evolve through the work of human institutions, their practices and traditions, as people try creatively to resolve the conflicts which arise within a living tradition as it adapts to a changing environment. I see an understanding and acceptance of this thought as central to everything else I have discussed.[1] It is also an attempt to understand the ways in which definitions of sin and forgiveness, once anchored securely within a Judaeo-Christian tradition of human relationships with God, are moving out into uncharted waters, and leads on to a discussion of the courses we may follow in future. How should sin and forgiveness be understood in a post-Christian society? This is the question I am exploring.

In this concluding chapter I outline the main themes I have dealt with. Chapter 1, consisting of four case studies, described specific moral dilemmas concerning the nature of sin, forgiveness and punishment which erupt in a society in a process of transition. Chapter 2 recorded a range of possibilities drawn from literature and art which may help us to understand how our responses to such dilemmas have evolved over time. The following two chapters charted recent changes in our attitudes to sin and forgiveness. In Chapter 5, I examined the idea of structural sin as a facet of our continuing journey as members of the human race from a local to a global economy.

In this concluding chapter, I draw together the threads that run through the whole book and try to formulate some ideas that may help us – intellectually, spiritually and in our daily lives.

The Transition to New Paradigms

Since this is a work concerned with changing attitudes to sin and forgiveness it may be helpful to outline the way in which I see these changes developing within social structures – particularly the structures underpinning Christian thought. It has been argued that 'changing ... systems is a process, not an event: a kind of drama that passes through successive acts which often take a long time to unfold'.[2] An existing ideology is normally based in a well-established regime, defended by those who

---

[1] For detailed discussion of this view see Alasdair MacIntyre, *After Virtue: a study in moral theory*, Duckworth: London 1981.

[2] David Donnison, 'The Academic Contribution to Social Reform', *Social Policy & Administration*, Vol. 34, March 2000, No. 1. This article also outlines the general theory behind my argument.

have a vested interest in it. Isaiah Berlin took the view that any organization which lasted for more than 25 years had already established such roots.[3] New ideas rarely begin in the large, well-established groupings of a structure. It is not normally from the pulpits that one first hears demands for change. Deviations within traditional Christianity began either with individual radical thinkers or in small groups, sometimes setting up as new sects. More recently, as with the liberation theologians and with women's groups, some reformers are trying to work within, and thereby influence, the wider structure. Others, picking up on the new thinking, simply abandon the structure and seek individual personal or secular developments of the new ideas being offered. The structure has lost meaning for them.

The ideas of the 'reformers' may begin to penetrate the power structure. This is a crucial point in the process since there may be too strong a conflict, between the interests of the establishment and the new ideas, to make it possible for the establishment to absorb them. If this is the case either new ideas or the structure will collapse, one or the other will wither away, or, as happened in the Reformation, new, strong opposing structures will emerge from the struggle. But often a slow accommodation is possible. This appears to be happening currently with new perceptions of the nature of God. The radio programme, *Thought for the Day*, presents a range of views on this subject, although the central issue is never directly addressed. The shock and horror which greeted Bishop David Jenkins'[4] public rejection of a range of earlier beliefs in hell, miracles and the Virgin Birth has subsided into a wry acceptance that attitudes on these matters have shifted.

By outlining the acts of this drama we can begin to understand the processes which have led to the current view that we are living in a post-Christian society. This description has been popularly interpreted as meaning a fully secular or non-religious society. I do not accept this thought. Christians appear, in a variety of ways, to have questioned only some basic tenets of the Christian belief system and some of these they have rejected. In doing this they have been influenced by new scientific knowledge, changing social values and a new democratic reluctance to accept authority without question. They have shown this by their rejection of church attendance while maintaining some regard for the value of rituals and what I have described earlier as the religious impulse, although this is not always expressed in conventional ways.[5] In a general rather than a specific sense they accept the Christian tradition, letting go what they see as implausible and adhering to what they see as reasonable or useful. Some see themselves as redefining Christianity. There are others who, over the 150 years in which this process has most dramatically been seen, have moved to a fully secular view.

According to Blumenberg,[6] everyone is familiar with the description of secularization as a long-term process 'by which a disappearance of religious ties, attitudes to transcendence, expectations of an afterlife, ritual performances and

---

[3] I heard Berlin discuss this in a radio programme in the 1950s. It made a very powerful impression on me.

[4] See David Jenkins, *God, Miracle and the Church of England*, SCM: London 1987.

[5] Examples of this are concerns for animal welfare and environmental campaigns.

[6] Hans Blumenberg, *The Legitimacy of the Modern Age*, trans. Robert M. Wallace, Massachusetts Institute of Technology: Boston, MA 1983.

firmly established terms of speech is driven onward in both private and daily public life'. But, he adds, we are still 'within the horizon' of the operation of this process:

> ... we are describing something that would not even exist for us if we were not still in a position to understand what had to precede it, what hope of salvation, what the next world, transcendence, divine judgement, refraining from involvement in the world and falling under the influence of the world once meant – that is, to understand the elements of that 'unworldliness' that must after all be implied as a point of departure if we are to be able to speak of secularization.[7]

Sometimes the questions which threaten the established values of the wider structure can be reformulated in ways that make it possible for them to be discussed and for the structures to change in order to accommodate them. This can be a slow process and again some members, impatient at the delay, will leave. If change is too slow, only a rump will be left holding on to the earlier beliefs. But even if the wider structure does change there will be people left within who disagree with that change and try to hold on to the old values. This was very clearly seen in the reformation of the service of the Mass in the Catholic Church where a group still claiming to be members of the Church – in fact claiming to be the true members of the Church – continued to celebrate the earlier form.

Conflict of some kind is a normal part of these changes. In the West now, religious reformulations are not likely to be associated with violence but will be expressed in more muted forms. Apathy is more likely to be the response to religious disagreement, even within families where it was once an overwhelming issue.[8] Serious conflict is more likely to arise in situations where the earlier formulation is linked with fundamental attitudes which serve other community needs. Forgiveness is an interesting example of this since in spite of being in theory a fundamental tenet of Christianity, in practice it has only operated in restricted areas of life. Few priests or ministers, with the exception of those courageous people like the one I mentioned in the first chapter, have felt it possible to preach forgiveness from the pulpit in the cases of Myra Hindley, the boys who killed James Bulger or the paedophile who killed Sarah Payne. Such clerics can themselves be seen as dangerous and not 'a safe pair of hands' for future promotion. The appointment of the radical Anglican priest, Rowan Williams, as Archbishop of Canterbury, in itself a statement of a changing paradigm, was greeted with a mixture of delight and anxiety.

There has been less hesitation to preach against sin, but here the changing nature of the public perception of sin has led to modification of the discourse, particularly in the area of sexual behaviour.[9] Forgiveness has been seen as a mechanism for an

---

[7] Ibid., pp. 3–4.

[8] Benito Perez Galdos, arguably the greatest Spanish writer since Cervantes, describes this vividly in his novel *Dona Perfecta*, trans. A.R. Tulloch, Phoenix House: London 1999, an exploration of 'the religious question' during a period of social change in nineteenth-century Spain.

[9] Some of the smaller sects are less inhibited and of course the Roman Catholic Church preaches powerfully on what it sees as the sin of abortion.

individual to gain forgiveness from God, either directly in Protestantism or through an intermediary in Catholicism. Although, again in theory, forgiveness of the self is linked with the requirement to forgive others, this requirement does not appear to be recognized by many people who would describe themselves as Christians. They would defend their right not to forgive others. Perhaps we need to recognize that the human tendency not to forgive, indeed to get an emotional charge from blaming and scapegoating, has been so strong that the Christian message has not been able to affect it and in some cases has reinforced it.[10]

Yet there has been in recent years an outbreak of acceptance of the importance of forgiveness among heads of State. The Pope asked forgiveness for the Church's treatment of the Jews, Prime Minister Blair asked forgiveness of the Irish for British oppression, New Zealand and Australia are expressing guilt about their treatment of indigenous peoples. We saw in Chapter 2 how forgiveness became a central issue of debate for survivors of the Holocaust. Chapter 4 discussed the new emphasis on forgiveness in the discipline of psychology and in widely read books where the emphasis is on the physical and emotional benefits of forgiveness to the victim. There are also constant demonstrations in television 'soaps' of quarrels followed by forgiveness and reconciliation and American television presents shows whose aim is to reconcile feuding families and friends.

This confusion, this variety of ways of addressing the question, appears always to take place when there is a paradigm shift of the kind described by Kuhn – when an old order is giving way to a new. The next stage of the process appears to be a reformulation of the original question raised by the reformers and then a narrowing of the possible responses. The pure Christian position on forgiveness, so movingly expressed in the biblical parable of the prodigal son and in the Rembrandt painting of the same title, appears to have degenerated into a confused muddle which satisfies no one. Throughout Christianity it has only been truly effective in the dyad of the one-to-one relationship with God under strict conditions which involve repentance and atonement linked to the mysterious and wondrous quality of grace. In our much more complex society, where for many God has been relegated to an abstraction, the question we need to ask is not why you should not forgive but what are the conditions in which forgiveness is appropriate to the wider requirements of a moral society?

This stage has been reached only as a result of a re-examination and reformulation of an understanding of what constitutes sinful behaviour which in the past might have required forgiveness. The Christian Church took ownership of the Ten Commandments with which Moses had stated the religious and ethical demands laid by God on the people of ancient Israel.[11] They later added the Seven Deadly Sins,[12] which reflected the needs of a more complex society. The Ten Commandments have diminished in the hold they once had on the lives and imagination of Europeans; the Seven Deadly Sins of pride, envy, anger, lust, gluttony, greed and sloth, while still highly relevant, are in some cases, as with lust

---

[10] See Dan Cohn-Sherbok, *The Crucified Jew: Twenty Centuries of Christian Anti-Semitism*, Erdmans: Grand Rapids 1997, p. 73.

[11] Exod. 20.1–17 and Deut. 5:6–21.

[12] Solomon Schimmel, *The Seven Deadly Sins*, Oxford University Press: Oxford 1997.

and greed, glorified. On the other hand new sins have been created as a result of the changed moral sensitivity we have developed since the Victorian era. In this country abuse of children in the workplace is no longer tolerated,[13] it is illegal to abuse one's marriage partner; nor, at a different level, is drunk driving tolerated. Sin has been largely secularized. Fenn argues that, at least in American society, 'The Church has clearly lost its monopoly on the production of sin and has been relegated to a relatively minor role ....' He relates this to the increasing identification of corporate sin – what I have described as iniquities. The sins he identifies are 'to poison the water supply, falsify information on the dangerous consequences of drugs and chemicals ... buy politicians, finance death squads, refuse sanctuary to refugees, or drive whole groups of people to despair'.[14]

Earlier definitions of sin were dependent on the accompanying concepts of repentance, atonement and redemption. These are also being reinterpreted and all are being seen as operating within a constantly changing relationship with one's fellow humans. One aspect of this is the new concept of secular mediation[15] and what could be described as a rediscovery of restorative justice.[16] These changes are taking place within a wider shift of changes in our perception of the relevance of the Judaeo-Christian tradition to life in the twenty-first century. The formal institutions of the Christian Church are no longer the only source of our society's view of moral behaviour. Meanwhile thoughtful people have pointed out that what some describe as the process of secularization can also be described as a redefinition of religion.[17]

Rather than accepting an authoritarian view of right and wrong behaviour, individuals appear to be choosing to create a personal morality, or in some cases a collective secular morality. What we have seen in the previous chapters is a steady drift in personal attitudes to sin and forgiveness towards this post-Christian stance. Underlying this has been a movement of secularization in public affairs, combined with a consistent and possibly growing interest in what are loosely described as 'spiritual' matters. This apparent contradiction is part of the Kuhn thesis which describes the nature of paradigm shift. Issues of sin and forgiveness can be seen as central in this process.

What Secularization Has Offered

In its initial sense, 'secular' had a singular meaning. It meant 'non-religious', that which opposed the sacred.[18] Toynbee offered his interpretation of the process:

---

[13] We continue to tolerate it in the countries which supply us with cheap goods made by children.

[14] Richard K. Fenn, *The Secularization of Sin: an Investigation of the Daedalus Complex*, Westminster/John Knox Press: Louisville, KY 1991, p. 62.

[15] Marian Liebmann, ed., *Mediation in Context*, Jessica Kingsley Publishers: London 2000.

[16] Howard Zehr, *Changing Lenses*, Herald Press: Scottdale, PA 1995.

[17] See Blumenberg, *Legitimacy of the Modern Age*.

[18] Bernard Eugene Meland, *The Secularization of Modern Cultures*, Oxford University Press: New York 1966, p. 9.

From the beginning of the eighteenth century ... the leaven of secularization and the zest
for technology spread progressively from one stratum of Western society to another till it
had permeated the whole mass, culminated in the discrediting of the West's Christian
heritage and the elevation of a technical civilization that has only tenuous connections at
best with the Christian heritage and ethos.[19]

We can read this quotation now as an oversimplification; secularism has emerged as
a much more complex set of issues. But it is important to understand why Toynbee
used the word 'leaven', which means a pervasive and transforming influence.[20] The
leaven he describes was in part the attempt to resist the uncontrolled passions of
religious cults and individuals. 'The prime motive', he says, 'was a horror at the
wickedness and destructiveness of religious fanaticism.'[21] Meland describes this
kind of secularist as being 'in the spirit of the Renaissance man or of the eighteenth-
century liberal ... dedicated to the freedom and refinement of the human spirit'.[22]
This suspicion of religious enthusiasm and the attempt to replace it with reason is
still understandable when we look at the continuous use of religion as a battle cry in
Northern Ireland and the Middle East, even though it is increasingly being
recognized that religious hysteria is often a way of expressing deeper economic and
social problems.[23]

One aspect of those uncontrolled passions has been the fierce adoption of the
concept of the scapegoat. The essence of scapegoating is the rejection of personal
responsibility for sin or a range of other problems which might lead to blaming of
the self. The 'other' becomes the whipping boy, the rejected, the excluded, the one
for whom we have no responsibility and whom we can attack with impunity.[24]
Central to this is the belief that the scapegoat, being driven out of the community,
carries away with it all the evils placed upon it. Stern describes this as 'the riddance
of something profoundly unwanted'.[25] Following Leviticus, Andrea Dworkin sees
murder and exile as the two paradigmatic fates of the scapegoat. She suggests
however that 'Murder can be intimate, exile can be internal, being separated from
the common life, one's human dignity and social legitimacy denied.'[26] It is in other
words a more subtle process than is commonly assumed.

It is also assumed by most who refer to the concept of the scapegoat that this is
somehow built into the human genetic makeup, rather than being a response to a
certain set of social circumstances. In the setting described in Leviticus in early

---

[19] Arnold Toynbee, *An Historian's Approach to Religion*, Oxford University Press: Oxford 1978,
p. 180.

[20] cf. Matt. 13:33.

[21] Arnold Toynbee, *Historian's Approach*, p. 182.

[22] Meland, *Secularization of Modern Cultures*, p. 17. Folk memory recalls a popular toast of the time
which expresses this idea: 'Prosperity to the Established Church and death to all enthusiasm'.

[23] A major change in secularism is a new recognition of the importance of religious sensibility and
the human sense of wonder.

[24] This is a very crude interpretation. For more detailed discussion see Rene Girard, *The Scapegoat*,
Johns Hopkins University Press: Baltimore, MD 1986.

[25] Philip Stern, *The Oxford Companion to the Bible*, eds Metzger and Coogan, Oxford University
Press: Oxford 1993, p. 69.

[26] Andrea Dworkin, *Scapegoat: The Jews, Israel and Women's Liberation*, Virago: London 2000, p. 16.

Israel, the use of the scapegoat was a very sophisticated device, making possible the restoration of order and balance in the community. Its translation by Girard into an understanding of stereotypes of persecution was a very important intellectual step. Later work, particularly the work of historians, has helped us to see the social and economic, rather than only the innate, wellsprings of persecutory massacres.[27] That may open up possibilities of preventing their occurrence rather than accepting their inevitability. This view seems not yet to have entered a wider consciousness, but what has been clearly accepted since the Second World War is the deadly quality of scapegoating in our unsettled times. The genocides in Armenia, Germany and Rwanda are classic examples.

The concept of scapegoating is closely tied in with the notion of purity which is in turn linked to notions of perfection. Mary Douglas concludes from her study of Leviticus that 'holiness is exemplified by completeness. Holiness requires that individuals shall conform to the class to which they belong. And holiness requires that different classes of things shall not be confused.'[28] This may have been a valid position for a community in early Israel but is untenable in the ethnically and culturally mixed society of the planet we see as home and the community of nations we are in the process of creating. In this task occasional failures are to be expected. Far from holding to the goal of perfection we are going to have to be content with 'good enough-ness', a concept borrowed from psychotherapy. In essence this means 'doing the best one can with what one has'. What becomes important is that one does the best one can while recognizing the limitations inherent in the situation one is dealing with.

For many citizens it was questions of personal human dignity and entitlement to social legitimacy within a democratic structure, and therefore the rejection of scapegoating, that led to the development of the modern secular State. The 1948 Universal Declaration of Human Rights by the United Nations can be seen as a response to the horrors of the Second World War, where scapegoating took on a new dimension.[29] A major role of this multicultural, secular organization has been to regulate and mediate between the institutions of a civil society and also between contending interest groups within communities. In order to do this it is necessary to put aside the concept of the scapegoat. Under the regulations each member state is required to combine its regulatory and mediating role with allowing a degree of freedom for the expression of what may be critical differences in attitudes within and between these groups.

These ideals have not always been reflected in practice, but the statement of intentions has been an important step forward in human history. It is dependent on a

---

[27] Ian Kershaw, *Genocide, Religion and Modernity*, Holocaust Memorial Lecture, University of Glasgow, 23 January 2001.

[28] Mary Douglas, *Purity and Danger*, Ark Paperbacks: London 1966, p. 53.

[29] The European Convention on Human Rights (ECHR 1950) followed. This is now enforceable in British Courts. It includes the right to life, the prohibition of torture and treatment or punishment which is inhuman or degrading, the prohibition of slavery and forced labour, the right to liberty and security, the right to a fair trial, no punishment without law, the right to respect for private and family life, the right to freedom of thought, conscience and religion, the freedom of expression, the freedom of assembly and association, the right to marry and start a family, the prohibition of discrimination.

tolerant democracy which is not always available in member states: democracy can be highly intolerant. Even in Britain this entire agenda is complicated by racial, gender, class and educational differences which in turn affect attitudes to issues like sin, forgiveness and the understanding of justice. This has led us to question many features of our conventional justice system. As a result we see the setting up of more informal mediation processes, some highly creative,[30] to help in situations of conflict which seem inappropriate to be dealt with by courts. The steady secularization of structures of the State has made it possible for us to stand back and examine traditions like scapegoating which conflict with modern concepts of human rights and human dignity in democratic societies.

Retributive or Restorative Justice?

In this process the concepts of repentance and redemption have had to be revisited. One view is that where mediation is used in the criminal justice system we would do better to leave aside the concept of redemption in either its theological or secular sense and focus on restorative justice. The focus here is on future behaviour, not past misdeeds, on reconciliation – or at least mutual tolerance – not punishment; on the needs of the victims and the community, not the offender's guilt; on mutual agreement rather than imposed authority, and on the people directly involved, not the lawyers and other professionals. These are secular attempts to find ways of reconciliation between individuals and groups for whom religious concepts of forgiveness and redemption appear to have little or no meaning. It involves an acceptance that no one is or can become totally pure.

Howard Zehr, a practising Mennonite, is a writer and consultant on criminal justice issues. He is best known for examining assumptions about 'retributive' justice and finding alternatives in history, biblical tradition and common practice. When crime is responded to with retributive justice it is seen as 'a violation of the state, defined by lawbreaking and guilt. Justice determines blame and administers pain in a contest between the offender and the state directed by systematic rules.' In restorative justice, on the other hand, crime is seen as 'a violation of people and relationships. Justice involves the victim, the offender and the community in a search for solutions which promote repair, reconciliation, and reassurance.'[31]

Zehr rejects a narrow vision of what we label as crimes, considering it not biblical. He sees the Bible as holding out for us a vision 'of how people ought to live together, in a state of shalom, of right relationship'. Behaviours we call crime violate such relationships, but so do a variety of other harms, including acts of oppression by the powerful against the powerless. He goes on to argue that to see injustice holistically, without artificial lines between crimes and other injustices, we have to see the whole continuum of harms: 'The Old Testament prophets remind us that structural injustice is sin, and that such injustice in turn breeds more injustice.'[32]

---

[30] Marian Liebmann, ed., *Arts Approaches to Conflict*, Jessica Kingsley Publishers: London 1996.

[31] Howard Zehr, *Changing Lenses, A New Focus for Crime and Justice*, Herald Press: Scottdale, PA 1995, p. 181.

[32] Ibid., p. 186.

We saw in Chapter 4 how Lapsley asked that restitution be made. John Lampen of Northern Ireland believes that restitution is at least as basic a human response as retribution.[33] While it represents recovery of losses its real importance is symbolic since it implies an acknowledgement of the wrong and a recognition of responsibility. Zehr says that for many an experience of justice is a necessary precondition for forgiveness to occur but for some forgiveness will not seem possible. He also makes the point that we ignore the important need for rituals. We can see the ritual of the trial with its drama and theatrical setting, but we also need rituals of closure, what has been described as 'rituals of reordering'.[34] These ideas hark back to notions of justice in communities before the concept of the state developed.[35]

Clearly, for those 'sinners' described in Chapter 1, retributive justice seems to have been the only option considered. In none of the cases have we seen any restoration of balance. There is a sense from press reports of public reaction to the offenders that a belief in demonic powers is stronger than what might have once been seen as the power of grace. We appear to have a strong concept of evil but no concept of redemption. Myra Hindley and the other offenders discussed have been dealt with in what can be seen as either a religionless world devoid of hope or else a Manichaean world where good and evil are in equal combat.

An Alternative to Retributive Justice

The capacity to choose whether or not to sin and the capacity to choose whether or not to forgive are essential components of our human characteristics. But what do we mean by being human? We should not glamorize it or sentimentalize it. Our strength as a species, our ability to spread and survive over the face of the planet, appear to lie precisely in a combination of fragility and flexibility. We can adapt and adjust to any situation, have an astonishing range of behaviour from barbaric cruelty to exquisite tenderness, and will develop whatever attitudes and beliefs appear helpful to ourselves and our species. Today, in the global village the planet has become, we are seeing some of the effects of the divergent and sometimes contradictory sets of attitudes and values we share as different groups of humans encounter each other. The most fragile of our capacities seem to be love, compassion and empathy for anyone other than those close to us. But both to achieve them and, as important, to maintain them, depend, like a plant, on them having the appropriate soil in which to grow and flourish. It is when empathy in particular fails that we are driven into the world of demonic powers.

The last verse of 'Dover Beach' seems an appropriate comment:

> Ah, love, let us be true
> To one another! For the world, which seems
> To lie before us like a land of dreams,
> So various, so beautiful, so new,

---

[33] John Lampen, *Mending Hurts*, Quaker Home Service: London 1987, p. 57.

[34] Zehr, *Changing Lenses*, p. 209.

[35] See Simon Roberts, *Order and Dispute: An Introduction to Legal Anthropology*, Martin Robertson: London 1979, Chapter 3.

> Hath really neither joy, nor love, nor light,
> Nor certitude, nor peace, nor help for pain;
> And we are here as on a darkling plain
> Swept with confused alarms of struggle and flight,
> Where ignorant armies clash by night.[36]

Empathy does not always fail. During the controversy over the release date for the boys who killed Jamie Bulger, one broadsheet newspaper published the story of a similar incident which had taken place in Norway.[37] In the small town of Trondheim, two 6-year-old boys had kicked, stripped, beaten and stoned a 5-year-old girl and left her in the snow to die. The two boys were regarded as victims rather than criminals and treated accordingly – they were back at school in a few weeks accompanied by a psychologist at all times and were supported by the Child Support Agency for the next four years. The girl's mother, asked by the British journalist if she hated the boys, seemed astonished by the question. 'No', she says, 'of course not.' The questions were pursued: '... should they have been punished, locked up?'

The quiet, humane response shocks the journalist: 'No, they were punished enough by what they did. They have to live with that. I think everybody has got to be treated like a human being. The children had to be educated, had to learn how to treat other people so they could get back into society ... I have forgiven the boys for a long time.'

The local community was involved from the beginning. The day of the murder was a Saturday so the police and the local child administrator decided to open the school to give information to the public and reassure them. They wanted to meet them before the media had the news. The result of this involvement meant that local people felt collective shame, grief and responsibility. There was no question of a public trial for these children. The age of criminal responsibility in Norway is fifteen, unlike Britain where it is ten.

Why the Norwegian response was so different in its humanity from the British is not something easily explained, but the fact that it is possible for it to be different in this way offers hope. The two most important factors appear to be an acceptance that children are entitled to understanding and respect *as children* rather than as either innocent angels or potentially evil beings, and the recognition of collective responsibility for the children along with a sense of community. What in the British cases were the factors that deterred the neighbours of Mary Bell and the boys Thompson and Venables from paying attention to the abuses these children were enduring and reacting to them? The Norwegian response shows that it is possible for there to be an alternative within neighbouring groups of Europeans to the punitive, retributive approach we appear to have developed in Britain.

Calling in the Scapegoat

Allowing for the fact that between individuals, one of whom has harmed the other, there are important issues which have to be settled, we have to consider on each

---

[36] Arnold, 'Dover Beach'.
[37] *The Guardian*, G2, 30 October 2000.

occasion what the relevant response could be. There are no simple rules that define what must be done. Murder, particularly of a child, is an attack, not only on the person who was killed, but also on the whole community. The community is forced back into an understanding that children are the inheritors of the future, a sacred role. In Britain this unfortunately seems only to come into consciousness when the child is killed. The victim becomes sanctified. In a society which has only a fractured understanding of ritual, where people conjure up a crude mixture of superstition, within a Judaeo-Christian vocabulary of revenge and post-Christian cynicism, the killers are natural scapegoats. Scapegoats, we must remember, cannot be redeemed.

The main difference between today's practices and the Hebrew Bible's description of the scapegoat who carried away the sins of the children of Israel[38] and then disappeared into the desert is that we are baffled about what to do with our scapegoats. No longer able to exile them to distant colonies or to kill them as a sacrifice, our only solution is to lock them up and try not to let them out. That was the fate of Myra Hindley. But we have a number of groups who fit the concept of 'syphilitics of the soul', described by Margaret Atwood.[39] They include prostitutes, paedophiles, drug addicts and, in the eyes of Christian fundamentalists, homosexuals. Each group represents the way in which human urges, once called sins and still sometimes defined as 'unnatural', find a place in our world. If we are to talk about community we have to recognize that this has to be totally inclusive, not the anaemic form of inclusion where the good allow a few reformed characters to join them. We are in fact all in this together, the good, the bad and the ugly. The drug dealers, the money launderers, the paedophiles, the murderers, the prostitutes, they are in us and we are in them in the sense that they act out the potential found in many people.

We have said that the world in which Myra Hindley found herself is a religionless world which rejects this inclusive view. It offers neither release through forgiveness nor a future through salvation or redemption. Even her death was not a release for the families of the children who were killed. They wound their lives round their hatred of her and without her the meaning she gave their lives was gone. They live in a cold despairing world from which there is no exit. The various Secretaries of State who rejected the possibility of her release fed into this unhappy near-Jacobean drama, taking on the role of avenger. What happens to us in a world which has no rituals for recognizing repentance, atonement and forgiveness? Even if we accept that pure forgiveness cannot be offered we need to have some system of closure, of completion and restoring balance. We have not yet addressed the lacunae left by the abolition of the death sentence. We are left only with a confused mixture of guilt, hatred and a degraded demand for perfection. We have reached a point in our history where we may no longer have the choice of projecting the faults in ourselves on to individuals or groups and expect them to be carried away. We know too much and we have to learn to live with who and what we are – no matter how uncomfortable that may be.

---

[38] Lev. 16:21–22.
[39] Margaret Atwood, 'The Sin Eater' in *Dancing Girls*, Vintage: London 1996, p. 213.

The Struggle to Know Ourselves: Truth and Reconciliation

In all of this work I have been referring to the quality of being human. The view of Antonio Damasio,[40] one of the group of neuro-biologists now exploring the so far inexplicable mystery of how human beings know who they are (in other words, consciousness), is that it is our capacity to know we have feelings that confirms our humanity. He believes that we are all engaged in a process of self-creation and that human identity is a sensational response – a way of coping not just with feelings but with our awareness of those feelings. This new acceptance that human consciousness is directly related to feeling can expand our understanding of our responses to disgust, guilt and anger, feelings of joy and of the sacred, but also of guilt and shame. Damasio believes this is what has created, among other abilities, conscience. Conscience is of course central to the whole process of having an awareness of sin and its link to forgiveness. What is clear is that we are only on the threshold of these mysteries. Another neuroscientist, Gerald Edelman, talks without anxiety about a process of discovery of the nature of being human that might take another five hundred years, such is its complexity.[41] He is offering us a lesson in humility. What we have to do in the meantime is to work out what being human means for us in practice, both as individuals and as members of a community.

The Truth and Reconciliation Commission

The Truth and Reconciliation Commission was a brave attempt to heal the wounds of apartheid in South Africa. The suffering of the South African people had been the result of both individual sin and structural sin. In the sacrament of penance, some aspects of which Protestantism had rejected during the Reformation, a penitent was required to reconcile the self with God and the Church in three ways. The first was to confess error, then express contrition and finally make atonement in some way. The pattern this sacrament offered seemed to many Christians a necessity if the victims of apartheid were to forgive their oppressors. It was this view that led to the decision of the South African government, instigated by the Anglican Archbishop, Desmond Tutu, to set up the Truth and Reconciliation Commission in 1966. Tutu assumed that those brought before the Commission would accept their guilt, confess their sins and express contrition. This in turn would bring relief, particularly to those families whose loved ones had been tortured and murdered during the years of the apartheid regime.

The poet Antjie Krog, who followed the work of the Commission for the two-and-a-half years of their hearings, writes that reconciliation has formed an integral part of Tutu's theology since 1979. But, she goes on to say, Tutu has 'Africanized' the concept by basing it in the community in which he lives: 'The Church says: you must forgive, because God has forgiven you for killing His Son. You can only

---

[40] Antonio Damasio, *The Feeling of What Happens: Body and Emotion in the Making of Consciousness*, Heinemann: London 1999.

[41] Gerald Edelman speaking on Radio 4, 29 June 2000.

become human in a humane society. If you live with hatred and revenge in your heart, you dehumanize not only yourself, but your community.'[42] President Thabo Mbeki takes a different view, believing that true reconciliation can only take place when the continent and South Africa itself are transformed. He talks about an African renaissance. These two positions reflect a fundamental difference in views of reconciliation, but both are rooted in an understanding of the part played by the social context in which conflict and reconciliation take place.

Krog quotes a statement given to the Commission by Cynthia Ngewu, the mother of one of the victims, Christopher Piet: 'This thing called reconciliation ... if I am understanding it correctly ... if it means this perpetrator, this man who has killed Christopher Piet, if it means he becomes human again, this man, so that I, so that all of us, get our humanity back ... then I agree, then I support it all.'

On the other hand, in an interview after refusing to forgive her son's murderer for killing and 'braaing' (barbecuing) her son, one woman said, 'It is easy for Mandela and Tutu to forgive ... they lead vindicated lives. In my life nothing, not a single thing, has changed since my son was burnt by barbarians ... Therefore I cannot forgive.'

The word reconciliation is sometimes taken to mean the restoring of harmony, but one has to ask what kind of harmony could have coexisted with the ugly facts of murder and torture that underlay the apartheid system. Here harmony would have to be seen as a future possibility, not a return to the past. The problems of the Commission were compounded by the denial of so many whites, including Botha and de Klerk, former leaders of the ruling party, about the part they played in upholding the system and their refusal to appear before the Commission. They claimed they did not know of the horrors and therefore made it easier for others to say the same. Tutu's reliance on truth as a way to reconciliation was not shared by the guilty men.

The main attack on the Truth Commission was that it asked for forgiveness from the victims of apartheid without securing justice or any form of redress. This attack came from those operating within the paradigm of retributive justice, whereas Tutu had shifted to a paradigm of restorative justice. His problem was that restorative justice that leads to reconciliation demands two factors missing in the structure of the hearings. The first is that the victims, the offenders and the community have all to be involved in the search for solutions which promote repair, reconciliation and reassurance. The second is that the offence has to be understood in its full context, that is to say, moral, social, economic and political.[43] This obviously was not likely to be the case in the South African context but Tutu should nevertheless be acknowledged as a brave and imaginative man to have made the attempt.

Krog believes that the Commission did help most victims and those of their families who participated to find an emotional closure to their distress. We know that speaking our pain and knowing that it has been heard can be cathartic. Other oppressed peoples in Rwanda, Nicaragua and Australia have set up their own Truth

---

[42] Antjie Krog, *Country of My Skull*, Jonathan Cape: London 1999, p. 110.

[43] These ideas are expressed in the work, already mentioned, of the Mennonite consultant on criminal justice issues, Howard Zehr. He also discusses community justice and covenant justice. See *Changing Lenses: a new focus for crime and justice*, Chaps 7–10.

and Reconciliation Commissions, seeking to find their own form of closure in the expression of their truth. In initiating these processes Tutu was moving in advance of many of his compatriots into a new paradigm and possibly a new understanding of how one can make a more human and humane response to evil behaviour. I am left with the thought that these 'new' possibilities may be more likely to express themselves in societies which have not yet been exposed to the worst aspects of industrialization, in other words societies where the notion of community and its healing possibilities, not only vengeance, retain meaning.

The Power of Memory: Do We Forgive and Forget?

Lapsley, whose views on forgiveness we have already heard and who was a witness to the Commission, has also addressed the question of memory, a human capacity which has played a key part in faith traditions. It is important in this discussion to be aware that what was largely seen to be a comparatively uncomplicated but interesting function of the human brain has in recent years become a source of intense scientific interest and for some people of agonizing conflict. Primo Levi, for whom the task of remembering his own and others' experience was a central life task, described human memory as a 'marvellous but fallacious instrument'.[44] This thought has been particularly highlighted over the issue of sexual abuse of children where a small but significant number of adults, mainly women in therapy, believe they have recovered memories of being sexually abused by their fathers and occasionally by their mothers – abuse denied by their parents.[45] The difficulty here is that both parties, parents and children, are equally convinced of the correctness of their memories. They cannot both be correct.

Another example is the story of Binjamin Wilkomirski, who wrote a book describing his recovered memories of being a child in the Holocaust camps. Although the book was hailed as a classic, a journalist later uncovered the fact that there was no truth in the story. Yet Wilkomirski continues to believe in the truth of what he has written.[46] Levi takes the view that the initial substitution of fantasy for reality may be a conscious attempt to ease emotional pain and constant repetition of the story blurs the difference between the false and the true. By constant retelling, 'polishing and retouching here and there', there is a transition to total belief.[47]

It was Freud who first taught us about the power of the unconscious to protect us from unacceptable knowledge through the mechanism of denial. What scientists are now studying is our capacity for selective remembering and even of falsely

---

[44] Levi, *The Drowned and the Saved*, p. 11.

[45] See Mark Pendergrast, *Victims of Memory*, HarperCollins: London 1996. An opposing view that incest is a socially tolerated act of child rape by fathers is offered by Louise Armstrong, *Rocking the Cradle of Sexual Politics*, Women's Press: London 1995. This debate has led to some painful family confrontations in which the parents involved have absolutely denied the abuse and have accused the therapists involved of 'planting' these memories in the process of the therapy. The 'victim's' therapy, dependent it is thought on their forgiveness, is seriously compromised by the denial.

[46] Binjamin Wilkomirski, *Fragments*, Picador: London 1996.

[47] Levi, *The Drowned and the Saved*, p. 12.

remembering or fantasizing. This is part of the problem faced by Michael Lapsley and others engaged in the truth and reconciliation procedures in trying to come to terms with memories of past conflicts. Faith memories expressed in rituals such as the Jewish Passover dinner with its emphasis on the memory of being slaves in Egypt, and the Christian Eucharist, 'this do in remembrance of me', have given memory a transcendent significance – although recent scholarship suggests that these too may be false memories or myths. We have gone on creating rituals in the form of traditions and memorials ranging from pilgrimages to processions. We are becoming aware in many areas of the danger as well as the beauty of the memories we try to encapsulate. We see '1690' painted on a wall in a working-class district of Glasgow and we are reminded of three hundred years of hatred of Catholics by Protestants. The fact that in the Battle of the Boyne the Protestant army was supported by the Pope in what was a political rather than a religious dispute has been selectively forgotten.

Black South Africans are having to come to terms with the fact that the white population is selectively rearranging history in ways which relieve them of any necessity to seek forgiveness for their past behaviour. There is however one exception to the denial that they had any responsibility for what happened; the exception is the faith community. Michael Lapsley made the point that the Christian gospel was the main tool of oppression but it has also been a medium of liberation for those ministers of religion and members of the faith community who came to the Truth Commission to say 'Sorry'. Some positive results have emerged. The torturers, like the Nazis who said, 'Scream all you like, no one will hear you', have been proved wrong. The stories told have brought the memory of the torture and the screams into the light of day.

The disadvantage of memory, whether true or false, is that it freezes the story it is trying to tell. This has particularly been the case with the post-Holocaust responses of some members of the Jewish community, whose slogan, 'We must never forget', has been so abrasive and insistent that it has led to the equally distressing concept of 'Holocaust fatigue'. If the 'we' had included the whole community, if the authentic stories of the suffering in the camps had included the gypsies, the communists, the Poles, the German and other resisters of Nazism, it could have been a liberating message. Some Jews have understood this, but others have adopted an identity of victimhood which ironically has been embraced by the heavily armed nation of Israel and feeds into conflicts in the Middle East. This identity prevents any *rapprochement* with Palestinians who have in their turn experienced being victims of the Israelis.

The same problems about memory and forgiveness run through the massacres like those in Rwanda in Africa, and Bosnia and Kosovo in Europe. Five months after the war in Kosovo ended, a plea for ethnic tolerance on the part of the Albanians to the Serbs was made by President Clinton. He asked a packed public meeting, 'Will you be focused on hatred and getting even, or will you be thinking of new schools for your children, new homes? No one can force you to forgive what was done to you but you must try.' He received a polite but unconvinced reception. One young Albanian man said later, 'There's no way we can live together [with the Serbs]. We will never be able to live with them.' Clinton was trivializing the idea of forgiveness because he did not appreciate the painful, hard work which healing and reconciliation demand, or recognize that outsiders have no right to lecture those who have suffered outrageous pain and humiliation about their obligation to forgive. Primo Levi, because he tried to maintain a reasoned style of discourse, was at one point described by Jean Amery as being a 'forgiver'. His response was to say:

> I don't consider this either an insult or praise but an imprecision. I am not inclined to forgive, I never forgave our enemies of that time, nor do I feel I can forgive their imitators in Algeria, Vietnam, the Soviet Union, Chile, Argentina, Cambodia and South Africa because I know no human act that can erase a crime. I demand justice, but I am not able, personally, to trade punches or return the blows.[48]

We have seen in these stories, told in the Commission and resonating in the names of these countries, such pain and suffering for individuals and their families that we can only respect whatever defences of denial or anger individuals turn to in order to ease that suffering. But standing outside we can also see the danger to the wider community when that results in a cycle of pain followed by retribution. The next question is: how do you get the poison out of the memory and prevent the victim becoming the aggressor?

Lapsley's Approach

The miracle of the twentieth century is that the black communities of South Africa have not sought revenge. Lapsley is now Director of the Cape Town-based Institute for the Healing of Memories. This institute seeks to contribute to the healing journey of individuals, communities and nations. A basic assumption of the institute is that the staff also need to be on a journey. This view has its roots in the work of the Scottish psychiatrist Maxwell Jones, who saw patients and staff in therapeutic communities as being on the same journey towards personal growth; he believed every human being has a story.[49] Lapsley, trying to create a therapeutic community for all citizens, sees every South African as having a story. Everything focuses on the person's experience of the apartheid regime and he or she has to answer the three questions we have already heard: what did I do? What was done to me? What did I fail to do?[50]

They are then asked to do further work based on Karl Jaspers' identification of four kinds of guilt – criminal, political, moral (those who stood back and did nothing come into this category) and metaphysical (which embraces the response of the world community).[51] Guilt is seen as only helpful if it leads to action and is

---

[48] Ibid., p. 110.

[49] Maxwell Jones, *Social Psychiatry in Practice: the idea of the therapeutic community*, Penguin: London 1968.

[50] The cross-cultural similarities thrown up by new forms of therapy are always of interest. This three-question technique is also used in Buddhist Temple therapy with people seeking forgiveness and understanding of their lives. See K. Carmichael, *Ceremony of Innocence*, Macmillan: London 1991, p. 191 and D.K. Reynolds, *The Quiet Therapies*, University Press of Hawaii: Honolulu 1980.

[51] Karl Jaspers, *Basic Philosophical Writings – Selections*, ed., trans., with introductions by Edith Ehrlich, Leonard H. Ehrlich, George B. Pepper, Ohio University Press: Athens, OH 1986.

not to be valued for its own sake. A major aim is that people should not continue to think of themselves as victims since people who do this eventually become victimizers of others – sometimes in subtle ways. Lapsley's interpretation of the Greek word for forgiveness is that it means untangling a knot; and this is how he sees its role. The workshops he organizes may serve only to take one step forward towards that. He describes how one woman was enabled to say goodbye to her son who had been killed. Just to let her son go was an important step without forgiving anyone. Lapsley's attitude to forgiveness is very refreshing. He has drained it of romanticism and glamour and replaces its meaning with a tough practical vision. While having abandoned the purity of Christian pacifism and any trace of the Jesus of Holman Hunt,[52] he draws on the Hebrew Bible as his main theological source and seems to have developed a pragmatic Christianity which combines compassion for suffering with a passionate sense of justice. He comes close to Borg's description of the way in which Jesus modified the Jewish idea of holiness. No longer was holiness understood to need protection, but as an active force which overcame uncleanliness. The people of God had no need to worry about God's holiness being contaminated. In any confrontation it would triumph.[53] In abandoning pacifism and being willing to support the armed struggle of the African National Congress (ANC), much as Bonhoeffer accepted that Hitler should be killed, Lapsley was taking the view that contact with evil did not make Jesus unclean – rather, as in the case of the leper, it was the leper who was made clean.[54]

Lapsley's Christianity appears like a new, tougher, more pragmatic variety, drawing on whatever sources of the Hebrew and Christian Bibles he finds helpful in his compassionate search for justice. He has moved beyond Archbishop Tutu's theology and appears to be developing an individual vision, which could be described as post-Christian in that it rejects assumptions about the duty to forgive. Lapsley, perhaps as a response to the trauma of being left without hands, seems to look at the world with a clarity which takes nothing for granted – everything is seen as if for the first time. This enables him to look at the part played by memory and guilt but also to help those with whom he works to question their own experiences and take charge of their futures.

Looking to the Future

One aspect of the post-Christian era is the way in which theology can now be individualized. Everyone can be his or her own kind of Christian. There can be theistic, deistic or atheistic Christians, none of whom believe in the divinity of Christ. There are theists who reject Christianity because they see its institutions

---

[52] William Holman Hunt (1827–1910), co-founder of the Pre-Raphaelite Brotherhood, painted a picture of Jesus called *The Light of the World* which enjoyed a great sentimental success. Most of his works are now regarded as artistic failures. At the time they were successful representations of what is now a discarded set of attitudes.

[53] Marcus J. Borg, *Conflict, Holiness and Politics in the Teachings of Jesus*, Trinity Press International: Harrisburg, PA 1998.

[54] Mark, 1:40–45.

as sexist and repressive to women or homosexuals but respect its founder. Most important, the social undertone of secularism increases the level of toleration of a wide range of religious or non-religious views. This makes possible ecumenical links which would otherwise have been thwarted by a rigid interpretation of belief. Some of these ecumenical links have focused on the resolution of conflict, and we find in countries like Israel and Nigeria examples of Jews and Muslims, and Christians and Muslims, working together for peace. This is to some extent achieved by demoting the importance of the religious structures while retaining the rituals which lie at their heart and in some cases developing new ones which can be shared with other faiths.

This involves a high level of demanding, collective work. It also involves the capacity to trust and to respect those whom you may have previously seen as enemies or rivals. In South America and in South Africa, priests working with the people as partners in the struggle for change let go of any practices which stood between them and a full participation in and understanding of the economic and spiritual lives of local people. One Irish priest, with hundreds of square miles of the South African countryside as his parish, told me how he made it possible for women in the village to say Mass when he could not be there. At home, he would have been seen as a heretic.

Questions relating to consciousness, self and imagination have, until a recent surge of interest by neurobiologists, been seen as the preserve of the philosopher, the theologian or the poet, often without reference to the others' vision. Increasingly, with advances in understanding the complexity of neural processes and the uniqueness of each individual brain, and a recognition that there is increasingly less distinction between philosophy and science, theology and poetry, a multidisciplinary approach is emerging. Similarly, the religious impulse, which has led to a range of attempts to give meaning to the life of the most simple human being as well as those who, like Rembrandt and Mozart, create miracles, can no longer be contained in a narrow set of beliefs. It is being mobilized in support of the environment, of animal welfare, of justice, of the rights of citizens not to be exploited by commercial interests and increasingly against the worst excesses of global capitalism. Those involved may reflect a range of beliefs or none. It is not a religion that brings them together, nor is religion likely to divide them. It is rather what I am describing for want of a better phrase as the religious impulse, that mysterious human quality which makes us seek to be better than we are. The drive to do so is an aspect of the religious and creative impulses which are also aspects of being human.

Utopia may no longer be a dream we can find by escaping to another world or by following a charismatic leader in this world, but we can certainly create something better than the world we now inhabit. We cannot do this in isolation but only in relationship with each other. This is a lesson we can learn from the way in which the Norwegian village handled the murder of one of their children by another two of their children. They accepted from the beginning that all the children were theirs, none were to be excluded or scapegoated. This can also be seen as the ancient vision of the Kingdom which Don Cupitt, along with many others in our history, insists we have to create in this world – not in one of the imagination. But those who want this have to create a Kingdom on earth for everyone, not only those who see themselves as the children of God. This means that those issues of structural sin discussed in Chapter 5 must be confronted.

It is in the turning to the concept of community that I find fragments of hope for the dilemmas facing us. Thomas Fuller, the seventeenth-century royal chaplain and historian, said, 'If it were not for hopes, the heart would break.'[55] There are many definitions of community. Mine is one which is based on inclusion and rejects both scapegoating and tribalism, since tribalism depends for its survival on rejection of the 'other'. This means that what we call sin and what we describe as forgiveness are seen as being concerned with practical aspects of human behaviour, feelings and relationships, rather than abstract rules handed down by tradition and by those with the authority to interpret it. To achieve this requires more than preaching – indeed that may be counterproductive. If, as I have argued, our morality is collectively created and recreated with changing social and economic circumstances, it would imply that we can choose to change it by changing those circumstances. Certain individual 'sins' like street crime and burglary are shown to increase or decrease inversely with job opportunities. The iniquity of poverty shows the same relationship with jobs and is reflected in poorer health and educational opportunities. We have a human responsibility to work through our institutions to bring about such changes as would make our chosen morality easier to live by, at both an individual and structural level. Omitting to do that we are faced with Lapsley's third question: what did you fail to do?

Forgiveness is being recast as an emotional experience which can be relevant in interpersonal situations between offenders and their victims. It is increasingly seen as helpful to the victim's mental and physical health to choose to forgive; being forgiven can also be a way of helping the offender recover the loss of the human quality of empathy which led to the offence. But that is for the individuals themselves to decide. To forgive or not to forgive is increasingly being seen as a choice everyone is entitled to make; it may be a choice to forgive made out of a religious conviction or as a result of self-examination in psychotherapy;[56] it may be a choice not to forgive since that is not seen as helpful to the people involved or likely to change the situation that led to the offence.[57] Or forgiveness, as Lapsley said, may 'not be on the table' because no one has confessed to the offence or offered to put it right in any practical way.

Forgiveness is no longer relevant in the public arena. It is not for me or anyone else outside those involved in her crimes to say that they forgive Myra Hindley or that she should have been forgiven. As a concept of universal, authoritative, professionally or religiously administered ideas of morality, such attitudes are becoming less and less relevant to the kind of world we inhabit and the debates and dilemmas we face. What we can say as citizens who shared the world with her is that she should have both faced justice and been treated with justice. This applies to all the cases we looked at in Chapter 1. Our understanding of justice has also shifted. The retributive justice of the past is giving way to the notion of

---

[55] Thomas Fuller, *Gnomologia*, 1732: 2689.

[56] Examples of both these paths to forgiveness are described most powerfully in Eric Lomax's personal story of torture and reconciliation in *The Railway Man*, Vintage: London 1996.

[57] The most common example of forgiveness not changing the situation is found in domestic abuse.

restorative justice, which is forward looking rather than concentrating on the detail of the past; it is participative, inclusive and democratic,[58] rather than authoritative, religious or purely professional, evolving rather than fixed in past case law.[59] The response of the Norwegian community to the murder of one of their children has a great deal to teach us.

---

[58] Anthony Giddens describes us as living in 'a world of interrogation and dialogue' in *Beyond Left and Right: The Future of Radical Politics*, Polity Press: London 1994, p. 85.

[59] Some of these qualities emerged in the *Kilbrandon Report*, HMSO, 1966, which led to the creation of Children's Panels in Scotland which were designed to separate children from the adult judicial system.

Postscript

We have moved out of a period of history which could clearly be designated as Christian in an institutional sense of that word. What some see as the original Christian ethic may have been gradually abandoned from the beginning of the fourth century onwards when Christianity became the official religion of the State. The period in which we live now can be described as post-Christian, but it may be equally correct to use Giddens' phrase, 'the post-traditional society'. He makes the point about traditions that 'you don't really have to justify them: they contain their own truth, a ritual truth, asserted as correct by the believer'.[1] We have seen that we are all involved in a diverse, globally cosmopolitan order in which such a stance is no longer tolerable. Giddens believes that we are the first generation to live in a thoroughly post-traditional society, a term he prefers to post-modern. This is not a society in which traditions cease to exist; rather it is one in which tradition 'changes its status' since by being brought into contact with other traditions each is forced to 'declare themselves'.[2] This is what is happening in our examination of the traditions of sin and forgiveness.

I opened this work with two assumptions. The first was that there is no such thing as evil as an entity. I could not use it to describe a person, only as an adjective to describe that person's behaviour in certain situations. This meant that sin and forgiveness have to be assessed in the context of understanding, as far as is possible, the background and circumstances in which the offence has taken place. This conviction derives from my experience of working with men and women whom society had defined as evil and because of that had punished them, sometimes by giving them a life sentence of imprisonment. Of these people there were none who did not seem to me to have the potential, even the actuality, of goodness. Secondly I did not believe that there was any behaviour which we designated as evil, that in some other society would not have been seen in a different light either now or in the past. To kill and to rape and to torture are the three clearest examples of that. Nothing that I have read or discussed while undertaking this work has shifted those two assumptions but what has happened is that I have attempted to clarify some others:

- All definitions of sin are humanly constructed and vary from community to community and from time to time.
- To forgive or not to forgive is a choice anyone should be able to make without fear or favour. They should however be helped to understand the consequences of their choice.

---

[1] Giddens, *Beyond Left and Right*, p. 6.
[2] Ibid., p. 83.

- All religious texts are the work of fallible human beings and should be understood as reflecting their view of the world they lived in.
- It is important to value the rich heritage of human history and the poetic wisdom that these texts can offer us, but it is also important to distinguish between the time in which they were written and the time in which we live.
- Our moral behaviour and beliefs are intricately related to the social and economic circumstances within which we live and can be influenced by changes in those circumstances.
- We have a responsibility, along with our fellow citizens, to try to change those circumstances in ways that foster the morality to which we have chosen to adhere.
- The community has the responsibility to clarify and explain what it understands as virtuous behaviour as well as sinful behaviour and to make virtuous behaviour easier, sinful behaviour less tempting.

In these conclusions I have asked an ancient and unresolved question: how do we live together in non-damaging and creative ways? It is a question that has relevance for every human being as an individual, as a member of a family, a group or a nation. In this work we have recognized that dark forces of fear, greed and violence may lie within any of us. We have also seen remarkable examples of love and compassion which transcend these forces. It is these last examples that help us hold to the thought that we can find better ways of living together. Rembrandt's great painting, *The Return of the Prodigal Son*, holds that possibility before our eyes. Since I have repeatedly stressed the collective and social character of the morality in which sin and forgiveness are embedded, it may be fitting to conclude with a reminder that each of us has the right and duty to make our own stand on moral questions.

Cavafy posed the dilemma we face in his poem 'Thermopylae':

> Honour to those who in the life they lead
> Define and guard a Thermopylae.
> Never betraying what is right, consistent and just in all they do
> But showing pity also, and compassion;
> Generous when they are rich, and when they are poor,
> Still generous in small ways, still helping as much as they can;
> Always speaking the truth,
> Yet without hating those who lie.
>
> And even more honour is due to them
> When they foresee (as many do foresee)
> That in the end Ephialtis will make his appearance,
> That the Medes will break through after all.[3]

Each generation has had to confront the question of how we carry on while living with the possibility of the nightmare appearing – and this generation more than

---

[3] C.P. Cavafy, *Collected Poems*, trans. Edmund Kelley and Philip Sherrard, ed. George Savidis, The Hogarth Press: London 1984. Ephialtis is the name of the demon of nightmare among the Greeks.

most because of our capacity to destroy ourselves. But it can also, as we have seen, appear at an individual level. We all carry Ephialtis, demon of nightmare, within ourselves. It becomes more important that we work collectively towards constructing humane, constructive, peaceful moral processes so as not to slide back into the scapegoating and tribalism implicit in the moral debris left over from the traditions of sin and forgiveness which we are now abandoning.

Bibliography

This bibliography contains a number of titles not referred to in the text that I nonetheless regard as being significant for an understanding of the topic and, more generally, of the crisis of theistic belief and religious practice in which the topic has its place.

Adams, Robert P., *The Better Part of Valor: More, Erasmus, Colet and Vives, on Humanism, War and Peace*, University of Washington Press: Seattle 1962

Adorno, Theodor, *Prisms: Cultural Criticism and Society*, trans. Samuel and Shierry Weber, Neville Spearman: London 1967

Althaus-Reid, Marcella, *Indecent Theology: Theological perversions in sex, gender and politics*, Routledge: London and New York 2000

Altizer, Thomas J.J., *The Contemporary Jesus*, SCM Press Ltd 1998

Ancrene, Wisse, *Guide for Anchoresses*, trans. Hugh White, Penguin Classics, Penguin Books: London 1993

Anon., 'Comfort Women', *Trouble and Strife*, No. 41, p. 59

Anscombe, G.E.M., 'Modern Moral Philosophy', in *Ethics, Religion and Politics*, volume 3 of her *Collected Papers*, University of Minnesota Press: Minneapolis 1981

Arendt, Hannah, *Eichmann in Jerusalem: a report on the banality of evil*, Penguin Books: New York 1994

Arendt, Hannah, *The Human Condition*, University of Chicago Press: Chicago and London 1958

Arnold, Johann Cristoph, *The Lost Art of Forgiving*, The Plough Publishing House: Farmington, PA 1998

Arnold, Matthew, 'Dover Beach' in *The Penguin Book of English Verse*, ed. John Hayward, Penguin Books: Harmondsworth 1956

Atwood, Margaret, *Alias Grace*, Bloomsbury: London 1996

Atwood, Margaret, *Dancing Girls and other stories*, Vintage: London 1996

Atwood, Margaret, *The Handmaid's Tale*, Vintage: London 1996

Augustine, Saint, *City of God*, trans. Henry Bettenson, Penguin Classics, Penguin Books: London 1984

Augustine, Saint, *Confessions*, trans. Henry Chadwick, World's Classics, Oxford University Press: Oxford 1991

Babuta, Subniv and Bragard, Jean-Claude, *Evil*, Weidenfeld & Nicolson: London 1988

Bakan, David, *Sigmund Freud and the Jewish Mystical Tradition*, Beacon Press: Boston 1975

Balasuriya, Fr. Tissa, *Mary and Human Liberation: the story and the text*, ed. Helen Stanton, Mowbray: London 1997

Bales, Kevin, *Disposable People: New Slavery in the Global Economy*, University of California Press: London 1999

Ballard, J.G., *Crash*, Vintage: London 1995

Barker, Pat, *The Regeneration Trilogy*, Penguin Books: London 1998

Barrett, C.K. *A Commentary on the Epistle to the Romans*, Adam & Charles Black: London 1984

Barth, Karl, *Church Dogmatics*, ed. G.W. Bromiley and T.F. Torrance, 13 vols. T&T Clark: Edinburgh 1969

Bataille, Georges, *Literature and Evil*, trans. Alastair Hamilton, Marion Boyars: London and New York 1997

Bataille, Georges, *Story of the Eye by Lord Auch*, trans. Joachim Neugroschal, Penguin Books: London 1982

Becker, Ernest, *The Birth and Death of Meaning*, The Free Press: New York 1971

Becker, Ernest, *Escape from Evil*, The Free Press: New York 1975

Becker, Ernest, *The Structure of Evil*, The Free Press: New York 1968

Beckett, Samuel, *Waiting for Godot*, Faber & Faber: London 1959

Begg, Ean, *The Cult of the Black Virgin*, Arkana, Penguin Books: London 1996

Berrigan, Daniel, *Absurd Convictions, Modest Hopes: conversations after prison with Lee Lockwood*, Vintage: New York 1973

Berrigan, Daniel, *Ten Commandments for the Long Haul*, Abingdon Press: Nashville, TN 1981

Blake, William, *Complete Writings*, ed. Geoffrey Keynes, Oxford Paperbacks: Oxford 1972

Blessington, Francis C., *Paradise Lost: Ideal and Tragic Epic*, Twayne Publishers: Boston 1998

Bloom, Harold, *The American Religion: The Emergence of the Post-Christian Nation*, Simon & Schuster: New York 1993

Bloom, Harold, *Omens of Millennium: the Gnosis of Angels, Dreams, and Resurrection*, Riverhead Books: New York 1996

Bloom, Harold, *Shakespeare: The Invention of the Human*, Fourth Estate: London 1999

Bloomfield, Morton W., *The Seven Deadly Sins*, State College Press: Michigan 1952

Blumenberg, Hans, *The Legitimacy of the Modern Age*, trans. Robert M. Wallace, Massachusetts Institute of Technology: Boston, MA 1983

Boal, Augusto, *Theatre of the Oppressed*, trans. Charles A. and Martia-Odilia Leal McBride, Pluto Press: London 1979

Boccaccio, Giovanni, *The Decameron*, Penguin Books: London 1972

Bonder, Nilton, *The Kabbalah of Envy: Transforming Hatred, Anger and Other Negative Emotions*, trans. Julia Michaels, Shambala: Boston and London 1997

Bons-Storm, Riet, *The Incredible Woman*, Abingdon Press: Nashville, TN 1996

Borg, Marcus J., *Conflict, Holiness and Politics in the Teachings of Jesus*, Trinity Press International: Harrisburg, PA 1998

Boswell, John, *Christianity, Social Tolerance, and Homosexuality: Gay People in Western Europe from the Beginning of the Christian Era to the Fourteenth Century*, University of Chicago Press: Chicago and London 1981

Bowlby, John, *Child Care and the Growth of love; based on the report on Maternal Care and Mental Health; abridged and edited by Margery Fry*, Penguin Books: London 1953

Boyle, Jimmy, *A Sense of Freedom*, Canongate: Edinburgh 1977

Bradford, Richard, *Paradise Lost*, Open University Press: Milton Keynes 1992

Brink, André, *Imaginings of Sand*, Minerva: London 1996

Brock, Rita Nakashima and Susan Brooks Thistlethwaite, *Casting Stones: Prostitution and Liberation in Asia and the United States*, Fortress Press: Minneapolis, MN 1996

Broderick, J;., *Fall from Grace: the life of Eamonn Casey*, Brandon Book Publishers Ltd: Dingle, Co. Kerry, Ireland 1992

Brook, Barbara, *Feminist Perspectives on the Body*, Feminist Perspectives Series, Longman: London and New York 1999

Brown, Norman O., *Life Against Death*, Sphere Books: London 1970

Brown, Norman O., *Love's Body*, Vintage: New York 1966

Buber, Martin, *Ecstatic Confessions*, ed. Paul Mendes-Flohr, Harper & Row: San Francisco 1985

Bultmann, Rudolph, *Primitive Christianity*, trans. R.H. Fuller, Living Age Books: New York 1989

Bunyan, John, *The Pilgrim's Progress, a casebook*, ed. Roger Sharrock, Macmillan: London and Basingstoke, 1976

Burgess, Anthony, *A Clockwork Orange*, Ballantyne Books: New York 1963

Burnett, Anne Pippin, *Revenge in Attic and Later Tragedy*, University of California Press: London 1998

Cadoux, C. John, *The Early Christian Attitude to War: a contribution to the history of Christian ethics*, Headley: London 1919

Campbell, Beatrix, *Goliath: Britain's Dangerous Places*, Methuen: London 1993

Campbell, Joseph, ed. *Myths, Dreams and Religion*, Spring Publications: Dallas, TX 1970

Campbell, Joseph, *Myths to Live By*, Paladin Books: London 1985

Campbell, Joseph, with Bill Moyers, *The Power of Myth*, ed. Betty Sue Flowers, Doubleday: New York and London 1988

Camplisson, Joe and Hall, Michael, *Hidden Frontiers: Addressing deep-rooted violent conflict in Northern Ireland and the Republic of Moldova*, Island Publications: Newtownabbey, Co. Antrim 1996

Camus, Albert, *The Myth of Sisyphus*, trans. Justin O'Brien, Penguin Books: Harmondsworth 1975

Camus, Albert, *The Outsider*, trans. Joseph Laredo, Penguin Books: London 1982

Camus, Albert, *The Plague*, trans. Stuart Gilbert, Penguin Books: London 1948

Casey, Maurice, *Aramaic sources of Mark's Gospel*, Cambridge University Press: Cambridge 1998

Capra, Fritjof, *The Tao of Physics: An Exploration of the Parallels between Modern Physics and Eastern Mysticism*, Fontana/Collins: London 1975

Capra, Fritjof, *Uncommon Wisdom*, Flamingo: London 1988

Capra, Fritjof and Steindl-Rast, David, *Belonging to the Universe: New Thinking About God and Nature*, Penguin Books: London 1992

Carmichael, Kay, *Ceremony of Innocence: Tears, Power and Protest*, Macmillan: London 1991

Cavafy, C.P., *Collected Poems*, trans. Edmund Kelley and Philip Sharrard, ed. George Savidid, The Hogarth Press: London 1984.

Chadwick, Owen, *The Secularization of the European Mind in the 19th Century*, Canto, Cambridge University Press: Cambridge 1995

Chaucer, *The Canterbury Tales*, ed. Walker W. Skeat, Clarendon Press: Oxford 1894

Christ, Carol P. and Plascow, Judith, eds, *Womanspirit Rising: a feminist reader in religion*, Harper & Row: San Francisco and London 1979

Clark, Kenneth, *Rembrandt and the Italian Renaissance*, John Murray: London 1996

Clark, Ronald W., *Freud: The Man and the Cause*, Jonathan Cape and Weidenfeld & Nicolson: London 1980

Classen, Constance, Howes, David and Synnott, Anthony, *Aroma, The cultural history of smell*, Routledge: London and New York 1994

Claude-Pierre, Peggy, *The Secret Language of Eating Disorders*, Random House of Canada: Toronto 1997

Coetzee, J.M., *Disgrace*, Secker & Warburg: London 1999

Cohn-Sherbok, Dan, *The Crucified Jew: Twenty Centuries of Christian Anti-Semitism*, Eerdmans: Grand Rapids, MI 1997

Coleridge, Samuel Taylor, *Complete Poetical Works*, ed. Ernest Hartley, Oxford University Press: Oxford 1969

Coles, Robert, *The Secular Mind*, Princeton University Press: Princeton, NJ 1999

Conrad, Joseph, *Almeyer's Folly: a story of an Eastern river*, Everleigh, Nash and Grayson: London 1921

Conrad, Joseph, *Heart of Darkness*, Wordsworth Editions: London 1995

Conrad, Joseph, *Lord Jim*, Penguin Modern Classics, Penguin Books: London 1957

Cooper, David A., *Silence, Simplicity and Solitude*, Bell Tower: New York 1992

Currie, Thomas W., *Ambushed by Faith: The Virtues of a Useless Faith*, Pickwick Publications: London 1993

Cupitt, Don, *Mysticism After Modernity*, Blackwell: Oxford 1998

Cupitt, Don, *The Religion of Being*, SCM: London 1998

Cupitt, Don, *The Revelation of Being*, SCM: London 1998

Dabourne, Wendy, *Purpose and Cause in Pauline Exegesis*, Cambridge University Press: Cambridge 1999

Dale, Graham, *God's Politicians*, HarperCollins: London 2000

Damasio, Antonio, *The Feeling of What Happens: Body, Emotion and the Making of Consciousness*, William Heinemann: London 1999

Dante, *The Divine Comedy: The Portable Dante*, trans. Lawrence Binyon, ed. Paulo Milano, Penguin Books: London 1977

Davies, Nick, *Dark Heart*, Chatto & Windus: London 1997

Davis, Colin, *Levinas: an introduction*, Polity Press: London 1996

Deigh, John, *The Sources of Moral Agency, Essays in Moral Psychology and Freudian Theory*, Cambridge University Press: Cambridge 1996

Detweiler, Robert and Jasper, David, eds, *Religion and Literature: A Reader*, Westminster/John Knox Press: Louisville, KY 2000

Dickens, Charles, *The Life of Our Lord*, Simon & Schuster: New York 1999

Dickinson, Emily, *The Complete Poems of Emily Dickinson*, ed. Thomas H. Johnson, Faber Paperback, Faber & Faber: London 1977

Dostoevsky, *The Karamazov Brothers*, trans. Ignat Avsey, World's Classics, Oxford University Press: Oxford 1994

Douglas, Mary, *Purity and Danger: an analysis of the concepts of pollution and taboo*, Ark Paperbacks: London and New York 1966

Douglas, Tom, *Scapegoats: transferring blame*, Routledge: London and New York 1995

Dowrick, Stephanie, *Forgiveness and Other Acts of Love*, The Women's Press: London 1997

Dubos, René, *A God Within: a positive view of mankind's future*, Abacus: London 1976

Dutton, Kenneth R., *The Perfectible Body, The Western Ideal of Development*, Cassell: London 1995

Dworkin, Andrea, *In Harm's Way: The Pornography Civil Rights Hearings*, eds Catharine A. MacKinnon and Andrea Dworkin, Harvard University Press: Cambridge, MA and London 1997

Dworkin, Andrea, *Life and Death*, Virago: London 1997

Dworkin, Andrea, *Scapegoat: The Jews, Israel and Women's Liberation*, Virago: London 2000

Eckhart, Meister, *Selected Writings*, trans. Oliver Davies, Penguin Books: London 1994

Edelman, Sandra, *Turning the Gorgon: a meditation on shame*, Spring Publications: Woodstock, CT 1998

Edwards, David L., *Christianity: The First Two Thousand Years*, Cassell: London 1997

Eliot, George, *Janet's Repentance in Scenes from a Clerical Life*, Blackwood: Edinburgh 1913

Emery, F.E. and Trist, E.L., *Towards a Social Ecology: contextual appreciation of the future in the present*, Plenum Press: London 1972

Empson, William, *Milton's God*, Chatto & Windus: London 1961

Engels, Frederick, *Conditions of the Working Class*, Blackwell: Oxford 1958

Erdinast-Vulcan, Daphna, *Joseph Conrad and the Modern Temper*, Clarendon Press: Oxford 1991

Erikson, Erik H., *Young Man Luther: a study in psychoanalysis and history*, Faber & Faber: London 1958

Esslin, Martin, *The Theatre of the Absurd*, Pelican Books: London 1974

Estes, Clarissa Pinkola, *Women Who Run With The Wolves*, Random House: London 1993

Fairlie, Henry, *The Seven Deadly Sins Today*, University of Notre Dame Press: Notre Dame 1995

Fenn, Richard K., *The Secularization of Sin: An Investigation of the Daedalus Complex*, Westminster/John Knox Press: Louisville, KY 1991

Ferguson, Ian, *The Philosophy of Witchcraft*, George G. Harrap: London 1924

Fiedler, Leslie A., *Love and Death in the American Novel*, Paladin: London 1960

Finaldi, Gabriele, *The Image of Christ*, National Gallery Company Limited: London 2000

Fiorenza, Elisabeth Schussler and Copeland, M. Shawn, eds, *Feminist Theology in Different Contexts*, SCM: London 1996

Fish, Stanley, *Surprised by Sin*, Macmillan Press: New York 1997

Flanigan, Beverly, *Forgiving the Unforgivable*, Macmillan: New York 1992

Fleming, David Hay, *The Reformation in Scotland: Causes, Characteristics, Consequences*, Hodder & Stoughton: London 1910

Foucault, Michel, *Discipline and Punish: The Birth of the Prison*, trans. Alan Sheridan, Penguin Books: London 1991

Foucault, Michel, *The History of Sexuality, Vol. 1*, trans. Robert Hurley, Allen Lane, Penguin Books: London 1979

Fränger, Wilhelm, *The Millennium of Hieronymus Bosch*, trans. Eithne Wilkins and Ernst Kaiser, Faber: London 1952

Freedberg, David, *The Power of Images*, University of Chicago Press: Chicago and London 1989

Freud, Sigmund, *Civilization, Society and Religion*, The Pelican Freud Library, Vol. 12, ed. Albert Dickson, Penguin Books: London 1964

Fromm, Erich, *Escape From Freedom*, Rinehart & Co.: New York 1941

Fromm, Erich, *Man For Himself*, Routledge & Kegan Paul: London 1949

Fromm, Erich, *On Disobedience and other essays*, Routledge & Kegan Paul: London, Melbourne and Henley 1984

Fromm, Erich, *You Shall Be As Gods*, Jonathan Cape: London 1967

Fuller, Thomas, *Gnomologia: adages and proverbs, wise sentences and witty sayings. Ancient and modern, foreign and British; compiled by Thomas Fuller*, printed for Thomas and Joseph Allman: London and John Fairbairn: Edinburgh 1816

Gaarder, Jostein, *Vita Brevis: a letter to St. Augustine*, trans. Anne Born, Phoenix House: London 1997

Gaita, Raymond, *A Common Humanity: thinking about love and truth and justice*, Routledge: London and New York 2000

Galdos, Benita Perez, *Dona Perfecta*, trans. A.R. Tulloch, Phoenix House: London 1999

Garrett, Catherine, *Beyond Anorexia: Narrative, Spirituality and Recovery*, Cambridge University Press: Cambridge 1998

Gellner, Ernest, *Conditions of Liberty*, Penguin Books: London 1996

Gellner, Ernest, *Postmodernism, Reason and Religion*, Routledge: London and New York 1992

Gellner, Ernest, *Saints of the Atlas*, Weidenfeld & Nicolson: London 1969

George, Elizabeth, *In Pursuit of the Proper Sinner*, New English Library, Hodder & Stoughton: London 1999

Gibbon, Lewis Grassic, *A Scots Quair*, Penguin Books: London 1986

Gibson, Walter S., *Hieronymus Bosch*, Thames & Hudson: London 1973

Giddens, Anthony, *Beyond Left and Right: The Future of Radical Politics*, Polity Press: London 1994

Girard, René, *Violence and the Sacred*, trans. Patrick Gregory, Johns Hopkins Paperbacks edition: London 1979

Girard, René, *The Scapegoat*, trans. Yvonne Freccero, Johns Hopkins University Press: Baltimore 1986

Glicksberg, Charles I., *The Tragic Vision in Twentieth Century Literature*, Southern Illinois University Press: Illinois 1963

Glover, Jonathan, *Humanity: A Moral History of the Twentieth Century*, Jonathan Cape: London 1999

Goldberg, Michael, *Why Should Jews Survive?*, Oxford University Press: Oxford 1995

Goodwin, James, *Autobiography: The Self Made Text*, Twayne Publishers, Macmillan: New York 1993

Gosse, Edmund, *Father and Son*, Windmill Library, Windmill Press: Kingsmill, Surrey 1938

Greene, Graham, *The End of the Affair*, Penguin Books: London 2000

Groeschel, Benedict J., *Augustine: Major Writings*, Crossroad: New York 1995

Grof, Stanislav, *Books of the Dead*, Thames & Hudson: London 1994

Gutierrez, Gustavo, *Essential Writings*, ed. James B. Nickoloff, SCM Press: London 1996

Hallman, Ralph J., *Psychology of Literature*, Philosophical Library: New York 1961

Hampson, Daphne, *After Christianity*, SCM: London 1996

Hampson, Daphne, *Theology and Feminism*, Basil Blackwell: Oxford 1990

Harding, M.P., *Priest*, The Blackstaff Press: Belfast and Wolfeboro, NH 1987

Hardy, Alister, *The Biology of God*, Jonathan Cape: London 1975

Hardy, Thomas, *Jude the Obscure*, Macmillan: London 1896

Hardy, Thomas, *Tess of the D'Urbervilles*, Penguin Popular Classics, Penguin Books: London 1994

Harris, Lynda, *The Secret Heresy of Hieronymus Bosch*, Floris Books: Edinburgh 1995

Harrison, Kathryn, *The Kiss: a secret life*, Fourth Estate: London 1997

Hawthorne, Nathaniel, *The Scarlet Letter*, The World's Classics, Oxford University Press, Oxford 1990

Haynes, Stephen R. and Roth, John K., eds, *The Death of God Movement and the Holocaust: Radical Theology Encounters the Shoah*, Greenwood Press: Westport, CT and London 1999

Heasman, Kathleen, *Evangelicals in Action: An Appraisal of their Social Work*, Geoffrey Bles: London 1962

Heron, John, *Co-operative Inquiry: Research into the Human Condition*, Sage Publications: London 1996

Hill, Frances, *A Delusion of Satan*, Hamish Hamilton: London 1996

Hobsbawm, Eric, *Age of Extremes: The Short Twentieth Century 1914–1991*, Michael Joseph: London 1994

Hoeller, Stephan A., *The Gnostic Jung and the Seven Sermons to the Dead*, A Quest Book, The Theosophical Publishing House: Wheaton, IL 1982

Hogg, James, *The Private Memoirs and Confessions of a Justified Sinner*, Penguin Classics, Penguin Books: London 1987

Holloway, Richard, *Godless Morality: Keeping religion out of ethics*, Canongate Press: Edinburgh 1999

Horgan, John, *The Undiscovered Mind: How the Brain Defies Explanation*, Weidenfeld & Nicolson: London 1999

Horrocks, Chris and Jevtic, Zoran, *Baudrillard for Beginners*, Icon Books: Cambridge 1996

Howard, Keith, ed. *True Stories of the Korean Comfort Women*, Cassell: London 1995

Huxley, Aldous, *The Devils of Loudon*, Chatto & Windus: London 1952

James, Oliver, *Britain on the Couch*, Century: London 1997

Jasper, David, *Rhetoric, Power and Community: An exercise in reserve*, Macmillan: London 1993

Jasper, David, *The Study of Literature and Religion: an Introduction*, Macmillan: London 1992

Jaspers, Karl, *Basic Philosophical Writings–Selections*, ed. and trans. with introductions by Edith Erlich, Leonard H. Erlich and George B. Pepper, Ohio University Press: Athens, OH 1986

Jay, Martin, *Adorno*, Harvard University Press: Cambridge, MA 1984

Jenkins, David E., *The Contradiction of Christianity*, SCM: London 1976

Jenkins, David E., *God, Miracle and the Church of England*, SCM: London 1987

Johnson, Pamela Hansford, *On Iniquity: some personal reflections arising out of the Moors Murder trial*, Macmillan: London 1967

Jones, L. Gregory, *Embodying Forgiveness: A Theological Analysis*, William B. Eerdmans Publishing Company: Grand Rapids, MI 1995

Jones, Maxwell, *Social Psychiatry in Practice: the idea of the therapeutic community*, Penguin Books: London 1968

Joyce, James, *A Portrait of the Artist as a Young Man*, Wordsworth Editions Limited: Ware, Hertfordshire 1993

Jung, Carl G., *Man and His Symbols*, Aldus Books: London 1964

Kazantzakis, Nikos, *The Last Temptation*, trans. P.A. Bien, Faber & Faber: London 1975

Kee, Cynthia and Norton, Reggie, eds, *Guatemala: The Right to Dream*, The Association of Artists for Guatemala: London 1995

Kellner, Douglas and Baudrillard, Jean, *From Marxism to Post Modernism and Beyond*, Polity Press: Oxford 1989

Kempis, Thomas à, *Imitation of Christ*, trans. Leo Sherley-Price, Penguin Books: London 1959

Kenzaburo Oe, ed., *Fire From the Ashes: Short stories about Hiroshima and Nagasaki*, Readers International: London 1983

Kierkegaard, Søren, *Fear and Trembling*, Penguin Books: London 1985

Kierkegaard, Søren, *Purity of Heart is to will one thing*, Fontana Books: London 1961

Kingsley, Charles, *The Water Babies*, Penguin Popular Classics: London 1995

Klein, Martha, *Determinism, Blameworthiness, and Deprivation*, Clarendon Press: Oxford 1990

Klein, Naomi, *No Logo*, Flamingo: London 2001

Kolnai, Aurel, *Ethics, Value and Reality*, University of London, The Athlone Press: London 1977

Koltov, Barbara Black, *The Book of Lilith*, Nicolas-Hays: York Beach, ME 1987

Krog, Antjie, *Country of my Skull*, Jonathan Cape: London 1998

Kuhn, Thomas S., *The Essential Tension: selected studies in scientific tradition and change*, University of Chicago Press: Chicago 1997

Kuhn, Thomas S., *The Structure of Scientific Revolutions*, University of Chicago Press: Chicago 1996, 3rd edn

Kung, Hans, *Yes to a Global Ethic*, SCM: London 1996

Laing, R.D., *The Politics of Experience*, Penguin Books: Harmondsworth 1967

Lampen, John, *Mending Hurts*, Quaker Home Service: London 1994

Lampen, John, ed., *No Alternative?: nonviolent responses to repressive regimes*, William Sessions: York 2000

Larkin, Philip, *The Whitsun Weddings*, Faber & Faber: London 1964

Laski, Marganita, *George Eliot and her World*, Thames & Hudson: London 1973

Lawrence, D.H., *The Man who Died*, Secker: London 1931

Lea, H.C., *History of Sacerdotal Celibacy*, Vol. 1, Williams and Norgate: London 1907

Leach, Edmund, *Lévi Strauss*, Fontana Press: London 1985

Leach, Edmund, *A Runaway World?*, The Reith Lectures 1967, British Broadcasting Corporation: London 1968

Lee, David C.J., *Ernest Renan: In the Shadow of Faith*, Duckworth: London 1996

Liebmann, Marian, ed., *Arts Approaches to Conflict*, Jessica Kingsley Publishers: London and Philadelphia 1996

Liebmann, Marian, ed., *Mediation in Context*, Jessica Kingsley Publishers: London and Philadelphia 2000

Levi, Primo, *The Drowned and the Saved*, trans. R. Rosenthal, Abacus: London 1995

Levinas, Emmanuel, *Otherwise than Being or Beyond Essence*, trans. Alphonso Lingis, Martinus Nijhoff Philosophy Texts Vol. 3, Martinus Nijhoff Publishers: The Hague, Boston and London 1981

Levi-Strauss, Claude, *Tristes Tropiques*, trans. J. and D. Weightman, Jonathan Cape: London 1973

Loewenstein, David, *Paradise Lost*, Cambridge University Press: Cambridge 1993

Lomax, Eric, *The Railway Man*, Vintage: London 1996

Lowry, Malcolm, *Under the Volcano*, Picador: London 1993

McEwan, Ian, *The Innocent*, Picador: London 1990

McKenzie, Alasdair M., *The Reaction to Christianity in Pagan Thought*, Thesis 1635, University of Glasgow

MacLean, Sorley, *From Wood to Ridge: Collected Poems in Gaelic and English*, Vintage: London 1989

McLellan, David, *Utopian Pessimist: The Life and Thought of Simone Weil*, Poseidon Press: London and New York 1990

MacIntyre, Alasdair, *After Virtue, a study in moral theory*, Duckworth: London 1981

MacIntyre, Alasdair, *Secularization and Moral Change*, Oxford University Press: London 1967

MacIntyre, Alasdair and Ricoeur, Paul, *The Religious Significance of Atheism*, Columbia University Press: New York and London 1969

Macoby, Hyam, *The Sacred Executioner: Human Sacrifice and the Legacy of Guilt*, Thames & Hudson, The Pitman Press: Bath 1982

Maimonides, *The Book of Knowledge*, trans. H.M. Russell and Rabbi J. Weinberg, The Royal College of Physicians, Edinburgh 1981

Marx, Karl and Engels, Frederick, *The Communist Manifesto*, with an introduction and notes by A.J.P. Taylor, Penguin Books: London 1967

Masters, Brian, *Killing for Company: the case of Dennis Nilson*, Coronet Books, Hodder & Stoughton: Sevenoaks, Kent 1986

Mayhew, Henry, *London Labour and the London Poor*, Griffin, Bohn: London 1851

Meland, Bernard Eugene, *The Secularization of Modern Cultures*, Oxford University Press: New York 1966

Merton, Thomas, *Conjectures of A Guilty Bystander*, Burns and Oats: London 1968

Miller, Alice, *The Untouched Key: Tracing Childhood Trauma in Creativity and Destructiveness*, Virago: London 1990

Milman, H.H., *The History of Christianity: from the birth of Christ to the abolition of paganism in the Roman Empire*, John Murray: London 1963

Milton, *Paradise Lost*, ed. Alastair Fowler, Longman: London 1998

Minkin, Jacob S., *The Teachings of Maimonides*, Jason Aronson: London 1987

Mithen, Steven, *The Prehistory of the Mind: a search for the origins of art, religion and science*, Phoenix: London 1998

Monbiot, George, *Captive State: The Corporate Takeover of Britain*, Macmillan: London 2000

Monbourquette, John, *How To Forgive*, Novalis, St. Paul University: Ottawa, and Darton, Longman & Todd: London 2000

Moore, Brian, *The Statement*, Flamingo: London 1996

Moore, Stephen, *God's Gym: Divine Male Bodies of the Bible*, Routledge: New York and London 1996

Moore, Thomas R., *A Thick and Darksome Veil, The Rhetoric of Hawthorne's Sketches, Prefaces and Essays*, Northeastern University Press: Boston 1994

Morgan, Edwin, *A.D.: A Trilogy of Plays on the Life of Jesus*, Carcanet Press: Manchester 2000

Morris, Lloyd, *The Rebellious Puritan – Portrait of Mr Hawthorne*, Constable: London 1928

Morrison, Blake, *As If*, Granta Books: London 1997

Müller-Fahrenholz, Geiko, *The Art of Forgiveness: Theological Reflections on Healing and Reconciliation*, WCC Publications: Geneva 1997

Murk-Jansen, Saskia, *Brides in the Desert: The Spirituality of the Beguines*, Darton, Longman & Todd: London 1988

Murphy, A., *Forbidden Fruit*, Little, Brown and Company, New York 1993

Myers, Henry Alonzo, *Tragedy: a view of life*, Cornell University Press: Ithaca, NY 1956

Myss, Caroline, *Anatomy of the Spirit*, Bantam Books: London 1998

Nabokov, Vladimir, *Lolita*, Penguin Books: London 1995

Nadel, Jennifer, *Sara Thornton: The Story of a Woman who Killed*, Victor Gollancz: London 1993

Newlands, George, *Generosity and the Christian Future*, SPCK: London 1997

Niebuhr, Reinhold, *The Nature and Destiny of Man: A Christian Interpretation*, Vol. 1, Nisbet: London 1941

Nietzsche, Friedrich, *Twilight of the Idols/The Anti-Christ*, Penguin Classics, Penguin Books: London 1990

Noddings, Nel, *Women and Evil*, University of California Press: Berkeley and Los Angeles 1989

Norris, Pamela, *The Story of Eve*, Picador: London 1998

Nouwen, Henri J.M., *The Return of the Prodigal Son: a story of homecoming*, Darton, Longman & Todd: London 1944

Nutall, Geoffrey, *Christian Pacifism in History*, World Without War Council, Basil Blackwell & Mott: Berkeley, CA 1971

Ohly, Friedrich, *The Damned and the Elect*: *guilt in western culture*, Cambridge University Press: Cambridge 1992

Olivier, Richard, *Shadow of the Stone Heart: a search for manhood*, Pan: London 1995

Ormerod, Neil and Thea, *When Ministers Sin: Sexual Abuse in the Churches*, Millennium Books: Alexandria, NSW, Australia 1998

Pagels, Elaine, *Adam, Eve and the Serpent*, Penguin Books: London 1990

Pagels, Elaine, *The Gnostic Gospels*, Penguin Books: London 1979

Paine, Thomas, *Basic Writings of Thomas Paine: Common Sense, The Rights of Man, Age of Reason*, Wiley Books: New York 1942

Paris, Erna, *Unhealed Wounds: France and the Klaus Barbie Affair*, Grove Press: New York 1986

Park, Andrew Sung, *The Wounded Heart of God*, *The Asian Concept of Han and the Christian Doctrine of Sin*, Abingdon Press: Nashville, TN 1993

Pattison, George, *Agnosis: Theology in the Void*, Macmillan Press: London 1996

Pendergrast, Mark, *Victims of Memory*, Harper Collins: London 1996

Phillips, Adam, *Promises, Promises: Essays on Literature and Psychoanalysis*, Faber & Faber: London 2000

Plaskow, Judith, *Sex, Sin and Grace*, University Press of America: New York 1980

Plato, *Republic*, trans. Robin Waterfield, The World's Classics, Oxford University Press: Oxford 1993

Porte, Joel, *In Respect to Egotism: studies in American Romantic writing*, Cambridge University Press: Cambridge 1991

Pottinger, Morris, *Parish Life on the Pentland Firth*, White Maa Books: Thurso 1997

Prince, Alison, *The Necessary Goat and other essays*, Taranis Books: Glasgow 1992

Rawls, John, *A Theory of Justice*, Harvard University Press: Cambridge, MA 1971

Reed, John R., *Dickens and Thackeray: Punishment and Forgiveness*, Ohio University Press: Athens, OH 1995

Reik, Theodor, *Dogma and Compulsion: Psychoanalytic Studies of Religion and Myth*, International Universities Press: New York 1951

Reilly, Patrick, *The Literature of Guilt*, Macmillan: London 1988

Renan, Ernest, *The History of the Origins of Christianity. Book 1: The Life of Jesus*, translated from the 13th edn with modifications by the author, Mathieson: London 1864

Reynolds, D.K., *The Quiet Therapies: Quiet Pathways to Personal Growth*, University Press of Hawaii: Honolulu 1980

Ricoeur, Paul, *The Symbolism of Evil*, Beacon Press: Boston 1969

Riddell, Carol, *The Findhorn Community: Creating a Human Identity for the 21st Century*, Findhorn Press: Findhorn, Forres 1990

Ridley, Matt, *The Origins of Virtue*, Penguin Books: London 1997

Ritchie, J., *Myra Hindley: Inside the Mind of a Murderess*, Angus and Robertson: London 1988

Roberts, Simon, *Order and Dispute: an introduction to legal anthropology*, Martin Robertson: Oxford 1979

Robinson, Duncan, *Stanley Spencer*, Phaidon: Oxford 1990

Robinson, John, *Honest to God*, SCM Press: London 1963

Roose-Evans, James, *Passages of the Soul: Rediscovering the Importance of Rituals in Everyday Life*, Element Books: Brisbane 1994

Rorty, Richard, *Contingency, irony, and solidarity*, Cambridge University Press: Cambridge 1989

Rousseau, Jean-Jacques, *The Confessions*, trans. J.M. Cohen, Penguin Classics, Penguin Books: London 1953

Sack, John, *An Eye for an Eye: The Untold Story of Jewish Revenge Against Germans in 1945*, Basic Books: New York 1993

Sangharakshita, *Transforming Self and World*, Windhorse Publications: Birmingham 1995

Sawday, Jonathan, *The Body Emblazoned: Dissection and the human body in Renaissance culture*, Routledge: London and New York 1995

Sayers, Dorothy L., *Creed or Chaos and other essays in popular theology*, Methuen: London 1947

Scarry, Elaine, *The Body in Pain*, Oxford University Press: Oxford 1985

Schimmel, Solomon, *The Seven Deadly Sins*, Oxford University Press: Oxford 1997

Schlink, Bernhard, *The Reader*, trans. Carol Brown Janeway, Phoenix: London 1997

Sereny, Gitta, *Albert Speer: His Battle With Truth*, Macmillan: London 1995

Sereny, Gitta, *The Case of Mary Bell*, Pimlico: London 1998

Sereny, Gitta, *Cries Unheard: The Story of Mary Bell*, Macmillan: London 1998

Sewall, Richard B., *The Vision of Tragedy*, Yale University Press: New Haven 1959

Shakespeare, William, *King Lear*, ed. Kenneth Muir, The Arden Shakespeare, Routledge: London and New York 1994

Shelley, Mary, *Frankenstein or The Modern Prometheus*, ed. M.K. Joseph, World's Classics, Oxford University Press: Oxford 1980

Shelley, Percy Bysshe, *The Complete Poetical Works of Percy Bysshe Shelley*, eds Thomas Hutchinson and Humphrey Milford, Oxford University Press: London 1940

Shorter, Bani, *Susceptible to the Sacred – The Psychological Experience of Ritual*, Routledge: London 1996

Shriver, Donald W., Jnr, *An Ethic for Enemies*, Oxford University Press: Oxford 1995

Silberman, Shoshana, *A Family Haggadah*, Kar-Ben Copies: Rockville, MD 1987

Sinnott, Anthony, *The Body Social: Symbolism, Self and Society*, Routledge: London 1993

Slovo, Gillian, *Every Secret Thing: my family, my country*, Little, Brown and Company: London 1997

Smart, Ninian, *Dimensions of the Sacred: an anatomy of the world's beliefs*, Fontana Press: London 1997

Smedes, Lewis B., *Forgive and Forget: Healing The Hurts We Don't Deserve*, HarperCollins Paperback: New York 1996

Smiley, Jane, *A Thousand Acres*, Flamingo: London 1992

Smith, David James, *The Sleep of Reason: The James Bulger Case*, Century: London 1994

Smith, Roger W., *Guilt: Man and Society*, Anchor Books, Doubleday and Company: Garden City, NY 1971

Söelle, Dorothy, *Political Theology*, trans. John Shelley, Fortress: Philadelphia 1974

Sölle, D., Kirchberger, J.H. and Haag, H., *Great Women of the Bible in Art and Literature*, Mercer University Press: Macon, GA 1994

Sophocles, *The Three Theban Plays*, trans. Robert Fagles, Penguin Classics: London 1984

Soyinka, Wole, *The Burden of Memory, The Muse of Forgiveness*, Oxford University Press, New York, Oxford 1999

Steinberg, Leo, *The Sexuality of Christ in Renaissance Art and Later Oblivion*, University of Chicago: Chicago 1996

Stephen, Martin, ed., *Never Such Innocence*, Buchan and Enright: London 1988

Strauss, David Friedrich, *The Life of Jesus: critically examined*, trans. George Eliot, Swan Sonnenschein: London 1902

Styron, William, *Sophie's Choice*, Corgi Books: London 1980

Tarnas, Richard, *The Passion of the Western Mind*, Pimlico: London 1996

Tawney, R.H., *Religion and the Rise of Capitalism: a historical study*, Penguin Books: London 1980

Telfer W., *The Forgiveness of Sins*, SCM Press: London 1959

Teresa of Avila, Saint, *The Autobiography of St. Teresa of Avila*, trans. Kieran Kananaugh and Otilio Rodriguez, Book of the Month Club by arrangement with ICS Publications: New York 1995. Originally published as *The Collected Works of St. Teresa of Avila*, Volume One.

Thomson, Oliver, *A History of Sin*, Canongate Press: Edinburgh 1993

Thornton, Mark, *Do We Have Free Will?*, Bristol Classical Press: Bristol 1989

Tierney, Patrick, *The Highest Altar*, Bloomsbury: London: 1989

Tillich, Paul, *The Theology of Culture*, Oxford University Press: New York 1959

Townsend, Peter, *The Smallest Pawns in the Game*, Granada: London 1980

Toynbee, Arnold, *An Historian's Approach to Religion*, Oxford University Press: Oxford 1978

Treichel, Hans-Ulrich, *Lost*, trans. Carol Brown Janeway, Picador: London 2000

True, Michael, *To Construct a Peace*, Twenty-Third Publications: Mystic, CT 1996

Turner, Victor, *The Ritual Process: Structure and Anti-Structure*, Aldine de Gruyter: Hawthorne, NY 1995

Tutu, Desmond, *No Future Without Forgiveness*, Doubleday: New York 1999

Ulrich, Simon, *Pity and Terror*, St Martin's Press: New York, 1989

Updike, John, *A Month of Sundays*, André Deutsch: London 1975

van Alpen, Ernst, *Francis Bacon and the Loss of Self: essays in art and culture*, Harvard University Press: Cambridge, MA 1993

Vizinczey, Stephen, *In Praise of Older Women: the amorous recollections of András Vajda*, The University of Chicago Press: Chicago 1990

Walker, Alice, *Goodnight, Willie Lee, I'll See You in the Morning*, Women's Press: London 1995

Ward, Kevin, 'The Armies of the Lord: Christianity, Rebels and the State in Northern Uganda 1986–1999', paper presented to the British Association for the Study of Religion, Annual Conference, 6–9 September 1999, Stirling University

Waugh, Evelyn, *Brideshead Revisited: the sacred and profane memories of Captain Charles Ryder*, Chapman & Hall: London 1960

Webster, Richard, *Why Freud was Wrong: Sin, Science and Psychoanalysis*, HarperCollins: London 1995

Wiese, Jan, *The Naked Madonna*, trans. Tom. Geddes, The Harvill Press: London 1995

Wiesel, Elie, *The Testament*, Schocken Books: New York 1981

Wiesel, Elie, *Twilight*, trans. Marion Wiesel, Penguin Books: London 1991

Wiesenthal, Simon, *The Sunflower: On the Possibilities and Limits of Forgiveness*, Schocken Books: New York 1998

Wiles, Maurice, *What is Theology?*, Oxford University Press: Oxford 1976

Wilkomirski, Binjamin, *Fragments*, Picador: London 1996

Williams, Charles, *The Forgiveness of Sins*, The Centenary Press, London 1942

Williams, E., *Beyond Belief*, Paragon: London 1968

Williams, James G., ed., *The Girard Reader*, The Crossroad Publishing Company: New York 1996

Wilson, Edmund, *To the Finland Station: A Study in the Writing and Acting of History*, Secker & Warburg: London 1941

Winterson, Jeanette, *Oranges Are Not The Only Fruit*, Vintage: London 1985

Wood, Mrs Henry, *East Lynne*, Collins: London 1954

Woolf, Virginia, *Three Guineas*, The Hogarth Press: London 1952

Worsnip, Michael, *Michael Lapsley: Priest and Partisan, A South African Journey*, Ocean Press: Melbourne 1996

Worthington, Everett L., Jnr, *Dimensions of Forgiveness: Psychological Research and Theological Perspectives*, Templeton Foundation Press: Philadelphia and London 1998

Wright, Robert, *The Moral Animal: Evolutionary Psychology and Everyday Life*, Abacus: London 1996

Yarnold, Edward, *The Awe Inspiring Rites of Initiation: Baptismal homilies of the fourth century*, St Paul's Publications: Slough 1972

Young, Dudley, *Origins of the Sacred: The Ecstasies of Love and War*, Abacus: London 1992

Young-Bruehl, Elisabeth, *Hannah Arendt: For Love of the World*, Yale University Press 1982

Zehr, Howard, *Changing Lenses: A New Focus for Crime and Justice*, Herald Press: Scottdale, PA 1995

Catalogues and Paintings

Stanley Spencer R.A., Royal Academy of Arts, London 1980, in association with Weidenfeld & Nicolson: London

Stanley Spencer, The Astor Collection, text by Carolyn Leder, Thomas Gibson Publishing: London 1976

Rembrandt: Paintings, Drawings and Etchings: catalogue and notes by Ludwig Goldscheider, Phaidon Press: London 1960

Rembrandt, *The Return of the Prodigal Son*, in the Hermitage Museum, St Petersburg

Gabriele Finaldi, *The Image of Christ*, National Gallery Company Limited: London 2000

Prints and Drawings of Käthe Kollwitz, Selected and introduced by Carl Zigrasser, Dover Publications: New York 1969

The Rosenwald Collection, *The Downtrodden (Zertretene)*, The National Gallery of Art, Washington

Myra, Marcus Harvey, Royal Academy of Arts, *Sensation, Young British Artists from the Saatchi Collection* 1997

Photographic Collections

Peace Moves: Nuclear Protest in the 1980s, photographs by Ed Barber, text by Zoë Fairbairns and James Cameron, Chatto & Windus, The Hogarth Press: London 1984

Sebastiao Salgado, Photo Poche, introduction by Christian Caujolle, Centre National de la Photographie: France 1993

Reference Books

The Blackwell Encyclopedia of Modern Christian Thought, ed. Alister E. McGrath, Blackwell: Oxford 1993

A New Dictionary of Christian Theology, eds Alan Richardson and John Bowden, SCM: London 1983

The New Dictionary of Sacramental Worship, Gill and Macmillan: Dublin 1990

A New Handbook of Christian Theology, eds Donald W. Musser and Joseph L. Price, The Lutterworth Press: Cambridge 1992

The Oxford Companion to the Bible, eds B.M. Metzger and M.D. Coogan, Oxford University Press: Oxford 1993

The Oxford Dictionary of the Christian Church, eds F.L. Cross and E.A. Livingstone, Oxford University Press: London 1974, 2nd edn

The Shorter Oxford English Dictionary on Historical Principles, Oxford University Press: Oxford 1973

Reports

Child Abuse: Pastoral and Procedural Guidelines, A report from a Working Party to the Catholic Bishops' Conference of England and Wales on cases involving priests, Religious and other Church Workers, The Catholic Media Office: London 1994

Faith in the City: A Call for Action by Church and Nation. The Report of the
    Archbishop of Canterbury's Commission on Urban Priority Areas 1985
The Game's Up, Children's Society: London 1996
A Glimpse of Hell: Reports on Torture Worldwide, ed. Duncan Forrest, Amnesty
    International, Cassell: London 1996
Human Rights: Building a Safe, Just and Tolerant Society, Study Guide, Human
    Rights Act 1998, Home Office: London
Inquiry Into Income and Wealth, vols 1 and 2, Joseph Rowntree Foundation: York
    1995
Report of the Committee on Homosexual Offences and Prostitution, HMSO:
    London 1957, chaired by Sir John Wolfenden
Smyth, Marie, *Half The Battle: understanding the effects of the 'Troubles' on
    children and young people in Northern Ireland*, Incore: the Initiative on Conflict
    Resolution and Ethnicity: Londonderry 1998
Testimonies, compiled by the Korean Council for Women drafted for Military
    Sexual Slavery by Japan and the Research Association on the Women drafted for
    Military Sexual Slavery by Japan, trans. Young Joo Lee, ed. Keith Howard.
    Published as *True Stories of the Korean Comfort Women*, Cassell: London 1995

Journal Articles

Althaus-Reid, Marcella, 'Do Not Stop the Flow of My Blood: A Critical
    Christology of Hope amongst Latin American Women', *Studies in World
    Christianity*, 1/2, 1995, pp. 143–59
Althaus-Reid, Marcella, 'The Indecency of her Teaching', *Concilium*, 1996/7,
    pp. 124–13
Anon., 'Comfort Women', *Trouble and Strife: the radical feminist magazine*, No. 41
Coyle, Catherine T. and Enright, Robert D., 'Forgiveness Intervention with
    Postabortion Men', *Journal of Consulting and Clinical Psychology*, Vol. 65,
    1997, No. 6
Donnison, David, 'The Academic Contribution to Social Reform', *Journal of
    Social Policy & Administration*, Vol. 34, March 2000, No. 1, pp. 26–43
Duquoc, Christian, 'The Forgiveness of God', *Concilium*, Vol. 184, pp. 35–44
Elizondo, Virgil, 'I Forgive but I Do Not Forget', *Concilium*, Vol. 184, pp. 69–79
Freedman, Suzanne R. and Enright, Robert D., 'Forgiveness as an Intervention Goal
    with Incest Survivors', *Journal of Consulting and Clinical Psychology*, Vol. 64,
    1996, No. 8, pp. 983–92
Hebl, John H. and Enright, Robert D., 'Forgiveness as an Intervention Goal with
    Elderly Females', *Psychotherapy*, Vol. 30, Winter 1993, No. 4, pp. 658–67
Jasper, David, 'Theology and Postmodernity: Poetry, Apocalypse and the Future of
    God', *Svensk Teologisk Kvartalskrift*, Arg. 73, 1997, pp. 97–103
Peters, Jan, 'The Function of Forgiveness in Social Relationships: the social
    dimension', *Concilium*, Vol. 184, pp. 3–4
Rubio, Miguel, 'The Christian Virtue of Forgiveness', *Concilium*, Vol. 184, pp. 80–94
Saiving, Valerie, 'The Human Situation: A Feminine View', *Journal of Religion*,
    No. 40, April 1960

Studzinski, Raymond, 'Remember and Forgive: Psychological Dimensions of Forgiveness', *Concilium*, Vol. 184, pp. 12–21

Sobrino, Jon, 'Latin America: Place of Sin and Forgiveness', *Concilium*, Vol. 184, pp. 45–56

Tulip, Marie, 'Women Church', *Australian Journal of Feminist Studies in Religion*, August 1987, quoted in *Concilium* 1996/1, p. 17

Warner, Marina, 'Peroxide Mug-Shot', *London Review of Books*, Vol. 20, 1998, No. 1

Index